Hiking
Colorado's Summits

A Guide to Exploring the County Highpoints

John Drew Mitchler and Dave Covill

FALCON®

HELENA, MONTANA

*A*FALCONGUIDE®

Falcon® Publishing is continually expanding its list of recreation guidebooks. All books include detailed descriptions, accurate maps, and all the information necessary for enjoyable trips. You can order extra copies of this book and get information and prices for other Falcon® books by writing Falcon, P.O. Box 1718, Helena, MT 59624 or calling toll free 1-800-582-2665. Also, please ask for a free copy of our current catalog. Visit our website at www.FalconOutdoors.com

1 2 3 4 5 6 7 8 9 0 MG 04 03 02 01 00 99

All photos by John Mitchler and Dave Covill unless otherwise noted.

Mapping and Autocad drafting expertise provided by Rick Nies.
Thanks to Whitestar Corportation of Englewood, Colorado for help with digital graphics.

Library of Congress Cataloging-in-Publication Data

Mitchler, John Drew
    Hiking Colorado's summits : a guide to exploring the county highpoints / by John Drew Mitchler and Dave Covill.
        p. cm. -- (A Falcon guide)
    Includes index.
    ISBN 1-56044-715-X
    1. Hiking—Colorado—Guidebooks. 2. Mountaineering—Colorado—Guide-
books. 3. Trails—Colorado—Guidebooks. 4. Colorado—Guidebooks. I. Covill,
Dave. II. Title. III. Series.
GV199.42.C6M58 1999
796.51'09788—dc21   98-32352
                                                        CIP

CAUTION

Outdoor recreational activities are by their very nature potentially hazardous. All participants in such activities must assume the responsibility for their own actions and safety. The information contained in this guidebook cannot replace sound judgment and good decision-making skills, which help reduce risk exposure, nor does the scope of this book allow for disclosure of all the potential hazards and risks involved in such activities.

    Learn as much as possible about the outdoor recreational activities in which you participate, prepare for the unexpected, and be cautious. The reward will be a safer and more enjoyable experience.

Contents

Acknowledgments

This guidebook is an expansion of the groundbreaking research of David Olson, who spent hours of tedious map research to prepare a complete list of the highest point in every Colorado county. Andy Martin reviewed David's work and published it as part of a unique compilation of county summits in the United States, titled *County High Points*. Without their detailed work, our fieldwork and the writing of this guidebook would not have been possible. In addition to David and Andy, we must thank Jack Longacre, who created the Highpointers Club that has for the past decade been the social focus of the hobby and has been directly responsible for bringing us all together.

We would like to thank the editors at Falcon Publishing for believing in our ideas and for their patience in the preparation of this guide. Rick Nies, an Autocad expert if ever there was one, breathed life into our maps and drawings and provided much needed technical expertise. Hats off to our field team who independently double-checked our routes and descriptions: Ken Akerman, Beckie Covill, Dawn Howard, Jim Lightner, Steve Mueller, Lisa Nickens, and Walt O'Neil. Elena at the Denver Public Library helped us access USGS quads and Don at Cain T-Square in Denver assisted our map production efforts. As members of the Colorado Mountain Club, we were able to draw on the wealth of knowledge of fellow members and the extraordinary library of the American Alpine Club.

We are especially grateful to our manuscript reviewers; David Olson, Bob Packard, and Ken Akerman.

From John

I thank my parents, Bob and Helen, for supporting my ideas and providing a sound background to pursue my goals. The years spent at our homestead, Hill Spring Oaks, infused me with a deep appreciation of nature. My brother, Kurt, has been my closest friend through the years and has always been there, without fail, to help me on the difficult climbs in life. I give a very special thank you to Dawn for her skills, persistence, and companionship on and off the trail. A final thanks is due to all my hiking partners and to Frank Ashley, whose guidebook first inspired me to pursue highpoints.

From Dave

I'm indebted to my parents, Ruth and Ray Covill, for introducing me to the outdoor world and to my son, Chris Covill, for always inspiring me on a gloomy day. Appreciation is duly noted for my coworkers, Paul Pendleton and Jim Lightner; a little overtime on my part is in order. I would also like to thank Steve Doppler, my first hiking partner, and everyone else who has ever shared a trail with me. Most of all, thank you, Beckie, for sharing my dreams.

Preface

In April 1976, a table appeared in an issue of the Colorado Mountain Club's magazine, *Trail and Timberline*, which listed the highest point of land in each of 43 mountainous counties of Colorado. Two decades later, David Olson of Littleton, Colorado, performed a detailed review of the topographic maps of Colorado and created an updated version of the list, one that included the 20 plains counties. Andy Martin reviewed this list of the highest point, or summit, in each of Colorado's 63 counties and included it in his landmark book, *County High Points*. This guidebook of the highest point in every county of the United States, sorted by state, was what energized us in the spring of 1995 to begin a quest to visit the summits of every Colorado county.

At the time, we knew very little about these county summits and we did not know who else was pursuing this goal, although we assumed many climbers had reached the highest peaks of all of Colorado's mountainous counties. Research was required to locate each highpoint on United States Geological Survey (USGS) quads and determine suitable routes and access. Many weekends and vacations were spent over the following two years as we sought out each summit and recorded the information presented in this book. The quest ended for John on September 14, 1996, when he became the first person to have visited every county highpoint in the state, thus establishing a new goal for Colorado hikers and climbers. Dave followed suit by reaching the summit of Teller County.

Map Legend

Interstate	00	Cabins/Buildings	■
U.S. Highway	00	Highpoints	▲ 9,782 ft.
State or Other Principal Road	00 000	Topography	
Interstate Highway	⟹	Elevation	△ 9,782 ft.
Paved Road	⟹	Gate	•—•
Gravel Road	⟹	Mine Site	✗
Unimproved Road	=====⟹	Railroad	+++++++++++
Trailhead	○	County Line Boundary	
Main Trail(s) /Route(s)	- - - -	Continental Divide	— — — —
Bushwhack	....		
Parking Area	Ⓟ	Fence Line	•—•—•—•—
River/Creek/Waterfall		Powerline	•———•———•
County Road	CR		
Forest Road	FR	Snowfield	
Forest Trail	FT		
Four-Wheel-Drive	4WD	Glacier	
Two-Wheel-Drive	2WD	Map Orientation	N ▲
Campground	⛺	Scale	0 0.5 1 Miles

Colorado County Highpoints Locator Map

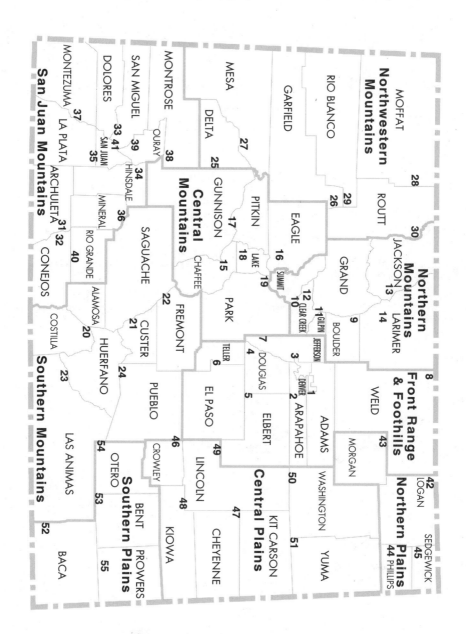

The Hobby of Highpointing

CLIMBING

Climbing mountain peaks has always fascinated the human race, and until this century it was considered more dangerous than challenging to reach the summit of even the easiest peaks. As time has gone by, however, specialized equipment has been invented, maps and directions have become more reliable, and the body of knowledge in the climbing community has improved to such a point that more and more of us can participate in this extraordinary pastime. By the early twentieth century, many of our nation's peaks had been scaled. First ascents had become fewer and fewer. In a natural quest for achievement, climbers started developing lists of similar climbing objectives so that individuals and groups could aspire to reach a common, recognized testament of their abilities.

Much has been written about the inner desire that some of us have to climb a mountain. You've heard of the exchange "Why do you climb the mountain?" "Because it's there!" Jim Wright of the *Standard-Examiner* wrote an article about the value of reaching a summit and wondered why no one asks bowlers why they bowl. Perhaps we enjoy the physical labor involved in reaching the summit of a mountain, or maybe we simply enjoy the view.

HIGHPOINTING

The same mystery surrounds our desire to create a list and accomplish each entry. We organize the routine of our daily lives into a series of achievable tasks by making lists of things we need or want to do. It feels good to complete a daily "to do" list, and it feels even better to make progress on completing a list dealing with the outdoors. "Listing" enthusiasts sport all manner of lists, such as those of state lowpoints or of junctions where three states come together. Your list could be expanded to visiting covered bridges, lighthouses, or the highest waterfalls in each state. The list of lists, so to speak, is endless. There are as many different experiences available as there are individuals willing to use their imagination.

If a list is composed of summits, or the highest points of a given set of geographical features, this is a list for peakbagging. Today, for example, the most popular climbing goal in Colorado is to visit the 54 peaks over 14,000 feet, known as the Fourteeners. When a list involves visiting the highest point in a given political or geographical area—for example, in a county, national forest, state, country, or continent—the activity is referred to as highpointing. Some of the highpointing lists we've heard about include the 54 Fourteeners in Colorado, the apexes of each mountain range in a state, the 8,000-meter peaks in Asia, the Adirondack Fortysixers, the highpoints of each Canadian province, and the highest point in each continent, known as the Seven Summits.

There are 3,142 counties in the United States. (This number changes every few years, as counties are formed or abolished by statewide mandates or votes.) Over the past decade, a growing number of enthusiasts have taken to this form of highpointing, which combines hiking and climbing with traveling to and locating less-visited locales in our countryside. Guidebooks for county summits have been published for California and Utah, and highpointers have completed the list of county summits for many states, including Arizona, Colorado, Connecticut, Maine, New Hampshire, New Mexico, Nevada, Rhode Island, Vermont, Washington, and, just recently, Wyoming. There are still over 30 states yet to be completed, so there is plenty of opportunity out there! At the close of 1998, 72 people had reached the summit of all 50 states, and 136 people had stood on the highest point of each of the 48 contiguous states. The Highpointers Club, started in 1987, recognizes these achievements and promotes communication between like-minded individuals.

Despite highpointing's popularity, a debate rages in hiking circles about whether it is ethical to catalog and rank every rise in nature's landform. On one side are the hiking purists who prefer the act of hiking over the goal. Their focus is on the overall experience, including the sights, sounds, and smells of the outdoors. Some who follow this school of thought will hike a mountain only to stop short of the summit to prove the point that the absolute peak is of little importance. At the other extreme are the peakbaggers, who are driven to create a list of goals and achieve them, sometimes within time limits, often with little appreciation of the hike itself. Peakbaggers also should not be confused with speed hikers. The latter are mainly concerned with the time required to visit a site, while the former may be slow in stride, as long as the goal is eventually reached. Peakbaggers do receive some satisfaction from the physical effort of climbing and much satisfaction when they plan their conquests; however, their greatest reward is the simple act of lining through the objectives on their lists. Many of us prefer to think of ourselves as a balance between the two, driven yet appreciative.

IN SEARCH OF DIFFERENT EXPERIENCES

A number of recent magazine articles lament the shrinking availability of a "wilderness experience." The 54 Colorado Fourteeners receive 200,000 visits annually, which represents a 300 percent increase in ten years! While hiking Fourteeners will always be popular, a growing number of hikers are channeling their attention to more remote, less glamorous peaks. The majority of county highpoints in Colorado offer a quality alternative for those willing to look past the Fourteeners. We have stood in line at switchbacks while hiking Longs Peak, Mount Elbert, and Grays Peak, and somehow we enjoyed the experience in the company of dozens of other peakbaggers. For every day like that, however, a week's worth of days have been spent hiking 11,000-foot mesas covered with wildflowers, climbing remote and exhilarating 13,000-foot peaks, and exploring buttes and ridges with panoramic views west to the Rocky Mountains. The list of county summits includes several stellar peaks in the eastern San Juan Mountains, an even less widely known mesa in northwestern Colorado, and unusual knobs and buttes near the Comanche National Grassland. We hope this guidebook helps ease the pressures on some of the more popular destinations and allows you to discover a different side of Colorado. By visiting each county, you can gain an appreciation for the incredible geographic diversity of the state.

PRIVATE OWNERSHIP

Access to the high mountains of Colorado is generally through federally owned national forests, but the county highpoints encompass more than just mountains. These summits are found not only in high terrain but in agricultural regions as well. As would be expected, much of the land in the plains counties is privately owned. Therefore, the county highpointer must secure permission to visit those summits on private land before arriving at the trailhead. We cannot stress the importance of this enough. The rural land is the means of sustenance to ranchers and farmers, and it must be treated the same as the backyard in suburbia and the front porch in the city; it serves as both "office" and a means of survival.

We have researched and provided all necessary information to contact the caretakers or owners of the 11 privately owned county highpoints. If you truly desire to visit a privately owned summit, please do not wait until the last minute before the trip to make contact with the owners; as many of them are difficult to reach during the hours that you may ordinarily call them. Also many ranchers and farmers work very long hours, so do not contact them much later than the dinner hour. If the owner is unwilling to grant permission for the time you request, please respect this and plan an alternate outing. Be courteous and understanding. Do not trespass!

Some owners have granted access to their property without specific permission. Others would like to know of your visit so they can recognize an unfamiliar vehicle on their land. Several owners request an interview in advance of any visit and may restrict access due to ranching activities.

When on ranch- or farmland, whether you are visiting a highpoint or not, please observe the following rules:

- Do not bother livestock in any way and do not climb fences. Leave gates as you found them, whether open or closed.

- Do not litter or deface private property.

- Collecting and hunting are certainly out of the question.

- Avoid trampling range vegetation; keep to the roads instead, however faint they may be.

- If possible, walk to a highpoint in order to minimize impact and to more fully experience the wide-open splendor of the plains.

IS THIS HOBBY FOR YOU?

We have written this guidebook for all those outdoor enthusiasts who can't wait to get out and see something they haven't seen before; to go somewhere new; to find a special place that few have found before; and generally not to follow in the footsteps of the rest of the weekend warriors. It is for those who like to keep track of their accomplishments, to shoot for a goal, to check off new places visited on the infinite list of the great outdoors as they go along. You know who you are: You make a list when you go to the grocery store. You write down directions when you need to drive to an unfamiliar neighborhood. You aren't afraid of a road trip, and you've camped out before just to save money. You keep track of who sent you a Christmas card. Most important, you remember all the mountains you've climbed and all the trails you've hiked. In short, you're a peakbagger, but you're tired of eating the dust of other hikers on the more popular peaks in Colorado, particularly on the Fourteeners. You yearn for the solitude of the plains mesa and the rugged splendor of a seldom-visited Thirteener. You anticipate the day, not too far from today, when you will jump in your car and make a quick escape to the trailhead of a nearby hill or peak that isn't famous, isn't difficult, isn't awe inspiring, but it's all yours for that day. You are now a county highpointer. This book is for you. Don't forget to sign the register.

Summiting in Colorado

THE CENTENNIAL STATE

The land that is now the state of Colorado, Spanish for "colored," the name first applied to the major river flowing through the state, was originally part of a larger territorial government established in 1859, which was then replaced by the Territory of Colorado on February 28, 1861. It is interesting to note that in 1858 present-day Colorado was included with parts of Nebraska, Utah, and Wyoming in an attempt to create a state called Jefferson. The actual state of Colorado came into being on August 1, 1876, the centennial year of the United States, hence Colorado's nickname of the Centennial State. The outline of the state is an unremarkable rectangle, in part unique because its southwest corner joins Arizona, New Mexico, and Utah in the only point where four states touch. The state's eastern border is a perfectly straight line; the other three borders have slight jogs in them due to surveying errors.

The rectangular shape of Colorado also does not reveal its diverse landforms and ecological zones. Though Colorado was once referred to as the "highest state" and is still thought of by many as mountain country (Colorado has 54 of the 70 highest peaks in the lower 48 states and also has the highest low point of any state), its eastern half is characterized by relatively flat, grassy high plains, a part of the Great Plains, so monotonous and arid

Columbine, the state flower, in Yankee Boy Basin near Mount Sneffels.

that it was referred to as the Great American Desert by early explorer Stephen Long. This region slopes eastward and supports a scattered assortment of mesas, buttes, and hills with relatively shallow drainages in between. The central quarter of the state is dominated by the famous Rocky Mountains, interrupted by great open areas known as parks. Colorado's western quarter slopes away from the mountainous center. This region, referred to as the Western Slope, is a land of rugged beauty with mountains, mesas, and deeply incised rivers. Overlain on this landform is a network of county outlines that carve Colorado into 63 political units ranging in size from Las Animas County at 4,771 square miles to diminutive Gilpin County at 149 square miles. Thus is the setting for a varied collection of county summits ranging from towering granite pinnacles to lowly rises amid rangeland. This is Colorado.

On a highway map you'll notice that Colorado is bisected by Interstate 25, running north to south from Trinidad to Fort Collins. Except for the highpoint of Denver County, all county summits west of I-25 are mountains or over 8,000 feet in elevation. All county summits east of I-25 are under 8,000 feet in elevation and are mesas, buttes, or gentle hills.

Peaks over 14,000 feet high, or Fourteeners, are responsible for 20 of Colorado's 63 county highpoints. These glamour peaks are the most popular of the state's hiking destinations and their routes have been analyzed and described in many fine guidebooks by world-renowned authors. Because of this, we have chosen to provide each peak's simplest route to the summit, although we highly recommend the reader research and evaluate other routes that may provide a more personally satisfying ascent.

COLORADO COUNTY EVOLUTION

Originally, the Territory of Colorado had 17 counties plus the Arapaho and Cheyenne reservations. By 1874, six additional counties had been carved out, two of which (Greenwood and Platte) would later be dissolved. As the state matured and as mining booms created the need for smaller, more functional counties, the number increased to 63. Of the first 17 counties, only Boulder, Clear Creek, and Gilpin have retained their original boundaries.

In 1902, the city of Denver was designated a county by a state amendment. The last counties to be created were Crowley in 1911 and Alamosa in 1913. As of this writing, the Front Range cities of Aurora and Broomfield are considering a statewide vote to allow them to become counties. This, of course, would add two additional highpoints to visit!

COLORADO'S CLIMBING HISTORY

Colorado has a long and colorful climbing history. It has been generally accepted that Native Americans, who occupied the land for centuries before white explorers arrived, were the first to climb many of the peaks and use them as lookouts. Many peaks, including Longs Peak in Rocky Mountain National Park and Blanca Peak in the Sangre de Cristo Range, were climbed by white explorers hoping to claim a first ascent, only to have their hopes dashed by evidence of past climbers, including pits, stone rings, and artifacts.

In the sixteenth and seventeenth centuries, the Spaniards were the first Europeans to explore Colorado. They journeyed north from New Mexico, but they do not appear to have ventured far into the mountain valleys. No evidence exists that any highpoints were first conquered by the Spaniards, although it is highly likely that most of the highpoints in the plains counties were summited by Indians or Spaniards long before the arrival of French trappers and American settlers in the early nineteenth century. Of course, the counties did not exist then, but the highpoints were there!

The nineteenth century was an era of exploration, highlighted by the famed surveys of the 1870s. Zebulon Pike, an early explorer, first reported finding Pikes Peak in 1806, but he was unsuccessful in his attempt to climb it. It remained a great challenge until 1820, when Dr. Edwin James, a member of the Long Expedition, conquered the peak with a small support party. Not long after, a woman, Julia Holmes, climbed Pikes Peak. Soon the exploits of other women, most notably on Longs Peak, had opened the mountains to a whole new breed of mountain women, previously not included in most alpine-style climbing. Pikes Peak was eventually named for the earlier exploits of Zebulon Pike. Dr. James was rewarded with his own peak, which is now the highest point in present-day Gilpin County. He proclaimed Pikes Peak to be the highest point in the United States, and the rush was on to find higher and more challenging peaks in the vast, uncharted wilderness of Colorado. Explorers such as John Fremont, Kit Carson, and Jim Bridger were instrumental in leading climbers into the mountains, and soon entire ranges became known to the outside world.

Pikes Peak was just the first in a long series of mountains claimed to be the highest in Colorado. Longs Peak, Grays Peak, Mount Lincoln, Mount Harvard, Mount Massive, Uncompahgre Peak, and Blanca Peak were all thought at one point to be the highest. It wasn't until the early 1920s that Mount Elbert was properly anointed as the state highpoint.

Longs Peak was first climbed by white adventurers in 1868, and the great decade of mountaineering and, indirectly, highpoint summiting was about to begin. In 1873 the government commissioned two parties, the Hayden and the Wheeler surveys, to explore and map the west, primarily in Colorado. The Wheeler Survey concentrated on mapping mountains from the valleys, but they did record a few first ascents, mainly in the Sangre de Cristo Range and the San Juan Mountains. The Hayden Survey concentrated on the mountains and was responsible for many first ascents, including a large number of what are now county highpoints. Among the unclimbed peaks to fall to this team from 1873 to 1876, although trappers or miners may have been there first, were the highest points in the Elk Range near Aspen, including Castle Peak. The Hayden team went on to summit Mount Wilson and Wilson Peak, near Telluride, in the San Miguel Range; numerous other peaks in the San Juans including Vermilion Peak, summit of San Juan County, West Spanish Peak near Walsenburg, and many of the easier crests of the Sawatch Range near Buena Vista.

7

In the following years, the conquest of other peaks would be added to the records. Hagues Peak in Rocky Mountain National Park was summited by a Mr. Chapin in 1880. By 1900 Mount of the Holy Cross had been sighted, visited, and suffered the indignity of having climbers ascend its famed cross couloir straight to the top. Most of the massive, broad-shouldered peaks in the Sawatch Range had been climbed by 1910, and soon the era of the great mountaineers and rock climbers began. Albert Ellingwood, Robert Ormes, and Dwight Lavender were among the wave of mountaineers who were climbing with better equipment, ropes and pitons, and improved European techniques. In 1916 Ellingwood and his party claimed Crestone Peak, the last Fourteener, and by the 1930s most of the major peaks in Colorado had been climbed. Carl Blaurock soon became the first person to climb all of the Fourteeners, a feat now claimed by over 900 persons. Blaurock is reputed to have performed a headstand on the summit of each peak he visited. Anyone who has been to Sunlight Peak, sister to Mount Eolus, the La Plata County highpoint, would question this man's sanity!

The Colorado Mountain Club (CMC), formed in 1912, began to record the events of the day, and sponsor many outings to Fourteeners and other interesting mountains. Other mountain clubs from out of state, including some from the Midwest, arrived with a hundred or more persons in search of a high alpine experience. Today, the CMC encourages limited group size on outings and minimal impact on the environment. Imagine the damage back then to the fragile lakes, woods, and tundra, as scores of horses and hundreds of feet invaded the valleys!

Lists were submitted to the CMC for publication, including a list of the 100 highest peaks, known as the Centennial Peaks. Spencer Swanger finished that list in 1977, a rather late date for such an important accomplishment. Shortly thereafter, climbers had visited all the Bicentennial Peaks, and eventually the Tricentennial Peaks, that is the 200 and 300 highest named summits in the state, respectively. Next to fall were the Thirteeners, more than 600 peaks above 13,000 feet in elevation.

Bob Martin, a retired oilman and author of climbing articles, is the ultimate Colorado peakbagger. He has done the highest 1,800 peaks in the state! Never one to climb just to merely summit, he revisits many favorite areas and enjoys hiking high passes and ridges. He is the premier student of Colorado peaks.

Climbing all the Colorado county highpoints was first achieved by author John Drew Mitchler in September 1996. Bob Martin, who had previously visited all the mountainous county highpoints, finished the plains counties in 1997; with a visit to Black Mountain in Moffat County, David Olson completed them in 1997 as well. Bob Packard and author Dave Covill reported climbing their last county highpoints, and many others are making progress on the list. Those who have accomplished the 54 Fourteeners already have 20 counties to their credit. It is interesting to note that there are an equal number of plains counties and Fourteener counties, leaving the remaining 23 counties with summits between 8,000 feet and 14,000 feet.

How to Use This Guide

Colorado offers 63 counties with 59 summits, all different in one aspect or another. Some require top physical condition and a moderate amount of mountaineering experience, others require advanced map and compass skills, and still others require excellent ability reading a highway map and a keen road sense. To help sort all this out, we have included a Trail Finder chart that categorizes the county summits by several popular sought-after features and sorts them by relative difficulty. In addition, each chapter provides a quick overview of the nature of the approach and the hike required to reach the actual highpoint. Study the general description, elevation gain, distance to hike, and difficulty, and you'll have a good idea of what to expect once you set out on the trail. Once you have hiked a variety of these county summits, you'll be able to judge any hike by its relative category of difficulty.

ESTIMATING DISTANCES

Distances along highways and roads have been determined by actual odometer readings, and to the extent possible, we had these mileages double-checked by field crews. We suggest, however, that you do not blindly follow only the road mileages but rely also on the lay of the land to aid your approach to the trailhead. In some cases, we took mileages from highway maps and confirmed them on maps of a smaller scale using map measurement wheels. (Note that distances on highway maps are usually designated in small black or red numbers between tick marks or significant landmarks.) Distances along interstate highways can also be verified since exit numbers reflect the nearest milepost, and this sometimes gives a clue to determine distances. Remember that mileage on interstate highways is calculated from south to north and from west to east, and that state and U.S highways are even numbered if they generally run east to west and odd numbered if north to south. If a map does not give distances, use the map scale to approximate the distance on the map. If the road is winding, use a multiplier of 1.2 to 1.5 to account for the added distance.

Whenever possible, trail mileages were gleaned from maps or trail signs in parks and national forests; otherwise, we estimated distance by employing a Silva map odometer to trace the route, or by using a clear ruler and marking each quarter of an inch on the map. On a USGS quad, each quarter of an inch represents about 500 feet, or a tenth of a mile. When estimating distance for a bushwhack, the tendency is to assume that you can hike straight up a ridge or across a slope. This is rarely the case, so we accounted for curves in the trail and switchbacks by measuring the likely route and using a multiplier of 1.5.

RATING A HIKE'S DIFFICULTY

We have categorized the difficulty of Colorado's county summits into drive-up, easy, moderate, and strenuous. All hikes within one category should be similar in nature. Easy hikes generally have less than 1,000 feet of elevation gain and are less than 2 miles long. Moderate hikes require up to 4,000 feet in gain and 5 miles of hiking. Strenuous hikes are over 5,000 feet in gain and require over 6 miles of hiking. Note, however, that there are obvious exceptions to the above generalizations due to the physical nature of a route. Leon Peak of Mesa County is a good example of the exception because, while this peak requires only 830 feet of gain, we list it as a moderate hike because of the tedious and dangerous jumble of boulders lining the way to the top.

Distance and elevation gain are most important in classifying a summit's difficulty rating. We provide one-way distances because our hiking goals are singular points. Although many of the county summits could be visited during a loop hike, few are likely to be done in that manner; therefore, we simply provide the one-way distance to meet the goal. For elevation gain, it is critical that you know the total gross (cumulative) gain, not just the summit minus trailhead elevation difference. Several county summits have downhill sections of trail on the route to the highpoint, and we have made every effort to provide the cumulative elevation required to reach the peak. Comparison of elevation gains with other sources may reveal slightly different numbers. We have attempted to use the most up-to-date information for trail and trailhead location, and it is sometimes at odds with the latest USGS quadrangle but always the result of field observation.

Each climb has been analyzed to determine the climbing difficulty under dry conditions and a class designation assigned, usually representing the most difficult stretch of the easiest route to the summit. The county highpoints do include some class-3 and class-4 climbs. Class 1 is simple hands-in-pockets walking. Class 2 is a hike requiring the use of your arms for balance. Class 3 requires the use of handholds and footholds to negotiate the route, and class 4, requires strong, confident moves with some exposure to a drop of 10 feet or more. Class 5 is technical climbing with rope and harness; it is not required on the easiest route up any Colorado county highpoint. In addition to the class, distance, and elevation gain, we arrived at our overall rating of a county highpoint by considering the exposure to vertical drops at any point on the route. The more demanding county summits have some scary sections that may call for the comfort of rope and harness. You must also consider the most difficult move, or crux maneuver, that the route requires. The exposure and crux combine to define the technical difficulty of the climb and weigh in heavily when ranking a summit's overall difficulty rating. Finally, you may also throw in other variables, such as the remoteness of the area and the distance traveled above timberline where you are exposed to weather.

MAPS

The maps in this guidebook were designed to assist in your overall preparation for reaching Colorado's highpoints. They are *not* intended to be used in place of topographic or other detailed maps, which are a critical part of any backcountry adventure.

For many of the Colorado counties, a well-known, named peak is the highest point. However, the summit for many counties is an unknown rise in the countryside and a USGS quad is essential for identifying the highest point. We have used the USGS 7.5-minute topographic quadrangles, scale 1:24,000, as the primary maps for this guide. Another must-have tool for every serious explorer and highpointer is the Colorado Atlas and Gazetteer, produced by DeLorme Mapping. This atlas will guide you to the trailhead of every county summit, whether mountain or plains. We consider the USDA Forest Service's national forest maps an important source for the identification of road names, trail names, campgrounds, and trailheads. As for state highway maps, those produced by the Colorado Department of Transportation are accurate and descriptive, and those produced by the American Automobile Association often contain road mileages not found elsewhere.

In the Denver area, most outdoor-recreation stores sell these maps and atlases. You can photocopy USGS quads at the main branch of the Denver Public Library, as well as at the larger universities in the area. However, clean original maps must be used for serious backcountry hikes to ensure you have all the color features of the map. In the past year, we have purchased maps from Maps Unlimited, REI, EMS, Mountain Miser, Grand West Outfitters, Neptune Mountaineering in Boulder, and other outdoor-recreation stores.

ELEVATION PROFILES

To provide you with an idea of the nature of each hike, we have profiled the elevation for every significant hike with a gain in excess of 300 feet. To prepare these, we took elevation readings every tenth of a mile, or 528 feet, from trails drawn on the USGS quads. The distances measured from the maps were cross-checked with the distances provided on maps and official trail signposts. All elevation and distance data were entered into a spreadsheet and graphed, using a smoothing function to better approximate actual trail conditions. Key features noted in the text are shown on the profiles. Use the profiles in each chapter for anticipating physical exertion during a hike, planning rest stops, and identifying key points. *Pay attention to the horizontal and vertical scales.* Profiles should be used as relative, not absolute, indications of a trail's inclination.

REGIONS OF COLORADO

We have divided this guidebook into nine regions, grouping the counties in each region by similarity of terrain, as well as by geographic proximity, in order to help you understand their diversity. Each region is accompanied by a map, illustrating the counties and highpoints involved and their relationship to roads and highways. We also note which hikes can best be combined into one-day or weekend excursions, and which can be done as warm-ups to more difficult hikes.

A map and compass are essential tools for all peakbaggers.

Being Prepared

MAKE IT A SAFE TRIP

The Boy Scouts of America have been guided for decades by what is perhaps the single-best piece of safety advice—be prepared! For starters, this means carrying survival and first-aid supplies, proper clothing, a compass, and a topographic map—and knowing how to use them.

Perhaps the second-best piece of safety advice is to tell somebody where you're going and when you plan to return. Pilots must file flight plans before every trip, and anybody venturing into the backcountry should do the same. File your "flight plan" with a friend or relative before taking off.

Close behind your flight plan and being prepared with proper equipment is physical conditioning. Being fit not only makes wilderness travel more fun, it also makes it safer.

To whet your appetite for more knowledge of wilderness safety and preparedness, here are a few more tips:

• Keep your party together.

• Check the weather forecast. Be careful not to get caught by a bad storm or along a stream during a flash flood. These events can occur in all Colorado counties whether on the eastern plains or western mountains. Watch cloud formations closely so you don't get stranded on a ridgeline during a lightning storm.

• Be fully prepared if you intend to travel during cold weather. Avoid exposing skin to cold wind and do not neglect food and water. Travel on snow, especially on steep terrain, only if you are experienced.

• Travel with companions. It's safer until you've gained the substantial experience and skills needed for solo treks.

• Study basic survival and first aid before leaving home.

• Don't eat wild plants unless you can positively identify them.

• Before you leave for the trailhead, find out as much as you can about the route, especially the potential hazards, the physical exertion expected, and a true estimate of the time required.

• Don't exhaust yourself or other members of your party by traveling too far or too fast. Let the slowest person set the pace. All should participate in route finding and decision making.

• Don't wait until you're confused to look at your maps. Follow them as you go along, from the moment you start moving up the trail, so you have a continual fix on your location. Get into the habit of plotting your progress on your map by using a pencil to sketch your route. Add useful information such as the time you reached a landmark and compass bearings you may have taken.

- If you get lost, don't panic. Sit down and relax for a few minutes while you carefully check your topo map and take a reading with your compass. Confidently plan your next move. It's often smart to retrace your steps until you find familiar ground, even if you think it might lengthen your trip. Lots of people get temporarily lost in the wilderness and survive— usually by calmly and rationally dealing with the situation.

- Stay clear of all wild animals.

- Take a first-aid kit that includes, at a minimum, the following: sewing needle, snakebite kit, aspirin, antibacterial ointment, two antiseptic swabs, two butterfly bandages, adhesive tape, four adhesive strips, four gauze pads, two triangular bandages, two inflatable splints, Moleskin or Second Skin for blisters, one roll of 3-inch gauze, a CPR shield, rubber gloves, and lightweight first-aid instructions.

- Take a survival kit that includes, at a minimum, the following: compass, whistle, matches in a waterproof container, cigarette lighter, candle, signal mirror, flashlight, fire starter, aluminum foil, water purification tablets, space blanket, and flare. If you find yourself in an emergency situation, remember to inventory what you have so that helpful tools aren't forgotten in the fright of the moment.

- Last but not least, don't forget that the best defense against unexpected hazards is knowledge. Read up on the latest in wilderness safety information in *Wild Country Companion* by Will Harmon (Falcon Publishing). Check the back of this guidebook for ordering information.

REMOTE PLAINS COUNTIES

Don't be fooled into thinking that outdoor dangers are reserved for only the mountains. The eastern plains counties of Colorado are as remote and exposed to nature as any area found in the high country, including the western slope of Colorado. A few simple suggestions will lead you on a safe and enjoyable visit.

- Plan your trip to the plains by studying the drive and acknowledging the distances involved. Take note of sizable towns.

- Always take a vehicle in good working condition. Check all vehicle fluids before you leave and never enter the countryside without a full fuel tank. In many areas of the plains counties, services are more widely scattered than in the mountains and there are far fewer people around to assist you in the event of a problem.

- Understand that many of the towns identified on the maps are mere ghosts of their former selves. Don't expect services at any but the largest cities and even then only during standard daytime hours.

- Carry a CB radio or cell phone in the event of an emergency or to stay in touch with other vehicles in your caravan, but don't count on your cell phone to work in all locales.

- Heed the weather reports and take immediate steps should a strong thunderstorm or snowstorm develop. A remote county road is no place to be during a spring or fall blizzard. There are monuments scattered across the region in memory of those who thought differently.

- Perhaps most important, remain aware and awake during the long monotonous stretches of highway, not only on the eastern plains but also on the western slope. If sleepy, do not attempt behind-the-wheel gymnastics to stay awake. Stop your vehicle to change the routine. Take a nap. Don't be fooled into thinking you're superhuman and can beat the need for sleep!

- Finally, stay alert as you travel the long straight stretches of highway; sharp jogs and curves in the road are common. These sharp, small bends reflect offset political boundaries not apparently linked to the monotonous landscape and can take the daydreaming driver by total surprise.

YOU MIGHT NEVER KNOW WHAT HIT YOU

Mountains are prone to sudden thunderstorms. If you get caught by a lightning storm, take special precautions, and remember the following:

- Lightning can occur miles from the storm center, so be watchful before the storm approaches and be sure to take cover before the storm hits.

- Don't try to make it back to your vehicle. It isn't worth the risk. Instead, seek shelter even if it's only a short way back to the trailhead. Lightning storms usually don't last long, and from a safe vantage point you might enjoy the sights and sounds.

- Be especially careful not to get caught on a mountaintop or exposed ridge. Also avoid large solitary trees, open areas, and standing water.

- Seek shelter in a low-lying area, ideally in a dense stand of small, uniformly sized trees. Avoid cave entrances, overhangs, and shallow depressions.

- Stay away from anything that might attract lightning, such as metal tent poles, graphite fishing rods, or pack frames.

- Get in a crouch position and place both feet firmly on the ground, next to each other, so as not to create a loop for electrical current to follow.

- If you have a pack (without a metal frame) or a sleeping pad with you, put your feet on it for extra insulation against shock.

- Don't walk or huddle together. Instead, stay 50 feet apart, so if somebody gets hit by lightning, others in your party can give first aid.

- If you're in a tent, stay there in your sleeping bag with your feet on your sleeping pad.

THE SILENT KILLER

Be aware of the danger of hypothermia—a condition in which the body's internal temperature drops below normal. It can lead to mental and physical collapse and death.

Hypothermia is caused by exposure to cold and is aggravated by wetness, wind, and exhaustion. The moment you begin to lose heat faster than your body produces it, you're suffering from exposure. Your body starts involuntary exercise such as shivering to stay warm and makes involuntary adjustments to preserve normal temperature in vital organs, restricting bloodflow in and to the extremities. Both responses drain your energy reserves. The only way to stop the drain is to reduce the degree of exposure.

As energy reserves are exhausted with full-blown hypothermia, the cold affects your brain, depriving you of good judgment and reasoning power. You won't be aware that this is happening. You lose control of your hands. Your internal temperature slides downward. Without treatment, this slide leads to stupor, collapse, and death.

To defend against hypothermia, stay dry. When clothes get wet, they lose about 90 percent of their insulating value. Wool loses relatively less heat; cotton, down, and some synthetics lose more. Choose rain gear that covers the head, neck, body, and legs and provides good protection against wind-driven rain. Most hypothermia cases develop in air temperatures between 30 and 50 degrees, but hypothermia can also develop in warmer temperatures.

If your party is exposed to wind, cold, and wet, think hypothermia. Watch yourself and others for these symptoms: uncontrollable fits of shivering; vague, slow, slurred speech; memory lapses; incoherence; immobile, fumbling hands; frequent stumbling or a lurching gait; drowsiness (to sleep is to die); apparent exhaustion; and an inability to get up after a rest. When a member of your party has hypothermia, he or she may deny any problem. Believe the symptoms, not the victim. Even mild symptoms demand treatment:

- Get the victim out of the wind and rain.

- Strip off all wet clothes.

- If the victim is only mildly impaired, administer warm drinks. Then get the victim into warm clothes and a warm sleeping bag. Place well-wrapped water bottles filled with heated water close to the victim.

- If the victim is badly impaired, try to keep him or her awake. Put the victim in a sleeping bag with another person—both naked. If you have a double bag, put two warm people in with the victim.

BE MOUNTAIN LION ALERT

Mountains lions (also known as pumas or cougars) are found throughout the West in desert, chaparral, forest, and even high mountain regions. Remnant populations are also scattered in pockets across southern Texas, Louisiana,

Alabama, Tennessee, and the southern tip of Florida. Rare sightings are reported in New England, upstate New York, and Canada's Maritime Provinces. Mountain lions are generally found anywhere deer and other large prey are plentiful.

Mountain lions are most active between dusk and dawn. They hunt by stalking their prey, then lunging or rushing from behind. The kill is made with a bite to the back of the neck or base of the skull. A mountain lion feeding on a kill may aggressively defend itself against all intruders. They are capable of leaping 20 feet and can outrun a deer over short distances. An adult male can reach 8 feet long and weigh 150 pounds.

When traveling or camping in mountain lion country, make lots of noise, especially around dawn and dusk when mountain lions are likely to be most active. Travel in groups of two or more.

Mountain lions may view children as prey because of their small size. Closely supervise children and do not let them roam out of sight. Also instruct them that running and high-pitched noises may attract a mountain lion and provoke an attack. Dogs are also attractive prey for hungry cats; it's best to leave dogs at home.

Frequently check on your pack animals, particularly at night if the horses seem nervous or spooked.

Sightings of mountain lions are rare, and even when a large cat is seen it's usually just a glimpse of disappearing fur and tail. Yet reports of mountain lion attacks are on the rise, particularly in California, Colorado, and Montana. Many of the recent attacks occurred near homes or rural residential areas, and most of the victims were small children. Experts say this trend is a result of residential sprawl overtaking mountain lion habitat and an increase in the mountain lion population. As young mountain lions are forced into new territory, they more often come into contact with people. Attacks in the backcountry are still relatively rare.

If you do happen to meet a mountain lion, heed the following guidelines (adapted from the Colorado Division of Wildlife):

- Do not approach a mountain lion, especially one that is feeding, appears injured, or has kittens in tow. Most big cats will flee on sight; give them room to escape.

- Stay calm, talking firmly in a monotone. Stand still or move slowly. Face the cat and remain standing. Do all you can to appear taller and larger— open a coat, raise your arms above your head. Pick up and hold small children so they won't run. Back away slowly if it seems safe to do so.

- Teach everyone in your group, and especially children, to stand still if a mountain lion is encountered. Running triggers a mountain lion's instinct to attack, and any cat can easily outrun a person.

- If a mountain lion lingers or acts aggressively, throw stones or branches at it. Do not turn your back on the cat. Continue to speak firmly and keep your arms outstretched. Try to convince the mountain lion that you are not prey and may in fact be a danger to it.

- If a mountain lion actually attacks, fight back with all your might. DO NOT play dead. Try to remain standing and facing the cat at all times. Hit it with rocks, branches, or walking sticks; punch and kick at the cat's face, neck, and belly. People have successfully fended off mountain lions with their bare hands.

- Report all mountain lion sightings immediately to a land management or wildlife official.

For more information, read *Mountain Lion Alert* by Steve Torres (Falcon Publishing, 1997).

Seasons and Weather

Colorado weather is notorious for being constantly changing and severe, on this you can depend. Plan for it. Consult a good source for weather information before going on any hike. Television and daily newspapers are timely, and the Internet also has outstanding sources, including real-time satellite and radar images (see, for example, www.weather.com). No matter what the forecast, use your own judgment, and turn back if there is a threat to your safety. Clouds can form in a matter of minutes on the opposite side of the mountain that you are hiking, and many hikers have been caught out in the open, high on a mountain in Colorado. This is a very real danger; each year hikers are hospitalized with hypothermia and succumb to lightning strikes. When hiking higher elevations, always plan on cold, wet, windy conditions even if the weather at the trailhead is sunny and warm.

The best season for hiking coincides, unfortunately, with the worst season for thunderstorms. You are likely to encounter a thunderstorm and a chance of precipitation on most midday hikes between June and early September. Actually some of the best hiking weather in Colorado can be had later, from mid-September through October, depending on the advent of snowfall. Many of the hikes listed in this guidebook can be enjoyed during this period.

Summer heat can be oppressive on the eastern plains of Colorado, and we encourage you to visit these highpoints in the spring or fall. The plains are usually free of snow by March, especially in the southeastern corner of

Young hikers should form good habits about watching the weather.

the state, although you should avoid the spring calving season if possible. Fall is thought of by many as the most scenic time of year, and indeed, with the aspens in full glow of golden splendor, it enhances any high country hike.

When winter sets in, consider snowshoeing or cross-country skiing on those summits with gentle slopes and less avalanche danger. Several county highpoints can be easily and safely enjoyed during the winter, and the experiences and views are completely different from what many hikers are used to seeing. We visited most of the county highpoints on the plains during the winter months and were surprised by the relatively dry conditions, especially during December and January. However, a severe snowstorm did spring up during one trip, making traveling very difficult even with a four-wheel-drive vehicle. Consult a weather forecast, and be prepared in the event of a major snowfall, something entirely possible in this state during spring and fall. Snows have come to Denver as early as September, and by mid-October most mountain peaks have received a troublesome amount of snow. The month with the most precipitation is March, followed by April.

Leave No Trace

Going into a wild area is like visiting a famous museum. You obviously don't want to leave your mark on an art treasure in the museum. If everybody going through the museum left one little mark, the piece of art would be quickly destroyed—and of what value is a big building full of trashed art? The same goes for pristine wildlands. If we all left just one little mark on the landscape, the backcountry would soon be spoiled.

A wilderness can accommodate human use as long as everybody behaves. A few thoughtless or uninformed visitors, however, can ruin it for everybody who follows. All backcountry users have a responsibility to know and follow the rules of no-trace camping.

Nowadays most wilderness users want to walk softly, but some aren't aware that they have poor manners. Often their actions are dictated by the outdated habits of a past generation of campers who cut green boughs for evening shelters, built campfires with fire rings, and dug trenches around tents. In the 1950s, these camping habits may have been acceptable, but they left long-lasting scars, and today such behavior is absolutely unacceptable. Although Colorado is fortunate to have received increased wilderness designations in recent years, popular wild places have become crowded. Many camping areas now show unsightly signs of heavy use.

Consequently, a new code of ethics is growing out of the necessity of coping with the unending waves of people who want a perfect backcountry experience. Today we all must leave no clues that we were there. Enjoy the wild, but leave no trace of your visit.

Three Falcon Principles of "Leave No Trace"

- Leave with everything you brought in.
- Leave no sign of your visit.
- Leave the landscape as you found it.

Most of us know better than to litter—in or out of the backcountry. Be sure you leave nothing, regardless of how small it is, along the trail or at your campsite. This means pack out everything, including orange peels, flip tops, cigarette butts, and gum wrappers. Also, pick up any trash that others leave behind.

Follow the main trail. Avoid cutting switchbacks and walking on vegetation beside the trail. Don't pick up "souvenirs," such as rocks, antlers, or wildflowers. The next person wants to see them, too, and collecting such souvenirs violates many regulations.

Avoid making loud noises on the trail (unless you are in bear or mountain lion country) or in camp. Be courteous; remember, sound travels easily in the backcountry, especially across water.

The authors lead a successful, if snowy, May summit climb for Colorado Mountain Club's Wilderness Trekking School.

Carry a lightweight trowel to bury human waste 6 to 8 inches deep at least 300 feet from any water source. Pack out used toilet paper.

Go without a campfire. Carry a stove for cooking and a flashlight, candle lantern, or headlamp for light. For emergencies, learn how to build a no-trace fire.

Camp in designated sites when they are available. Otherwise, camp and cook on durable surfaces such as bedrock, sand, gravel bars, or bare ground.

Finally, and perhaps most important, strictly follow the pack-in/pack-out rule. If you carry something into the backcountry, consume it or carry it out.

Leave no trace—and put your ear to the ground and listen carefully. Thousands of people coming behind you are thanking you for your courtesy and good sense.

Details on these guidelines and of "Leave No Trace" recommendations for specific outdoor activities can be found in the guidebook *Leave No Trace* by Will Harmon (Falcon Publishing, 1998). Visit your local bookstore, or call Falcon Publishing at 800-582-2665 for a copy.

Trail Finder

	EASY	MODERATE	DIFFICULT
To see a lake		27 Mesa 29 Rio Blanco	14 Larimer 20 Alamosa-Costilla-Huerfano 21 Custer-Saguache
To see a waterfall	55 Prowers	31 Archuleta 34 Hinsdale	21 Custer-Saguache 30 Routt 35 La Plata
To see interesting geology	26 Garfield 55 Prowers	23 Las Animas 36 Mineral 53 Bent	21 Custer-Saguache
To visit hot springs		10 Clear Creek-Summit 38 Montrose	15 Chaffee 17 Gunnison-Pitkin 30 Routt 39 Ouray
To be in true wilderness	26 Garfield	13 Jackson	14 Larimer 16 Eagle 30 Routt 35 La Plata
To view wildflowers		29 Rio Blanco 32 Conejos 34 Hinsdale	17 Gunnison-Pitkin 37 Montezuma 39 Ouray
To view wildlife	52 Baca	8 Weld 10 Clear Creek-Summit 25 Delta 36 Mineral	35 La Plata
For a gentle trail	6 El Paso-Teller 28 Moffat 43 Morgan 45 Sedgwick 54 Otero	8 Weld	
For a well-defined route	40 Rio Grande	10 Clear Creek-Summit 34 Hinsdale	9 Boulder 15 Chaffee 18 Lake

	EASY	MODERATE	DIFFICULT
For a bushwhack	55 Prowers	4 Douglas 36 Mineral 38 Montrose	7 Jefferson 22 Fremont
That are handicap accessible	1 Adams 3 Denver 6 El Paso-Teller 44 Phillips 50 Washington 51 Yuma		
If you want to climb high			9 Boulder 21 Custer-Saguache 33 Dolores-San Miguel 35 La Plata 41 San Juan
If you want to take a ridge walk		12 Grand 32 Conejos 36 Moderate	20 Alamosa-Costilla- Huerfano 22 Fremont 37 Montezuma
For an alpine environment		19 Park	9 Boulder 21 Custer-Saguache 33 Dolores-San Miguel 39 Ouray 41 San Juan
If you want to see a lot of other people	6 El Paso-Teller	10 Clear Creek-Summit 11 Gilpin	9 Boulder 18 Lake 39 Ouray
For kids	6 El Paso-Teller 24 Pueblo 28 Moffat 40 Rio Grande 54 Otero	29 Rio Blanco	
If you want to take pictures		34 Hinsdale 36 Mineral 53 Bent	9 Boulder 21 Custer-Saguache 39 Ouray
With good trailhead campgrounds	24 Pueblo 52 Baca	23 Las Animas 27 Mesa 34 Hinsdale	9 Boulder

	EASY	MODERATE	DIFFICULT
With scenic towns nearby		23 Las Animas 36 Mineral	9 Boulder 21 Custer-Saguache 39 Ouray 41 San Juan
For side trips along the trail	52 Baca	19 Park 36 Mineral	20 Alamosa-Costilla- Huerfano 35 La Plata 39 Ouray
For the best summit views		23 Las Animas	9 Boulder 15 Chaffee 21 Custer-Saguache 35 La Plata 41 San Juan
For a long hike (over 10 miles round trip)		36 Mineral	9 Boulder 14 Larimer 15 Chaffee 16 Eagle 17 Gunnison-Pitkin 20 Alamosa-Costilla- Huerfano 21 Custer-Saguache 30 Routt 35 La Plata

Colorado County Highpoints

Colorado County Highpoints That Might Require Orienteering and Mountaineering Skills

	County	Highpoint	Elevation	Skills Required
1	Adams	DIA Ridge	5,665	OM
2	Arapahoe	Smoky Hill Ridge	6,210	
3	Denver	Kipling near Belleview	5,680	
4	Douglas	Thunder Butte	9,836	O
5	Elbert	Elbert Rock	7,360	
6	El Paso	Pikes Peak	14,110	
6	Teller	Devil's Playground	13,060	
7	Jefferson	Buffalo Peak	11,589	O, M*
8	Weld	Buffalo Butte	6,380	
9	Boulder	Longs Peak	14,255	M*
10	Clear Creek / Summit	Grays Peak	14,270	
11	Gilpin	James Peak	13,294	O, M*
12	Grand	Pettingell Peak	13,553	
13	Jackson	Clark Peak	12,951	
14	Larimer	Hagues Peak	13,560	M*
15	Chaffee	Mount Harvard	14,420	M*
16	Eagle	Mount of the Holy Cross	14,005	M*
17	Gunnison / Pitkin	Castle Peak	14,265	M*
18	Lake	Mount Elbert	14,433	
19	Park	Mount Lincoln	14,286	
20	Alamosa, Costilla, and			
	Huerfano	Blanca Peak	14,345	M*
21	Saguache	Crestone Peak	14,260	M
21	Custer	East Crestone Peak	14,294	M
22	Fremont	Bushnell Peak	13,105	
23	Las Animas	West Spanish Peak	13,626	
24	Pueblo	Greenhorn Mountain	12,347	
25	Delta	Mount Lamborn	11,396	O, M*
26	Garfield	Flat Top Mountain	12,354	
27	Mesa	Leon Pk	11,236	O
28	Moffat	Black Mountain	10,840	
29	Rio Blanco	Orno Peak NW Ridge	12,027	O
30	Routt	Mount Zirkel	12,180	M
31	Archuleta	Summit Peak	13,300	O
32	Conejos	Conejos Peak	13,172	
33	Dolores	Mount Wilson	14,017	M
33	San Miguel	Wilson Peak	14,246	M
34	Hinsdale	Uncompaghre Peak	14,309	
35	La Plata	Mount Eolus	14,083	M
36	Mineral	Gwynedd Mountain	13,895	
37	Montezuma	Hesperus Mountain	13,232	O, M*
38	Montrose	Castle Rock	11,453	O
39	Ouray	Mount Sneffels	14,150	M*

	County	Highpoint	Elevation	Skills required
40	Rio Grande	Bennett Peak	13,203	
41	San Juan	Vermilion Peak	13,894	M
42	Logan	State Line Bluff	4,940	
43	Morgan	Judson Hills	4,935	
44	Phillips	County Line Rise	4,120	
45	Sedgwick	Sand Hill	4,120	
46	Crowley	Schubert Hill	5,220	
47	Cheyenne	Ranch Road	5,290	
47	Kit Carson	Ranch Road	5,255	
48	Kiowa	Selenite Bluff	4,690	
49	Lincoln	County Line Rise	5,960	
50	Washington	Presidents' Hill	5,420	
51	Yuma	Yuma Corner	4,440	
52	Baca	Carrizo Mountain	5,280	
53	Bent	San Jose Ranch Mesa	4,855	
54	Otero	Dry Bluff	5,260	
55	Prowers	Two Buttes	4,711	

Blank = No special skills required.

O = Orienteering skills required.

M* = Requires rock scrambling that may be uncomfortable to some hikers and may be dangerous in wet or snowy conditions.

M = Serious peak challenges; some parties may feel more comfortable with rope and harness.

Many of the peaks require rope, ice axe, and crampons during winter and the snow season.

Some climbers carry an ice axe on every Fourteener climb no matter the season.

Front Range and Foothills

1 Adams County—DIA Ridge

2 Arapahoe County—Smoky Hill Ridge

3 Denver County—Kipling and Belleview

4 Douglas County—Thunder Butte

5 Elbert County—Elbert Rock

6 El Paso and Teller Counties—Pikes Peak and Devils Playground

7 Jefferson County—Buffalo Peak

8 Weld County—Bison Butte

The Front Range and Foothills are where the two great regions of Colorado come together, geologically speaking. The granite mountains here form an interesting contrast to the upturned sedimentary rocks that underlie the plains, and the hikes are perhaps the most diverse of Colorado's nine regions. The foothills and plains are well represented, and massive Pikes Peak, a major mountain unto itself, is situated here. The highpoints can be reached by and large via interstate highway and paved secondary roads. This region includes some of the easiest summits, as well as perhaps the most difficult bushwhack, Buffalo Peak in Jefferson County. There are many other things to see and do in this area, and if you are visiting from far away, we recommend planning an extended stay in the Denver or Colorado Springs area. Pikes Peak and the Devils Playground can be combined as one excursion, and the Denver, Arapahoe, and Adams county highpoints also make for a nice half-day drive, with the possibility of adding Elbert County to that list. The Weld County highpoint requires advance notice.

Front Range and Foothills

▲ 8 Bison Butte

WELD

25

85

1

392

257 27

34

60

34

36

66

76

79

ADAMS

121

93 58

▲ 1 DIA Ridge

36

74 88

DENVER

ARAPAHOE

E-470

3 Kipling & Belleview

C-470

2 Smoky Hill Ridge

285

JEFFERSON

70

7 Buffalo Peak ▲

ELBERT

DOUGLAS

86

4 Thunder Butte

5 Elbert Rock ▲

67

83

24

TELLER

6 Pikes Peak

6 Devils Playground ▲

94

83

EL PASO

1   Adams County: DIA Ridge

General description: A short drive from downtown Denver, this summit is a gentle rise on a county road close to the new Denver International Airport (DIA).

Type of trip: Drive-up.

Distance: None.

Difficulty: Easy.

Elevation gain: No gain.

Summit elevation: 5,665 feet.

Maps: USGS Quad—Denver International Airport (formerly Box Elder School) (optional), DeLorme p. 41.

Access/permits: Adams County road right-of-way.

Best months: Year-round.

Location: North-central Colorado, about 10 miles east of Denver, and 6.5 miles south of the DIA terminal, and about 3 miles northeast of the Interstate 70 / E-470 interchange.

Finding the trailhead: The Adams County highpoint is located on rural 26th Avenue and can be approached from either westbound or eastbound I-70. If traveling east from I-25, I-225, or Pena Boulevard (the entrance to DIA), take exit 286 from I-70 south onto Tower Road (Colorado Highway 32). Proceed south across the railroad tracks and at 0.3 mile turn left (east) onto Smith Road. This takes you east back under I-70. After driving about 2 miles, turn left (north) on Piccadilly Road and cross the railroad tracks again. Continue another 0.3 miles, then take the next right (east) onto 26th Avenue, which turns from gravel to blacktop east of the new E-470 highway. Watch for Powhaton Mile Road (County Road 81) about 2 miles east of E-470. The highpoint is the rise 0.5 mile east of this road.

If traveling west on I-70, take Watkins exit 295 right (north) on County Road 24N. Cross over U.S. Highway 36 and take a jog to the left (west) around the railroad tracks. Continue north to 26th Avenue, a distance of 1.4 miles from US 36. Turn left and drive 3.5 miles west on 26th Avenue, passing by Monaghan Road (CR 21N) on your right (north) at 3 miles. The highpoint is the rise 0.5 mile west of Monaghan Road. The E-470 toll road, scheduled to open in 1999, is 2.5 miles west of the highpoint.

Upon reaching the highpoint, park safely off the county road and watch for vehicles as you admire the surrounding farmland. The highest elevation lies under the blacktop of the road. Although the land at the farmhouse about 1 mile to the north appears as high or higher, this is an optical illusion. By careful handlevel observations and backsighting, we have determined the land to the north to be lower.

The hike: This highpoint is on a county road with no hiking required. It is part of a ridge about 1 mile wide that extends north to Denver International Airport. From this summit you can gaze down at Watkins, about 3 miles southeast, and Manila, about 7 miles due east. The Amoco gas processing

Adams County: DIA Ridge

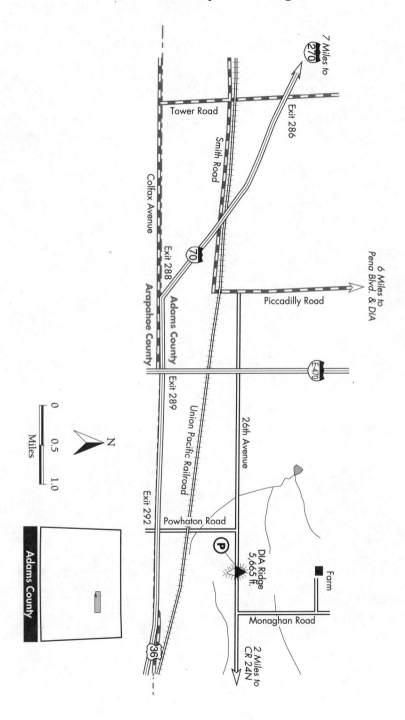

Jet airliners fly over the Adams County highpoint on approach to Denver International Airport, the world's largest airport.

plant commands your attention to the southwest. Try to spot the control tower of DIA poking above the northern horizon to the left of the farmhouse. We recommend you visit this site just before sunset as the evening light brings out the beauty of the gently rolling countryside. You can also watch airplanes fly overhead as they approach the airport. This highpoint requires driving gravel county roads that can cause steering difficulty. Don't speed! Be extra cautious of traffic traveling over the highpoint hill.

County highlights: Brighton, the county seat of Adams County, was established in 1901 and named for Alva Adams (1850–1922), the fifth, tenth, and fourteenth governor of the state of Colorado. Apparently, Mr. Adams needed some time off between terms to renew his gubernatorial vigor. Of the 3,142 counties in the United States, 203 are named in honor of presidents. This is one of the few counties, however, that seems to have a presidential namesake, but which in fact was named for someone other than a president.

Adams County is a mixture of residential, agricultural, and industrial characteristics. It is home to many who work in the county, but also to those who work in Denver and other nearby cities. Adams County was settled during the 1859 gold rush by Colonel Jack Henderson when he set camp on an island in the middle of the South Platte River, creating the town of Henderson.

Barr Lake State Park, a short distance north along I-76, is home to several nesting pairs of bald eagles, as well as numerous other species of birds. The Rocky Mountain Arsenal lies about 7 miles west of the highpoint. This former army installation manufactured chemical weapons and potent pesticides, but as a Superfund site it is now being converted into one of the nation's largest urban wildlife refuges. It will be administered by the U.S. Fish and Wildlife Service.

Camping and services: There are no camping facilities in the general area. Lodging and services can be found at various exits along I-70.

2 Arapahoe County: Smoky Hill Ridge

General description:	This grassy ridge on the plains requires the negotiation of a 10-foot road embankment.
Distance:	100 feet.
Difficulty:	Easy.
Elevation gain:	10 feet.
Summit elevation:	6,210 feet.
Maps:	USGS Quad—Piney Creek (optional), DeLorme p. 41.
Access/permits:	Arapahoe County road right-of-way.
Best months:	Year-round.

Location: North-central Colorado at the southeast edge of metropolitan Denver, on Smoky Hill Road and E-470, a mile northwest of the junction of Arapahoe, Douglas, and Elbert counties.

Finding the trailhead: From Interstate 25 in southeast Denver, take I-225 northeastward 4 miles past Cherry Creek Lake to exit 4 and exit right (south) onto South Parker Road. Zero your trip odometer. Go south 1.8 miles and take Quincy Avenue left (east). Proceed only 0.3 mile and turn right (south) onto Smoky Hill Road. Follow this four-lane road southeast for 6.5 miles to E-470, gaining the top of a pronounced ridge after 3.4 miles. Watch for good views of the Front Range after 3.8 miles. After passing over E-470, continue south on Smoky Hill Road past the radio towers on the hill at the milepost 10 sign and enjoy a view of your goal 1.2 miles away. The highpoint is at the junction of Smoky Hill Road and Otero Drive, 11.4 miles from I-225. Turn right (west) off Smoky Hill Road onto Otero Drive and park off the street out of traffic.

You can also reach Smoky Hill Road from E-470, which is a beltway being constructed around the Denver metropolitan area. (The stretch of E-470 from Smoky Hill Road to I-25 opened in July 1998 and is a toll road. The stretch of E-470 from Smoky Hill Road to I-70 to the north is scheduled to open July 1999.) From I-25, take exit 194 (E-470 exit 1) near Park Meadows Mall and proceed east on E-470 to exit 10, passing two tollbooths on the way. Go right (south) on Smoky Hill Road 2.8 miles to the highpoint. If coming from I-70, take exit 289 (E-470 exit 20, opening in summer 1999) and proceed south to exit 10 and pay a toll. Go left (south) on Smoky Hill Road 2.8 miles to the highpoint.

To avoid tolls, you may take exit 97 off I-25 onto Arapahoe Road. Proceed east for 4.5 miles to Parker Road. Continue straight across Parker Road (most lanes turn north or south) on Arapahoe Road, and continue another 4 miles to Liverpool Road (County Road 67). Turn left (north) and follow Liverpool Road north for 0.9 mile. Turn right (east) at the light onto Smoky Hill Road as it trends southeast for 4.6 miles to Otero Drive.

Arapahoe County: Smoky Hill Ridge

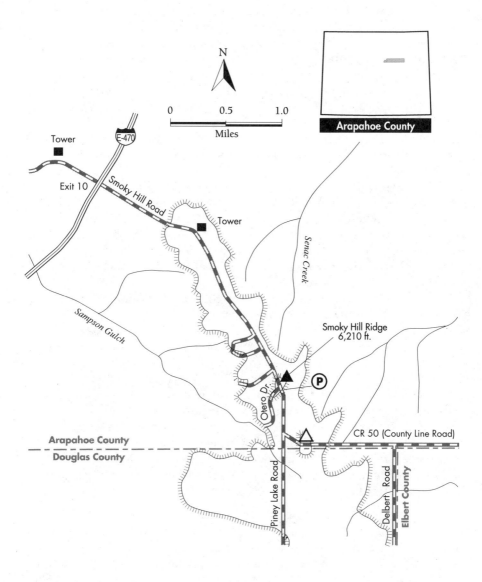

N

0   0.5   1.0
Miles

Arapahoe County

Tower

E-470

Exit 10   Smoky Hill Road

Tower

Senac Creek

Sampson Gulch

Smoky Hill Ridge
6,210 ft.

P

Otero Dr.

Arapahoe County
Douglas County

CR 50 (County Line Road)

Piney Lake Road

Delbert Road

Elbert County

The hike: At the intersection of Smoky Hill Road and Otero Drive, carefully cross to the east side of Smoky Hill Road and ascend the road embankment to the highest point of land in Arapahoe County. In this area, along Smoky Hill Road, three separate closed contours (areas of similar elevation) exceed 6,210 feet. Field observation using handlevels indicates that the northern area at Otero Drive is the highest. There is no benchmark or register. Watch for speeding rural traffic on this roller-coaster county road. Take care as you cross the road to the highpoint.

The other two contours of similar elevation are located just south of Otero Drive. Although lower in elevation, you may want to visit these two areas in case future widening of Smoky Hill Road wipes out the high hill at Otero Drive. To reach these two areas, go south on Smoky Hill Road toward Douglas County. After 0.4 mile you come to a stop sign at the junction of Smoky Hill Road (to the north), Piney Lake Road (directly south), and County Line Road (angling to the southeast). Turn left onto County Line Road and proceed 0.2 mile to the top of a hill where the road again bends slightly to the east. Pull completely off the road on the right (south) side. The area that lies directly across the county road to the north is one of the high contours. The other lies slightly farther north and appears to be a linear manmade dirt pile. Get close to the ground and observe that the hill near Otero Drive is slightly higher. This is why we carry handlevels, highpointers!

There is year-round access, but you might want to avoid this area in the winter if there is substantial snowfall, since the wind can cause drifts. Wait for a sunny day, as this is a good highpoint to bag in your off-season. The ridge is an erosional feature that extends for at least 10 miles to the southeast. There is a good view of the Front Range, 2.7 miles north of E-470 on Smoky Hill Road. You can spot Pikes Peak far to the south, Mount Evans to the west, and Longs Peak to the north. You can also spot the dark blue of Aurora Reservoir nestled in the gullies to the north. The plains roll off to the east and to the south the hills develop until they become the wooded area known as the Black Forest. Firmer siltstone layers of the Denver and Dawson formations form the ridge. Numerous prairie dogs make this area their home, and songbirds native to the plains can be seen in the summer when you get away from the main roads.

County highlights: Littleton, the county seat of Arapahoe County, was established in 1861. Note that the spelling of Arapahoe County is different from that of the Arapaho Indian tribe, who were once inhabitants on the plains in this area. Smoky Hill Road was named after the Smoky Hill Trail, which brought gold miners from Kansas along the Smoky Hill River. This trail was more direct than other routes, but the lack of game and water earned it the nickname "Starvation Trail." Note that Otero Street is the entrance to the Stage Run housing subdivision, named after the image of an old Smoky Hill stagecoach route. The land to the east and north of the highpoint is the 59,000-acre Lowry Bombing Range, which was used for military training from World War II through the Vietnam Conflict and which is now undergoing a munitions cleanup.

The Arapahoe County highpoint is a gentle but distinct rise on Smoky Hill Ridge.

Camping and services: There are no campgrounds available in the immediate vicinity. Motels can be found in the Parker Road and I-225 area. If you are interested in camping, try Cherry Creek State Park, a very popular summer destination for sailors, water skiers, and sun worshipers. There are two resevoirs a short distance from the highpoint. Aurora Reservoir, opened in 1991, allows swimming and electric motorboats, while Quincy Reservoir caters to fishermen. Although located just south of the county line in Douglas County, the new, ultrachic Park Meadows Mall may interest you. You can also brag of your highpoint exploits at our favorite spot for chicken wings, the Piper Inn, located a couple miles north of I-225 on Parker Road at Iliff Avenue. Ask for the Chinese style. The place has an incredibly eclectic clientele, ranging from businessmen to bikers. Bonus points if you arrive at the highpoint on your Harley!

3   Denver County: Kipling and Belleview

General description:	A suburban street in residential southwest Denver requires a short walk from side street parking.
Distance:	400 feet.
Difficulty:	Drive-up.
Elevation gain:	5 feet.
Summit elevation:	5,680 feet.
Maps:	USGS Quad, Fort Logan (optional)—DeLorme p. 41.
Access/permits:	City and county of Denver street right-of-way.
Best months:	Year-round.

Location: North-central Colorado, southwest Denver, half a block north of South Jellison Way (Jellison) near South Kipling Parkway (Kipling), 1 block north of West Belleview Avenue (Belleview).

Finding the trailhead: You may approach this highpoint from either the north or the south. If coming from the north, exit U.S. Highway 285, Hampden Avenue, south onto Kipling. Kipling is a four-lane avenue and gradually ascends a ridge. Travel south past an impressive federal correctional institution on the left (east) and proceed past West Quincy Avenue. Continue 0.6 mile south of West Quincy Avenue and watch for West Saratoga Place to the left (east), 1.6 miles from US 285.

If coming from the south, exit C-470, the beltway of metropolitan Denver, onto Kipling and proceed north on the four-lane avenue. Kipling traffic moves fairly fast for a street that winds through a residential area! After 4.5 miles, cross through the Belleview/Kipling intersection, which has retail outlets on the corners. Proceed through the Belleview light, to the second right, which is West Saratoga Place, 5 miles north of C-470. Turn right (east).

West Saratoga Place enters a fairly modern, moderately priced residential area. Proceed approximately 200 feet and take the first right onto South Johnson Street. After 0.15 mile the street makes a hard left and becomes West Chenango Avenue. Park along the curb in the bend formed by this hard left.

The hike: Once parked, walk the sidewalk on the right (west) side of the street and observe, between the two houses numbered 4895 and 4897, a straight sidewalk right-of-way lined with tall wooden fencing that extends west to Kipling. Walk this and upon reaching Kipling, turn left (south) on the sidewalk for approximately 200 feet to the end of the wooden fence that borders backyards. At this location there is an obvious phone junction box next to the sidewalk. This is Denver's highpoint.

At this point, you are standing at the extreme west edge of the city and county of Denver. If you walk to Jellison you have gone too far. Jefferson County, immediately south of the fencing, is where retail shops, a major home improvement store, and a gas station are located. Across Kipling is a

Denver County: Kipling and Belleview

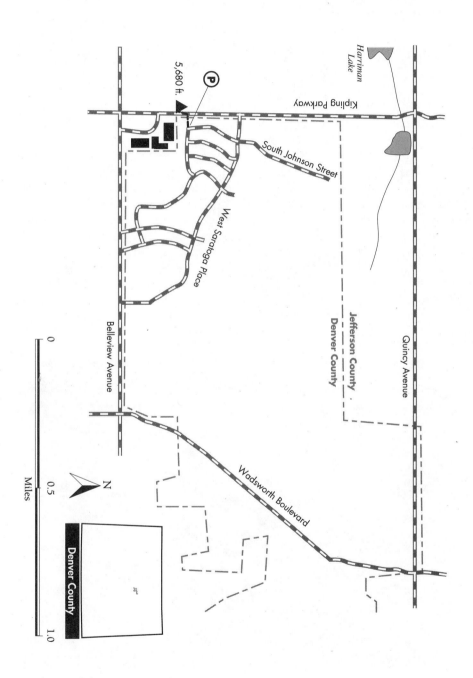

good vantage point from which to photograph the highpoint, but it may take five minutes or more to negotiate the traffic. Use the traffic lights at Belleview to cross Kipling. This highpoint can be visited year-round and offers a magnificent view of speeding suburban traffic.

The area originally consisted of gently rolling rangeland. Before Denver annexed land to the southwest in the 1970s during construction of the Southwest Plaza Mall, its highest point of land (elevation 5,480 feet) was located at 5005 West 33rd Avenue, adjacent to Pferdesteller Park near West 33rd Avenue and Yates Street. This area is immediately east of Sheridan Boulevard ten blocks north of Sloan Lake. A beautiful house sits at this location. In fact, homes and schools throughout the area display classic fancy Denver brickwork. The lowest point in Denver is located along the South Platte River under the bridge at East 52nd Avenue and Franklin Street, in the city's industrial area on the far northside.

Other locations that recently have been cited as being among the highest points in Denver include Inspiration Point (elevation 5,415 feet), just west of Regis University at Sheridan Boulevard and West 50th Avenue, and Mountain View Country Club (elevation 5,670 feet) at Belleview Avenue and I-25.

From Denver's highpoint, the foothills may be seen just a few miles to the west. The resistant layers of the Dakota Sandstone extend west to the foothills, where they are upturned and eroded to form the Hogback. In addition to numerous city parks, Denver has an extensive system of mountain parks, including nearby Red Rocks Amphitheatre where concerts are set against a spectacular red sandstone cliff backdrop. The growing bicycle

Look for the sidewalk right-of-way that provides convenient access from a side street to the Denver County highpoint.

and hiking trail system is being linked to systems in neighboring counties and is rivaled by few areas in the United States. Enjoy the quiet of Harriman Lake Park at Kipling and Quincy, just 0.5 mile north of the highpoint. Stop here for a few quiet moments and observe the birdlife in an area close to Denver, yet far removed from the urban setting. This is perhaps why many people move to Colorado. All the amenities of a fast-paced, high-tech world are here, with a quiet spot to enjoy the natural splendor just around the corner. Please respect the local property owners and park your vehicle in a legal zone in the neighborhood cul-de-sac, and come and go quietly, especially if you choose to visit during the evening.

County highlights: Denver is the county seat of Denver County, which was established in 1901. The county was named for General James William Denver (1812–1872), who was governor in 1858 of the Kansas Territory when most of Colorado was part of this territory. William Larimer and his partners hoped the governor, having a town named after him, would reward the new settlement by naming it the county seat of what was then Arapahoe County, Kansas. From such humble beginnings sprang the Queen City of the Plains. The Denver metropolitan area is now home to approximately two million people and a Superbowl champion football team.

Camping and services: This urban setting is not suitable for camping. Lodging is available in this area, and concentrated at the intersection of Wadsworth and Hampden northeast of the highpoint. Restaurants and gas stations are located along Kipling and Belleview south of the highpoint.

4   Douglas County: Thunder Butte

General description:	A half-day bushwhack through level forest and up a boulder hillside to a wooded peak with a grand view of Pikes Peak.
Distance:	2.3 miles, one-way.
Difficulty:	Moderate.
Elevation gain:	1,316 feet.
Summit elevation:	9,836 feet.
Maps:	USGS Quad—Westcreek (required), DeLorme p. 50, Trails Illustrated #135.
Access/permits:	Pike National Forest.
Best months:	May–October.

Location: Central Colorado, about 30 miles southwest of Denver, about 7 miles south of Deckers.

Finding the trailhead: Head southwest on U.S. Highway 285 from metropolitan Denver to Pine Junction. Turn left on Colorado Highway 126 and

Douglas County: Thunder Butte

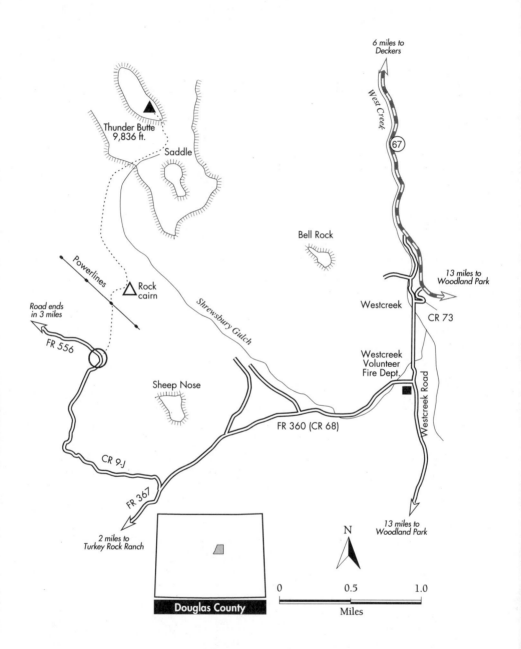

6 miles to
Deckers

West Creek

67

13 miles to
Woodland Park

Thunder Butte
9,836 ft.

Saddle

Bell Rock

Westcreek

CR 73

Powerlines

Rock
cairn

Road ends
in 3 miles

Shrewsbury Gulch

FR 556

Westcreek
Volunteer
Fire Dept.

Westcreek Road

Sheep Nose

FR 360 (CR 68)

CR 9-J

FR 367

2 miles to
Turkey Rock Ranch

Douglas County

N

13 miles to
Woodland Park

0   0.5   1.0

Miles

42

proceed 25 miles, through the towns of Pine and Buffalo Creek, to Deckers. Deckers consists of several buildings along CO 126, which ends at the South Platte River. Go straight across the river and onto County Road 67, and drive about 9 miles south to a sharp left curve, where the road turns east. To the right (west) at the outside of the curve is a small turnoff for the tiny hamlet of Westcreek. Follow this good gravel road, CR 73, 0.2 mile downhill to a junction with Westcreek Road; turn left (south) on Westcreek Road, also gravel, and go 0.6 mile to the Westcreek Volunteer Fire Department. Turn right (west) and go 2 miles on CR 68 (shown as Forest Route 360 on the Pike National Forest map) to a turnoff to the right (north). This is CR 9-J, which shortly becomes FR 556. Go sharply uphill at first, and then wind along on a wooded ridge crest for 1.5 miles until you reach a sharp left-hand turn. (If you miss this sharp turn you will notice a road off to the right [north] in 0.5 mile.) Look for a wire fence on the right (north) at the outside of the curve, and park here off the road. The fence ends at this point, and there is suitable parking for several cars. Passenger cars should have no trouble reaching the trailhead in good weather.

Key points:

0.3	Powerlines
0.7	Northwest-trending ridge
1.4	Base of steep hillside
1.9	South ridge
2.3	Summit

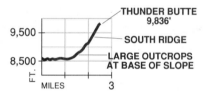

The hike: This is a good peak to practice your bushwhacking and orienteering skills. Plot your course on the USGS quad and measure compass bearings for use in the field. Starting just past the end of the fence, follow due north the faint road on the gentle but discernible ridge crest. The ponderosa and lodgepole pines are thinly spaced here, with little underbrush to confuse you. You pass under powerlines at mile 0.3. Look for shallow prospecting pits in the forest, evidence of the search for mineral wealth in the area.

At mile 0.7, the ridge you are on joins a narrower defined one, which trends northwest. Note the large rock cairn placed in this vicinity. You need to look for this on your return, or you might continue past this cutoff and wander down into Shrewsbury Gulch. Always stay high and orient yourself with the surrounding natural features. Follow this ridge northwest. There are a few small rock outcrops to orient you as you pass. The ridge gradually turns due north and then northeast as you approach Thunder Butte, and at mile 1.4, the terrain steepens considerably. Stay close to the large outcrops of Pikes Peak granite that form small towers and pancakelike formations, but pass below them to the right. Follow the drainage to the east, and bushwhack 0.4 mile up through a moderate amount of downed timber to mile 1.9 on a ridge above the saddle between Thunder Butte and its 9,440-foot subpeak to the south. From here a faint trail turns left (north) and climbs 0.3 mile up the south ridge of Thunder Butte. Be cautious as you approach the summit, as it is composed entirely of large, desk-sized boulders. There is a wood pole at the highpoint and a register in a can. Return by the same route. Take compass bearings. Because there is no trail to follow, be careful to orient yourself so you don't wander down into the drainages.

Boulder scrambling at the summit requires care, especially with rain or snow. Since most of the hike is along south-facing slopes, heat in the summer can also be a problem at this relatively low elevation. Be certain to bring sufficient water for your party. In the fall, there is a possibility of hunting in this area, so be cautious and wear orange.

The best time to visit is May through October. The gravel roads may be passable year-round, but the boulder scrambling at the summit would be difficult with any snow. Thunder Butte is an isolated peak, with a 360-degree view. Not a true butte, this peak's summit is very similar in nature to Jefferson County's highpoint, Buffalo Peak. Thunder Butte is actually 88 feet higher than 9,748-foot Devils Head. The summit is wooded in part, but a fine view of the Kenosha Mountains and Buffalo Peak will reward you for a scramble farther west a hundred feet along the summit crest. Sheep Nose is a prominent monolith to the south, near the fire station you passed on your way in. The May 1998 Turkey Creek fire, much smaller than the Buffalo Creek fire you passed through on the approach, is visible to the west. Pikes Peak looms grandly to the south, and Devils Head with its fire tower is about 8 miles to the northeast. Most people would answer "Devils Head" when asked what the highest point in Douglas County would be, but you know better. Devils Head is a prime locality for collecting smoky quartz, and we recommend taking the modest trail that leads to the lookout tower on the summit. The lookout is still occupied by rangers who are more than happy to chat with visitors.

A Colorado Mountain Club outing on a fine autumn day on the summit of Thunder Butte.

There is private property on all sides of Thunder Butte, and although historic access to Thunder Butte was across these lands, please respect the rights of property owners and do not attempt to access the peak through private drives. None will get you any closer or any higher than the trailhead described above. During your approach, north of Deckers, you pass directly through the devastating forest fire and flood damage from the May 1996 fire that consumed many square miles of the Pike National Forest, and several residences. You can't help but be impressed by the fury of a forest fire, and we can all learn from this lesson as we impose our presence upon the fragile wilderness.

County highlights: Castle Rock is the county seat of Douglas County, which was established in 1861 and named for Steven Douglas (1813–1861), the U.S. senator from Illinois and 1860 presidential candidate who was defeated by Abraham Lincoln. Douglas County is one of the fastest-growing counties in America, thanks in large part to the sprawling Highlands Ranch subdivision and others seeking to emulate it. Castle Rock is famous for the rock outcrop overlooking town, which resembles the tower of a medieval castle. It is also home to one of the largest factory outlet malls in Colorado.

Sedalia, just a few miles from metro Denver, is a quaint town but years removed from the hectic pace just to the north. Bud's is an interesting stop for lunch, while Gabriel's is a fine place for upscale dining.

The South Platte River at Deckers is quietly regarded by anglers as a great trout-fishing locality. Many families take a mini-vacation from the bustle of the city at this quiet junction just an hour away. The Deckers Resort is a great place to stop for lunch or dinner, and it serves as a general store for the community as well. Farther south on CO 67, just a few miles from Westcreek, is the Horse Creek KOA Camp, which also has a small restaurant.

Camping and services: Camping is available at any of several campgrounds along CO 126 and CO 67, but not in the vicinity of the trailhead. No services are available at Westcreek. Full services are available at Woodland Park to the south.

5   Elbert County: Elbert Rock

General description: An almost imperceptible rise near a county road.
Distance: None.
Difficulty: Drive-up.
Elevation gain: None.
Summit elevation: 7,360 feet.
Maps: USGS Quad—Cherry Valley School (recommended), DeLorme p. 51.
Access/permits: Elbert–El Paso county-road right-of-way.
Best months: March–November.

Location: Central Colorado on the Palmer Divide, about 25 miles northeast of Colorado Springs, and 10 miles east of Monument.

Finding the trailhead: The highest point of Elbert County appears to lie several hundred feet off a county road on private property, but the elevation difference from the county road to the actual highpoint is only a few feet at most. We consider it successful to simply reach the fence line along the county road right-of-way. Visitation of the actual highest ground would be by appointment only. Respect the owner's property by not harming fences, vegetation, or livestock.

Leave Interstate 25 at exit 163 and go east on County Line Road (Palmer Divide Road). After the interstate, the road passes south of a prominent feature known as Bald Mountain. The paved road ends after 1.7 miles and becomes a good gravel road. At 5 miles you reach Colorado Highway 83. Cross it and continue east, bending slightly south at mile 8.5 around a tree-covered hill, passing by Black Forest Road to the right (south). (The road is paved again from CO 83 to this bend at mile 8.5.) At mile 9.5 the road jogs north for 0.25 mile, east for 0.25 mile, and then south for 0.25 mile to rejoin the county line. You will pass Cherry Creek Road during this jog. Continue east on County Line Road, passing the Douglas–Elbert–El Paso county tri-junction at mile 11.3. At mile 11.5 the road jogs sharply south for about 0.1 mile around a large sandstone outcrop. Continue east, passing another small jog to the south at mile 12.3. As you enter the trees, continue to mile 12.6 and park your vehicle safely on the shoulder of the road. The road crests here and descends to the east. There is a flat meadow extending north from the county road into Elbert County. This meadow is bordered by the 7,360-foot contour line. We have concluded by field inspection that the relative relief of the four other areas where the terrain penetrates the 7,360-foot contour is insufficient to match the elevation in the meadow.

The hike: Walk over to the fence line on the north side of the county road, take your photo, and mark off this county on your checklist.

This highpoint can be visited year-round although the best time to visit is March through November. The gravel roads are usually passable year-round,

Elbert County: Elbert Rock

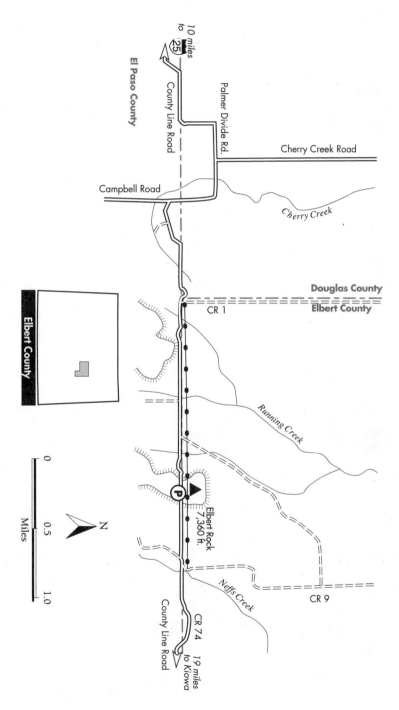

but locating the highpoint area might be difficult if there is substantial snow in the meadow. There is no view to speak of from this high ground. We named the highpoint of Elbert County in recognition of the exposed rock at the very highest ground in the meadow. Use caution when parking and crossing the gravel road. The famed Black Forest of Colorado extends southeast from here and is well worth driving through. Access this area via Black Forest Road, about 2 miles west of the tri-county junction. Please respect the rights of the property owners and do not cross the fence line into Elbert County north of the road without permission of Harmony Land and Cattle Company.

County highlights: Kiowa, named for the Kiowa Indian tribe, is the county seat of Elbert County, which was established in 1874. The county was named for Samuel Hitt Elbert, the sixth territorial governor of Colorado (1873–1874) and the chief justice of the Colorado Supreme Court from 1880 to 1883. Although rural, Elbert County's proximity to the expanding Denver metropolitan area make its real estate attractive, and though there are no sizable towns in the county, the county did install its first stoplight in September 1998 in Elizabeth.

Camping and services: Numerous private campgrounds can be found throughout the Black Forest area, as well as to the northwest in the Palmer and Monument areas. The nearest services are at I-25 exit 161 in Monument.

Owner contact: Harmony Land and Cattle Company, c/o Greg Dryden, 303-760-5652.

Elbert County's summit is an open meadow along a county road.

6 El Paso and Teller Counties: Pikes Peak and Devils Playground

Pikes Peak

General description: This world-famous solitary mountain is heavily visited and the summit can be reached easily by automobile and cog railroad or as a long day hike.
Distance: None.
Difficulty: Drive-up.
Elevation gain: 10 feet.
Summit elevation: 14,110 feet.

Devils Playground

General description: There is a short walk up this small bouldered hill along the Pikes Peak Gateway near the summit of the famous Fourteener. This hillock is also on the Crags Trail.
Distance: 0.2 mile, one-way.
Difficulty: Easy hike.
Elevation gain: 130 feet.
Summit elevation: 13,060 feet.
Maps: USGS Quad—Pikes Peak (optional), DeLorme p. 62, Trails Illustrated #137.
Access/permits: Pike National Forest, varying fees per carload or per person for toll road and for cog railroad.
Best months: May–October.

Location: East-central Colorado, about 15 miles west of Colorado Springs, and 7 miles west of Manitou Springs.

Finding the trailhead: From Interstate 25 in Colorado Springs, take exit 141 and go west on U.S. Highway 24 for about 9 miles through Manitou Springs along Fountain Creek to the hamlet of Cascade. Turn left (west) in Cascade at the well-marked turnoff to Pikes Peak onto the Pikes Peak Gateway, formerly called Pikes Peak Highway and Pikes Peak Toll Road. We refer to this road as "Gateway."

Follow this road to the tollbooth and pay the fee, $10 per person with a $35 maximum, as of this writing, to proceed. About the first 7 miles past the tollbooth are paved, and then the Gateway becomes a good gravel road. Continue 16.2 miles up the steep, winding road to a turnout and parking

El Paso and Teller Counties:
Pikes Peak and Devils Playground

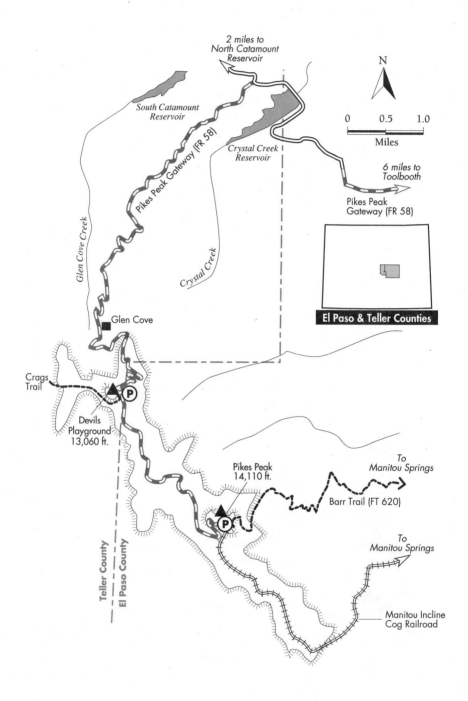

2 miles to
North Catamount
Reservoir

South Catamount
Reservoir

N

0   0.5   1.0

Miles

Pikes Peak Gateway (FR 58)

Crystal Creek
Reservoir

6 miles to
Toolbooth

Pikes Peak
Gateway (FR 58)

Glen Cove Creek

Crystal Creek

El Paso & Teller Counties

Glen Cove

Crags
Trail

Devils
Playground
13,060 ft.

Pikes Peak
14,110 ft.

To
Manitou Springs

Barr Trail (FT 620)

To
Manitou Springs

Teller County

El Paso County

Manitou Incline
Cog Railroad

area on the right (west). There is a sign on your left that explains the name "The Devils Playground." Park your vehicle on the right (west) side of the Gateway in the parking area. When you return from your hike in the Devils Playground, continue up the Gateway about another 3 miles to the large summit parking area where, with luck, you'll find a parking spot.

The hike: To reach the Teller County highpoint, follow the throngs of tourists up the side of the hill that forms the Devils Playground. There is no path per se; instead visitors leave their vehicles en masse at the large dirt parking lot and charge up the slopes to the boulder-strewn summit area. Although you can reach the summit with little effort by choosing a grassy route around the boulders, most people can't resist the temptation to do a little scrambling. Parents should exercise caution with youngsters, since many boulders can be walked up on one side and have a 20-foot drop-off on the opposite side. When returning to your vehicle, watch for traffic in the busy parking area and along the Gateway, if you elect to cross it to read the information sign about Devils Playground. The name is a reference to the electrical activity among the roadside boulders that is displayed during lightning storms.

To reach the El Paso County highpoint, which is the actual summit of Pikes Peak, look for the boulder pile within the parking area and scamper up to the highest spot. The rangers can direct you if needed. In the summit house is a large sign-in book that functions as a register.

Alternate routes to the top of Pikes Peak include the historic cog railroad, which leaves from Manitou Springs several times a day for a fare, as of this writing, of $22 for adults and $10.50 for children. The railway was constructed in 1890 and negotiates a 15 percent grade in its ascent. There are also two trails to the top. The popular Barr Trail, Forest Trail 620, leaves from a trailhead near the cog railroad in Manitou Springs and ascends 7,400 feet in about 13 miles along a relatively gentle path to the summit. This trail is the site of a marathon race each summer. The less popular Crags Trail leaves from the Crags Campground west of the Devils Playground, accessible from Colorado Highway 67 south of Divide. This trail ascends the western flank of Pikes Peak, passing the Teller County highpoint and continuing on to the summit, gaining 4,100 feet in about 6 miles.

The best time to visit is May through October. The Gateway, constructed for carriages in 1888 and improved for automobile use in 1915, opens as soon as the crew has cleared the snow from the road each spring, usually in May. The first significant snowfall in the fall generally marks the end of the season for vehicular access. Phone in advance if you are in doubt of conditions. Be careful of the long approach drive on the steep and winding road, which can result in serious engine or brake overheating. There is serious overcrowding at all points on the mountain, and patience is a virtue on the drive. There are only a few spots where you can pass. The Sierra Club is trying to require Colorado Springs to pave the road to end the dust and gravel pollution of this environmentally sensitive high country.

Lightning is a possibility on this exposed terrain, so refrain from leaving your vehicle at either highpoint if there are signs of a thunderstorm. Expect

The Teller County highpoint is a boulder-covered hill ahong the Pikes Peak Highway and Crags hiking trail.

the temperature to be substantially cooler than in Colorado Springs, so dress appropriately. The highpoints are easily reached via automobile or railway, and the quick ascent to 13,000 feet or higher will not give you any time for acclimatization. If you feel light-headed, descend immediately or seek medical attention at the summit house. There is an Olympic monument at the summit, and be sure to visit the summit house, with its extensive gift shop, five-cent coffee, and world-famous doughnuts. Denver is visible 75 miles to the north, and the Sangre de Cristo Range can be seen 100 miles to the southwest.

County highlights: Colorado Springs is the county seat of El Paso County, which was established in 1861. The county's name is Spanish for "the Pass," apparently in reference to Ute Pass, which leads west to South Park and beyond. Pikes Peak itself was named for Lieutenant Zebulon Pike, who first glimpsed the mountain in 1806 and called it Grand Peak. Before Pike, the Indians in the area called it "Tabihuache," meaning "Sun Peak." In 1820 Dr. Edwin James made the first recorded ascent of this majestic peak, formed 60 million years ago by local upthrusting. His name has particular significance to county highpointers, since the summit of Gilpin County bears his name. Katharine Lee Bates was inspired by the peak to pen the words to "America the Beautiful" shortly after visiting the summit. The economy of the area is heavily dependent on the prominent military presence. Fort Carson is a large army base to the south of Colorado Springs, and the air force has its primary training facility, the Air Force Academy, just north of the city. Deep within Cheyenne Mountain, just southeast of Pikes Peak, is

52

the central command post of NORAD established by the Pentagon as a defense warning system.

Teller County, established in 1899, was named for Henry Moore Teller, who served as a U.S. senator from Colorado from 1876 to 1882 and from 1885 to 1909 and in between these stints, as the Secretary of the Interior. Cripple Creek and the surrounding area were the site of a major gold rush in 1888. An estimated $12 billion in 1998 dollars in gold was mined; operations continue today in the town of Victor. With additional attractions too numerous to mention here, tourism is another important part of El Paso and Teller counties. Cripple Creek also received an economic boost in 1991 with the introduction of legalized gambling.

Camping and services: Camping is available at Pike National Forest's Crags Campground, accessed north of Cripple Creek. Food and gifts are available at the Pikes Peak summit house and at mile 14 on the Gateway at Glen Cove Inn (elevation 11,425 feet). Motels and camping are available along US 24, from the town of Divide down to Colorado Springs.

For more information: Pikes Peak Gateway (Colorado Springs operates the road under lease by the Forest Service), 719-684-9383, 1-800-368-4748; Cog Railway (access via Manitou Avenue), 515 Ruxton Avenue, Manitou Springs, CO 80829, 719-685-5401.

---

7   Jefferson County: Buffalo Peak

General description: A full-day, strenuous hike along a trail and boulder ridge to a remote summit, with views of the Front Range south of Denver.
Distance: 7.4 miles, one-way.
Difficulty: Strenuous.
Elevation gain: 3,489 feet.
Summit elevation: 11,589 feet.
Maps: USGS Quads—Green Mountain and Windy Peak (required), Cheeseman Lake and McCurdy Mountain (recommended), DeLorme p. 49, Trails Illustrated # 105.
Access/permits: Lost Creek Wilderness in Pike National Forest.
Best months: July–October.

Location: Central Colorado in the Kenosha Mountains, about 35 miles southwest of Denver and 15 miles southeast of Bailey.

Finding the trailhead: Head southwest on U.S. Highway 285 from Denver to Bailey. At milepost 227, you can see Buffalo Peak to the south. In Bailey, at the bottom of Crow Hill, turn left (east) onto County Road 68, and follow the North Fork of the South Platte River. After 1.3 miles this paved

Jefferson County: Buffalo Peak

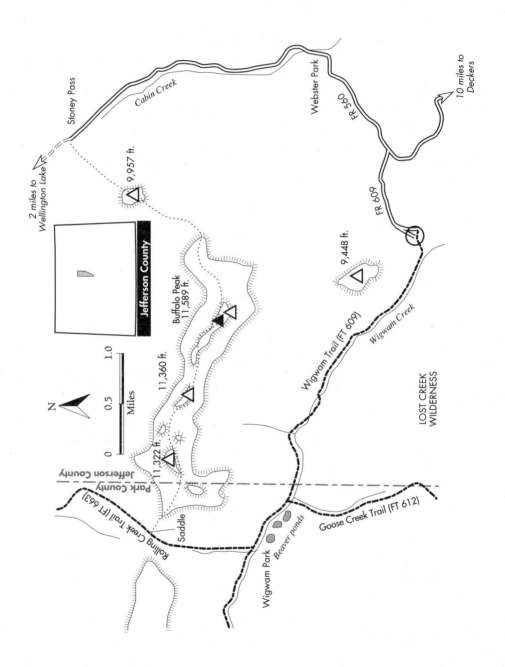

road becomes gravel. Stay to the right at the next two intersections, taking Forest Road 543 at mile 5.1 and continuing on it at mile 6.8. You cross the Colorado Trail and pass through the Jefferson County Outdoor Education Laboratory, before you reach the western end of Wellington Lake at mile 10.2, with a good glimpse to your right of Buffalo Peak and the Castle. At mile 10.9, again stay to the right, this time on FR 560, which becomes significantly rougher after it crosses the Wellington Lake dam. Passing through Stoney Pass and Webster Park, you reach FR 609 at mile 17.5. Watch for logging activity in this area. Turn right (west) onto FR 609 and proceed 1 mile to the parking areas of the Wigwam Creek Trailhead. This road has in the past been blocked off farther east than is indicated on the USGS quadrangle and Trails Illustrated maps. A passenger car can reach this trailhead in good weather.

To approach the trailhead from the south, travel north on Colorado Highway 67, about 23 miles from US 24 at Woodland Park, to Deckers. Go straight, crossing the South Platte River on CO 126 (CO 67 veers to the right). After about 12 miles, turn left (west) on FR 550, a gravel road. Proceed about 10 miles to Wellington Lake and follow the directions above from there.

Key points:
- 3.3   Goose Creek Trail (Forest Trail 612) in Wigwam Park
- 3.9   Rolling Creek Trail (FT 663)
- 5.0   Saddle
- 5.9   Blocky rise to 11,322 feet on ridge
- 6.6   Blocky rise to 11,360 feet on ridge

The hike: There is not an easy route to the summit of this mountain. Most parties elect to hike straight up the northeast slopes from Stoney Pass on FR 560, although this steep route has no trail and requires you to negotiate a maze of fallen trees. The route described here makes use of good trails but also requires a steep climb, is much longer in length, involves tricky route finding, and requires bushwhacking along the rocky ridge top. If backpacking appeals to you, seriously consider accessing the fine network of trails in the Lost Creek Wilderness by driving southeast on FR 77 and FR 127 from Kenosha Pass on US 285, about 20 miles west of Bailey. We have hiked all approaches, Stoney Pass, Kenosha Pass, and Wigwam Trail, and have elected to describe the Wigwam Trail hike to encourage a challenging alternative to reach this impressive peak.

From the two parking lots, walk southeast to the trailhead and sign the backcountry register. The first stretch of the Wigwam Trail (FT 609) is on a road that descends to

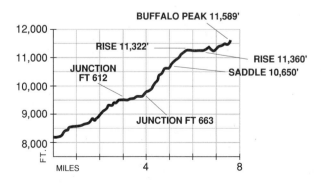

Buffalo Peak looking west form FR 560. Wigwam Trail is to the left and Stoney Pass is to the right.

Wigwam Creek, but don't be alarmed as you'll soon begin gaining elevation! Follow this trail northwest along Wigwam Creek as it hugs the south side of the major east-west ridge that forms the peak. The trail crosses Wigwam Creek several times using logs as bridges. At mile 3.3 you reach the junction with the Goose Creek Trail, which provides access to the southern reaches of the Lost Creek Wilderness. Continue on Wigwam Trail, passing a series of beaver ponds, until you reach the intersection with the Rolling Creek Trail (FT 663) at mile 3.9. You have ascended 1,480 feet. Take the Rolling Creek Trail right (north) steeply uphill until you reach a broad pine-covered saddle at mile 5. At this 10,650-foot saddle, you must turn right (southeast) and bushwhack 2.4 miles along the mountain's ridge to Buffalo Peak itself. The first 0.5 mile is very steep through open woods. Upon gaining the flat upper ridge, consult your USGS quad and take compass readings to keep headed toward your goal. There is some relief on this ridge, but take care not to stray off the sides onto the mountain's slopes. Where rock outcrops present an obstacle, stay to the left (north). Approach the final rise of Buffalo Peak on the left (north) side, although the scramble up the rocky south face of the summit is fairly easy in good weather. The peak itself is composed of two rock rises, the western rise being the true highpoint. We installed a new register at this summit so shout your triumph and record your achievement! Return via the same route but do not succumb to temptation and scramble down the south slopes of Buffalo Peak! There are numerous spots where you can cliff out, and the terrain is so steep it will take you longer. After leaving Wigwam Creek there is no source of water except for isolated snowbanks in late spring. Make no mistake: this is a long hike and you'll consume more than 2 quarts of water.

The best time to visit here is July through October. The gravel roads may be passable earlier, but scrambling along the ridge would be difficult with any snow. Buffalo Peak, also known as Freeman Peak, is the high terminus of a very long ridge, offering a 360-degree view. From the summit, the Castle, just west of Wellington Lake, is visible below you to the north. This impressive rock formation is attacked on a regular basis by technical climbers. Pikes Peak is visible to the south. Thunder Butte and Devils Head with its fire tower are a short distance to the east. This peak attracts large ravens that circle and swoop in the sky around you. Most people have absolutely no idea what the highest point in Jefferson County is, and now you have an opening line at your next social function. The summit is mostly open rock outcrop, with a few sparse, stunted evergreen trees. This is a fine example of a mountain that peaks at timberline—a bit higher and it would be truly alpine; a bit lower and it would be wooded on top with no view. The hike to Buffalo Peak lies entirely within the Lost Creek Wilderness that was established in the early 1980s. In this wilderness area, dogs are allowed but must be leashed at all times. There is private property along FR 560; please respect the rights of property owners by not attempting to access the peak through private property.

County highlights: Golden is the county seat of Jefferson County, which was established in 1861 and was named for Thomas Jefferson, the third president of the United States and the architect of the Declaration of Independence. Jefferson County is one of the most populous in Colorado, and its school district is the largest, exceeding the city and county of Denver. A large portion of the recent growth has come in the mountain suburbs, a trend that should continue into the next century as US 285 is widened to four lanes past Conifer toward Bailey.

Golden is also famous for the Colorado School of Mines and the Coors brewery, which offers tours every hour during the week. Check out the world-class pizza at Woody's across from Foss Drug, a general store that is a throwback to the time when Golden was the territorial capital. Morrison, another interesting town in this county, is home to the natural rock amphitheater known as Red Rocks, where nearly everyone who's anyone has played over the years. Bailey is far enough removed from the Denver metropolitan area to qualify as an honest-to-goodness mountain town and not a bedroom community. After your hike, pull in at the Bailey Station at the intersection of US 285 and CR 68 (FR 543) for a can't-miss burger. If you're the adventurous sort, we highly recommend the Bucksnort Inn in tiny Sphinx Park, just up CR 83 (South Elk Creek Road) from Pine toward Shaffers Crossing. People come from all over to this funky little hangout, nestled in a canyon with imposing rock cliffs on all sides. You may witness some high-level climbing activity on a nice day.

Camping and services: Camping is permitted along the forest roads north and south of the trailhead. The closest national forest campgrounds are Buffalo and Baldy, located several miles northeast from the Wellington Lake dam along FR 543. Additional campgrounds are found to the south by taking FR 560 to FR 211. There are campgrounds both east and west of this intersection. Primitive camping is allowed throughout the Lost Creek Wilderness provided that backcountry guidelines are followed. In national forests you are asked to locate your campsite 100 feet from water sources; in wilderness areas this is a rule that is enforced. If you choose to approach this peak from Kenosha Pass to the west, camp at Lost Creek Campground at the end of FR 127. The nearest services are in Bailey, although the towns of Deckers and Buffalo Creek offer some fuel and food on a limited basis.

8   Weld County: Bison Butte

General description:	A full-day's ride on horseback leads over treeless rangeland to a mesa at the Colorado-Wyoming border.
Distance:	4.5 miles.
Difficulty:	Moderate.
Elevation gain:	300 feet.
Summit elevation:	6,380 feet.
Maps:	USGS Quads—Carr East (required), Borrie WY (recommended), Carr West (recommended), and Cheyenne South WY (optional), DeLorme p. 20.
Access/permits:	State private lease; fee for full-day trail ride.
Best months:	April–May and October–November.

Location: North-central Colorado, about 25 miles northeast of Fort Collins, and 4 miles east of Interstate 25, near the Colorado-Wyoming border.

Finding the trailhead: The highpoint of Weld County is leased from the state of Colorado by the Terry Bison Ranch, which caters to the public, especially tourists, by operating a working dude ranch. Ranch staff will guide visitors to the highpoint by customizing the route of a full-day horseback ride, but advance notice is required to set up such a ride as they do not normally take visitors to this site. The ranch is concerned about the aggressive behavior of the bison herd and you should be, too. Do not enter bison rangeland unless you can run 35 miles per hour for at least a quarter of a mile because bison can!

To reach the Terry Bison Ranch, drive north from Fort Collins on I-25 for about 34 miles. The ranch is to your right as you pass the Colorado-Wyoming state line. Take exit 2, to Terry Ranch Road. The ranch's entrance is about 1 mile south on a paved road.

To get the best view of Bison Butte, we suggest you drive to a point along Terry Ranch Road, north of the highpoint. Turn left (east) on Terry Ranch Road after exiting I-25 and drive a couple miles north to view the mesa, which is now to your right. Bring your compass and USGS quadrangle map

Weld County: Bison Butte

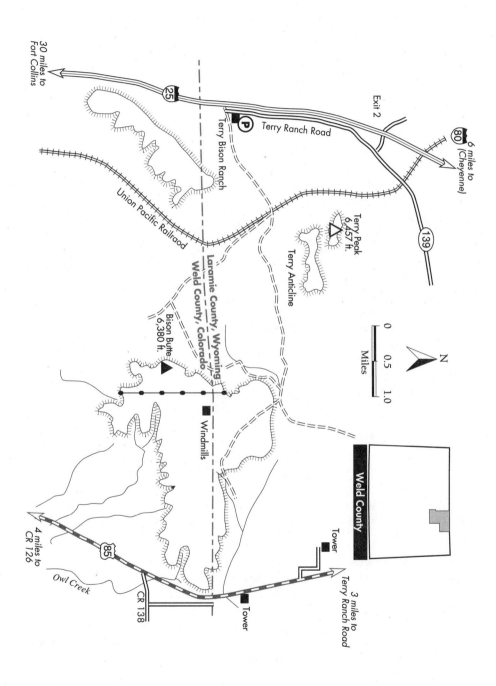

in order to locate features on this treeless land, such as conical Terry Peak and the long, uneven ridge of Terry Anticline. You should also be able to spot the bison herd on the range.

The eastern access to the highpoint is owned by the Lazy D Grazing Association. It, however, expressed concern about visitors disturbing the vegetation and wildlife habitat and the interaction of hikers with the cattle herds. As with private property anywhere, please respect the landowners' rights as you may not hunt, harvest, collect, or trespass on posted property. Besides, this land provides their livelihood and should be treated with respect.

The hike: Hiking to Bison Butte is restricted at this time, but horseback rides, or perhaps a guided nature walk, are available from Terry Bison Ranch. The highpoint is located at the western edge of the butte, where there are two rises that are noticeably about 10 feet higher than the surrounding area. By using a handlevel, it appeared to us that the southern of the two rises is the higher by a few feet. There is no register or cairn.

The best time to visit this area is spring or fall. The roads are winding and they can be snowy in the winter and may be hot in the summer. Avoid walking on range vegetation whenever possible, and don't climb on fences; leave all gates in the state you found them, whether open or closed. Under no circumstances should you bother the livestock. Bison are dangerous animals, wild in nature, and should be avoided at all costs. Bison are often referred to by their traditional name *buffalo*, although bison ranchers would like to distinguish their product from the true buffalo found in other parts of the world. Antelope are sometimes hunted on the mesa in organized forays by the landowners.

From the butte top, there is a sweeping view of the mountains from Pikes Peak to the south to Wyoming's Laramie Range to the northwest. In between are Mount Evans and the peaks of Rocky Mountain National Park. Bison Butte itself lies on a bluff on the edge of Wyoming's "Gangplank," the broad uneroded High Plains on which the transcontinental railroad was built. At the I-25 exit 296 rest area near the state line is a very interesting outcrop of Tertiary-age sedimentary rock. A patient birder may catch sight of hawks and other raptors riding the wind currents in search of their prey. There are power-generating windmills being erected on the mesa top by a Denver firm.

County highlights: Weld County, with Greeley as the county seat, was established in 1861 and named for Lewis Ledyard Weld, the first secretary of the Colorado Territory. At one time this whole area was part of an enormous cattle ranch known as the Vener Ranch, which spread over 10 miles in every direction. Pieces have been sold off over the years until only the present agricultural cooperatives and associations of today exist. James Michener made the area famous as the centerpiece of his novel *Centennial*.

John handlevels to determine the exact highest ground. PHOTO BY DAWN HOWARD

The Terry Bison Ranch offers, besides trail rides, a full range of activities including fishing, chuckwagon dinners, ranch tours, rodeos, and live entertainment. It even has Wyoming's first winery. The ranch also sponsors special events in the summer, one of which is a celebration held in July with a 5K run known as the Run in the Buff. Motorized tours of the 30,000-acre ranch are available and allow you to mingle safely with the bison herd, which currently numbers 3,000 head.

Nearby in Colorado is Loveland, famous for its Valentine's Day postmark, and home to a major factory outlet shopping center. The Anheuser-Busch brewery in Fort Collins, with tours available Wednesday through Sunday, should be another prime local destination.

Camping and services: The Terry Bison Ranch offers tent sites, RV hookups, and cabins as well as a restaurant and general store. Motels and full services can be found in Cheyenne to the north and Wellington and Fort Collins to the south. There is a restaurant in Rockport on U.S. Highway 85 southeast of the highpoint. Campgrounds are available 30 miles to the west in Roosevelt National Forest and in Rocky Mountain National Park.

Owner contacts: Terry Bison Ranch, Dan Thiel, General Manager, 51 I-25 Service Road East, Cheyenne, WY 82007, 307-634-4171.

Northern Mountains

The Northern Mountains are characterized by high, rugged peaks close to or on the Continental Divide, where snow comes early and stays late most years. Each of these are full-day hikes by themselves; do not try to combine any of them into one outing. We do, however, suggest making a long weekend of it in Rocky Mountain National Park and doing Longs Peak and Hagues Peak. None of these is particularly difficult, although there is some exposure and rock scrambling on Longs Peak.

Northern Mountains

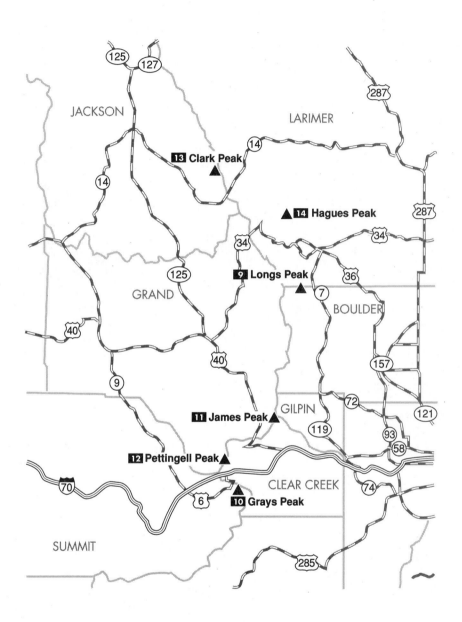

9   Boulder County: Longs Peak

General description: The most famous Colorado climb, this alpine peak
requires a long, strenuous hike on a trail and across
ledges and slabs with class 3 climbing at the summit.

Distance: 7 miles, one-way.

Difficulty: Strenuous.

Elevation gain: 5,255 feet.

Summit elevation: 14,255 feet.

Maps: USGS Quad—Longs Peak (recommended), DeLorme
p. 29, Trails Illustrated #200, national park maps.

Access/permits: Rocky Mountain National Park; no fee for a day hike.

Best months: August–September.

Location: North-central Colorado in the Front Range, about 70 miles northwest of Denver, and 10 miles southwest of Estes Park.

Finding the trailhead: Access to most routes on this peak is through the Longs Peak Ranger Station, located west of Colorado Highway 7 just inside the boundary of Rocky Mountain National Park. To reach this trailhead, drive about 9 miles south on CO 7 from its junction of U.S. Highway 34 near Estes Park. (From the south drive about 10 miles north from where CO 72 meets CO 7, about 14 miles west of the town of Lyons.) Turn west onto the paved, steeply winding road to the trailhead ranger station. On most prime hiking days, the parking lot is full and vehicles are parked along this approach road. If you begin your trek during office hours, check with the rangers for current conditions and study the displays about the mountain.

Key points:
- 0.5   Eugenia Mine Trail
- 2.5   Jims Grove (trail to Battle Mountain campsites)
- 3.1   Chasm Lake Trail
- 4.2   Granite Pass
- 6.0   Keyhole
- 6.4   Base of the Trough
- 6.7   Top of the Trough
- 6.8   Base of the Homestretch

The hike: The route described here is the popular Keyhole Route. Sign the trailhead register and take the East Longs Peak Trail west 0.5 mile, staying left (west) at the junction with the Eugenia Mine Trail. Continue on East Longs Peak Trail past Jims Grove Trail, which is on your right at mile 2.5, and past the trail to Chasm Lake, on your left at mile 3.1. At mile 4.2, where the North Longs Peak Trail splits off to the right, continue northwest to Granite Pass and go up the switchbacks to gain the Boulder Field that is a glacial valley layered with various sizes of rocks. Follow the streamside trail past the campground toward the head of this hanging valley and the trail's official terminus.

Boulder County: Longs Peak

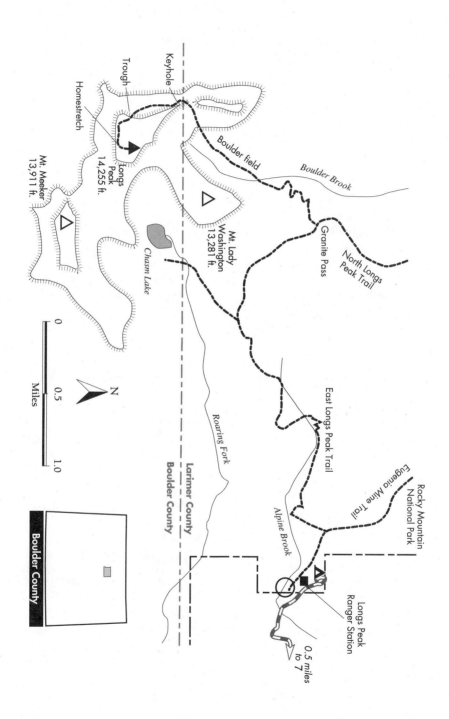

Homestretch

Trough

Keyhole

Boulder field

Boulder Brook

Longs Peak
14,255 ft.

Mt. Meeker
13,911 ft.

Chasm Lake

Mt. Lady
Washington
13,281 ft.

Granite Pass

North Longs
Peak Trail

0   0.5   1.0

Miles

N

East Longs Peak Trail

Roaring Fork

Larimer County
Boulder County

Eugenia Mine Trail

Rocky Mountain
National Park

Alpine Brook

Longs Peak
Ranger Station

0.5 miles
to 7

Boulder County

The last stretch of this trip requires boulder hopping without a trail. If you don't have several hundred fellow hikers to lead the way, scan the ridgeline to the southwest for a distinct gap with an overhang. That gap is the Keyhole and it provides access to a well-marked scrambling route to the summit. Look for the "bulls-eye," or "fried egg," symbols painted on the rocks. These mark the route, and if you always have one in sight ahead of you, you will probably not get lost. This sounds simple, but use discipline in the field and follow this advice. On several trips we have observed hikers go off route on the section from the Keyhole to the Trough. Pass through the breezy Keyhole gap and follow the level, broken ledges to the left (south), taking care when passing up a V-shaped chute. Continue on to mile 6.4 and the base of the Trough, a straight, steep, rock couloir that requires a difficult move past a boulder near the top. Upon reaching the top of the Trough, smile broadly since you have attained most of this route's elevation, although tricky spots still lie ahead. Proceed left and along cliff ledges called the Narrows that lead you to step up through a crack. The final hurdle is to bear left (north) after passing through a notch between two boulders to the base of the Homestretch and carefully scale the smooth steep slabs toward the summit, exploiting cracks for handholds and footing. The apex of Longs Peak is a boulder on the anticlimactic flat summit, 300 paces north of the Homestretch. Sign the register and return by the same route, exercising caution over the rocks and ledges, which can be very slippery if wet.

Allow 10 to 14 hours for this trip, and before taking on this mountain, consider whether you want to hike 14 miles as a one-day hike or as an overnight backpack. If you choose the former, plan to begin your day early, say 3:00 A.M., and if you choose the latter, plan to phone for backcountry camping reservations on the first day of March. No day hike fee is required to enjoy this route.

Since snow and ice make the rock ledges, boulders, and chutes treacherous, the best time to attempt this peak is mid-July through mid-September. The Longs Peak rangers do a very good job of monitoring the conditions and

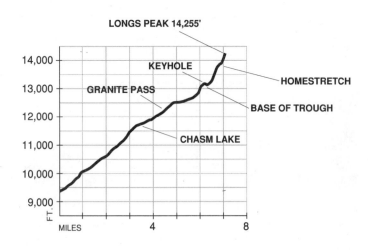

will let you know if the route is considered "technical." The ranger station is open, depending on the day's expected trail use, from 7:00 A.M. to 7:00 P.M. on busy summer days. A typical August Saturday in 1998 had 350 people on the summit. The route to the summit is on a good trail that is well-marked, but this peak does require a very long hike over rough terrain that is totally exposed to weather. Vast hordes of hikers, climbers, and tourists are on this route during the summer season in all manner of dress from those fully prepared for a high-altitude expedition to those ready for a shopping mall excursion. This is not a joke. The popularity of this peak allows many to believe it is an easy national park scenic tour, but it is not. Among the 47 who have died on this peak, 28 fell and 9 succumbed to exposure or lightning strikes. Considering the huge number of climbers on this peak, this is a remarkably low fatality rate. Heed the advice from the rangers and returning hikers, but always rely on your own assessment of the situation.

County highlights: Established in 1861, Boulder County derives its name from the abundance of these objects near Boulder City along Boulder Creek. In 1858, a group of prospectors pitched camp at the mouth of Boulder Canyon and the next year discovered gold about 12 miles to the west. The first organized mining district in the Rockies was formed here. Boulder, the county seat, served mainly as a supply center and farming community since then. This community dreamed of becoming home for the state university and in 1877 realized the dream with a freshman class consisting of nine men and one woman.

Longs Peak and its eastern neighbor, Mount Meeker, were called "the Two Guides" by Arapaho Indians. The current name for this Fourteener

A hiker surmounts the Homestretch, arriving at the expansive summit plateau of Longs Peak.

honors Major Stephen D. Long, who led an exploratory expedition through the area from 1819 to 1820.

Camping and services: Backcountry camping is allowed at primitive clearings in the Boulder Field, but it requires permits that can be obtained by phone from March through May or in person or by mail from June through September. The national park campground at the trailhead holds only 27 tent sites. Other campgrounds are available in the park through the entrances at Estes Park, located about 10 miles north. Commercial campgrounds, motels, and dude ranches can be found throughout the area and along CO 7. Estes Park, the eastern gateway to Rocky Mountain National Park, is a must-see tourist town waiting to take care of your every need, especially if that is eating, shopping for gifts, or drinking the local microbrew honey beer. Limited services are also available in the community of Meeker Park, about 2 miles south.

For more information: Rocky Mountain National Park, Estes Park, CO 80517, 970-586-1206 general information, 970-586-1242 backcountry permits, 970-586-4975 Longs Peak Ranger Station. Website: www.nps.gov/ romo.html.

---

10   Clear Creek and Summit Counties: Grays Peak

General description:	This day hike up a Colorado Fourteener, a very popular one due to its proximity to Denver, it is a straightforward hike on an established trail.
Distance:	3.4 miles, one-way.
Difficulty:	Moderate.
Elevation gain:	3,040 feet.
Summit elevation:	14,270 feet.
Maps:	USGS Quad—Grays Peak (recommended), DeLorme p. 38, Trails Illustrated #104.
Access/permits:	Arapaho National Forest.
Best months:	July– September.

Location: Central Colorado in the Front Range, about 40 miles west of Denver along Interstate 70 between Georgetown and Loveland Pass, on the Continental Divide.

Finding the trailhead: From I-70, about 6 miles west of Georgetown, take the Bakerville exit 221 and proceed south on unpaved Forest Road 189 (shown on some maps as County Road 321 and even CR 319) and watch for the Grays Peak sign and emergency phone box. From the Grays Peak sign, drive uphill on FR 189 1 mile south to a large Y-intersection and stay left. Proceed

Clear Creek and Summit Counties: Grays Peak

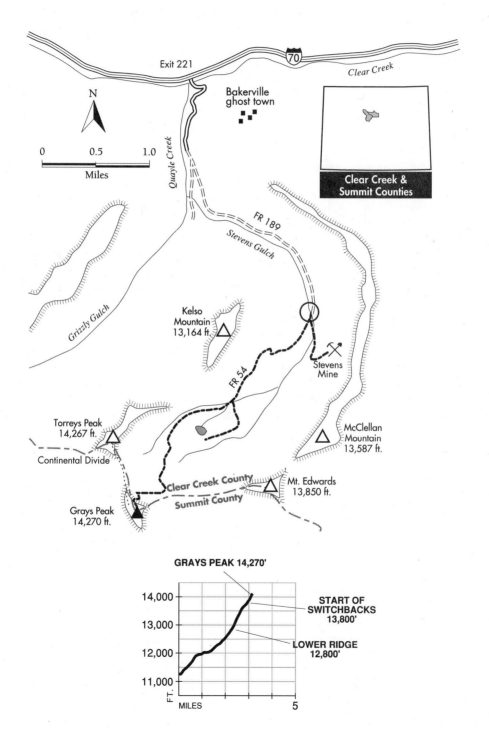

2.1 miles on FR 189 as it follows Stevens Gulch around the east side of Kelso Mountain. Follow this rough dirt and gravel road to the signed trailhead or until your vehicle can go no farther. FR 189 continues south for a short distance. If you stop short of the trailhead, be sure to park on the shoulder and not obstruct four-wheel-drive traffic. This route is generally passable after Memorial Day. A high-clearance two-wheel-drive vehicle can make it to the trailhead in good weather. The trailhead sign notifies you that you are at "Grays Peak Trailhead, 11,240'" and provides hiking information: "Grays Peak 4 miles (2 hours, hiking time) and Torreys Peak 4.5 miles (3 hours, hiking time)." The trailhead has wooden outhouses.

Key points:
   0.1   Wooden bridge
   2.2   Trail ascends out of basin
   2.9   Trail to Torreys Peak and beginning of final switchbacks

The hike: From the Grays Peak Trailhead, immediately cross the creek over a new wooden bridge and follow the heavily used Forest Trail 54. Continue southwest up the basin alongside the curving mass of McClellan Mountain, a 13,000-foot ridge that encircles the eastern flank of the approach trail. Once you pass Kelso Mountain to the northwest, continue curving to the southwest until you are above timberline and in the basin immediately below the Grays-Torreys saddle. Begin the steep climb up the north slope of Grays Peak. At the 13,800-foot level, at the beginning of the switchbacks, you may notice a trail to the right (northwest) that leads to Torreys Peak. Continue up the switchbacks to the summit. Wait in line to sign the register and enjoy a snack using the low rock walls as a windbreak. From the summit of Grays Peak, drop 563 feet north to the Grays-Torreys saddle and hike up to Torreys Peak, only 3 feet lower than its highpoint neighbor. Including Torreys Peak in your itinerary should only add an extra hour or so to your TRUBBLE (Time Remaining Until Beers, Burgers & a Leisurely Evening).

These peaks are only a one-hour drive from Denver and can be very crowded on summer weekends. Go on a weekday if you want fewer people or wait until after Labor Day. One interesting aspect of these peaks is that they are the only two Fourteeners directly on the Continental Divide. Grays Peak, Mount Zirkel in Routt County, James Peak in Gilpin County, Pettingell Peak in Grand County, and Summit Peak in Archuleta County are the only county highpoints directly on the Divide. In county highpointing circles, this peak is known as a "twofer" because its summit is the highest point for two counties.

The best season to climb here is after snowmelt in May or June through the first serious snow in mid-October, although these peaks are summited year-round by mountaineers. The route is north-facing and windswept and is not conducive to snowshoes or cross-county skis until late winter.

There is an impressive alpine panorama from Grays Peak. Numerous high peaks abound with Rocky Mountain National Park to the north, Mount Evans and Mount Bierstadt to the east, and Pikes Peak to the south. Pettingell

A crowd enjoys the summit of Grays Peak, typical of popular Colorado Fourteeners.
PHOTO BY BECKIE COVILL.

Peak, the highpoint of Grand County, can be distinguished about 8 miles to the northwest, just northeast of the Loveland Basin ski area. Mining activity dominates the slopes of most mountains in the area. The Grays-Torreys massif is composed of Precambrian igneous rock that was left in its present form by the Laramide Orogeny 65 million years ago. These peaks are on the western edge of the larger mountainous area known as the Front Range.

There is a higher concentration of Rocky Mountain goats and bighorn sheep in the Mount Evans–Loveland Pass area than anywhere else in the state. These critters are somewhat tame, especially the sheep, but use caution not to get too close to them, and never feed them. Domestication has become a major problem on the Mount Evans auto roads since the herds approach automobiles and will eat from hands held out of car windows. If you are lucky, you will spot the elusive ptarmigan, whose mottled colors blend in with the tundra to make them almost invisible. These alpine birds rarely venture below timberline and are known to remain completely still as hikers pass close by, a prime example of nature's camouflage systems.

County highlights: Georgetown is the county seat of Clear Creek County, and Breckenridge is the county seat of Summit County. Both counties were established in 1861. Clear Creek County was named for the major drainage that forms the heart of the county, and Summit County was named for the dominating high elevation in the region.

Georgetown is one of the oldest historic areas in the state. One can walk through what was once the third largest town in the state, see 200 of Georgetown's original buildings, and imagine the mining legacy that brought thousands of miners after the gold strike of 1859. Today, the town continues to draw thousands of tourists. Perhaps it's to take a self-guided walking tour of the town or to attend the annual Christmas market, held the first two weeks of December. Visit the many restaurants and shops or just enjoy the outdoor activities the area has to offer. Idaho Springs, about 12 miles east toward Denver, is home to several terrific bars, including the Pittsburg Mining Company, the Buffalo Bar, and Beau Jo's Pizza, that harken back to the mining days of yore.

With its beautifully restored buildings, Breckenridge also has that Victorian charm of days gone by and has earned a National Historic District designation. Check out the Breckenridge Brewery at the south end of town.

Summit County is best known for its skiing and offers the four terrific resorts of Arapahoe Basin, Keystone, Copper Mountain, and Breckenridge. Loveland Basin ski area is only about 5 miles west of Grays Peak on I-70.

Camping and services: There are no established campgrounds close to the trailhead, although you could camp there at a primitive site since it is in a national forest. Bear in mind that the trailhead is at 11,300 feet, higher and possibly colder than many peak baggers care to spend a night. Established campgrounds are available throughout Arapaho National Forest, the closest being south of Georgetown on FR 381. Lodging and full services are available along I-70, especially in Georgetown and Idaho Springs to the east and Dillon and Silverthorne to the west. The nearby ski areas provide services for daytime skiers only.

11 Gilpin County: James Peak

General description:	Map and compass are recommended for a half-day hike over a permanent snowfield and across tundra to an alpine peak on the Continental Divide.
Distance:	3.7 miles, one-way.
Difficulty:	Moderate.
Elevation gain:	3,300 feet.
Summit elevation:	13,294 feet.
Maps:	USGS Quads—Empire and Central City (required), DeLorme p. 39, Trails Illustrated #103.
Access/permits:	Proposed James Peak Wilderness Area in Arapaho National Forest.
Best months:	July–October.

Location: North-central Colorado in the Front Range, about 30 miles west of Denver, and 12 miles northwest of Idaho Springs.

Finding the Trailhead: From Denver, follow Interstate 70 west to exit 238, about 2 miles past Idaho Springs. (If traveling east on I-70 from Summit

Gilpin County: James Peak

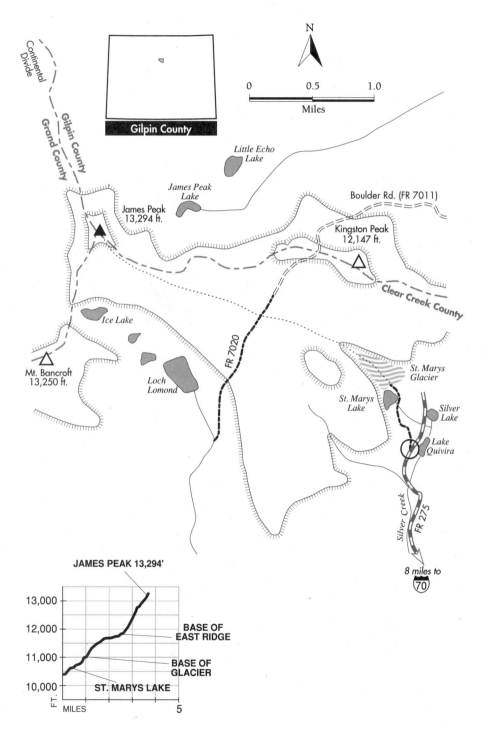

County, this exit is about 22 miles from the east portal of the Eisenhower Tunnel.) Turn north on the frontage road to Fall River Road (Forest Road 275), and take this winding paved road, passing Alice after about 8 miles. At mile 8.7, immediately after an abandoned ski lift, turn left (west) into a gravel parking lot. Several hundred feet past the large parking area is the trailhead, also on the left side of the road.

Key points:
　　0.8　St. Marys Lake
　　1.0　Foot of St. Marys Glacier
　　2.7　Base of east ridge

The hike: A large sign adjacent to a small fenced enclosure marks the trailhead to St. Marys Glacier. The trail climbs steeply up an abandoned road composed entirely of rocks. Continue for 0.8 mile, keeping to the left as other routes lead off to the north. When you reach St. Marys Lake, pause to take in the splendor of the cliffs towering above the tree-lined lake and look to the right for the snowfield curving up and out of sight to the west around the cliffs. Follow the dirt trail around the lake to the right (north), crossing the creek that empties the lake and reaching the foot of the glacier at mile 1. Don your sunglasses and climb the gentle snow slopes of St. Marys Glacier to mile 1.6, gaining 600 feet to the broad alpine meadow to the west. When you reach the top of the snow, cross the mile of flat tundra to the west, searching for higher ground to stay out of the swampy patches. Don't be surprised to see four-wheel-drive vehicles on these flats.

There are several high Thirteeners to the west, and James Peak is the one directly in front of you and farthest to the north in a row of peaks. Aim for the southeast basin at the foot of the peak, and wind your way up along a faint trail, turning north to a ridge that becomes the Clear Creek and Gilpin counties' boundary. The trail turns west and continues to the peak, skirting above the cliffs on the peak's east face. On the summit, Grays Peak and Torreys Peak are visible far to the south, Mount Evans dominates the southeast horizon, and the Denver metro area is clearly visible to the east. Sign the register and enjoy the sea of peaks and ridges around you.

You can glissade down from the peak in several steps, retreat across the tundra, and glissade again down St. Marys Glacier to the lake until July. Stay well away from the snow directly above the lake as it is steep and crowned with unstable snow cornices. Each year, injuries occur on these snowfields as inexperienced tourists emulate the seasoned hikers who are passing by them en route to the peaks beyond. The route to James Peak is above treeline and is exposed to weather and lightning, so monitor conditions constantly. Alternate routes to James Peak include a bushwhacking west approach off U.S. Highway 40 and a northeast approach on dirt roads from Central City, which we found to require a high-clearance vehicle.

The best time to visit the peak for non-snow hiking is July through September. From the trailhead on, the route is packed with deep snow until well into June each year. If you hike this summit before mid-July, bring an

Hiking James Peak in late spring allows you to practice glissading, sliding on the snow.

ice axe and know how to use it. If you don't mind crossing the tundra plateau during its soggy state, spring can be a terrific time to visit James Peak and practice the art of glissade, sliding down the snow. The Colorado Mountain Club uses the permanent snowfield for field practice sessions for the excellent hiking courses it offers. The summer scene is a party with countless tourists with picnic coolers and frisbees swarming over this snow novelty.

James Peak is one of six county highpoints in Colorado that lie directly astride the Continental Divide and is one of only three county highpoints in Colorado that mark a tri-county junction. The special nature of the James Peak Roadless Area is reflected in the current discussions to designate it a wilderness area. If successful, this could create a 50-mile continuous band of preserved mountain landscape stretching north from James Peak through the Indian Peaks Wilderness, Rocky Mountain National Park, and the Comanche Peak Wilderness.

James Peak is named for Edwin James, who in 1820 became the first person to record climbing a Colorado Fourteener, Grand Peak, near Colorado Springs. Major Stephen Long tried to rename this peak after Mr. James, but the peak was renamed instead after the more popular Zebulon Pike. Dr. Charles Parry fixed this oversight and gave the name James Peak to the 13,294-foot mountain and then humbly donated his own name to a higher southern neighbor, 13,391-foot Parry Peak. Edwin James gets the last laugh, however, as his peak is a county highpoint.

County highlights: Central City is the county seat of Gilpin County, which was established in 1861 and named for William Gilpin (1822–1894), the first territorial governor of Colorado. Although Gilpin County is one of the smallest counties in Colorado, with its 149 square miles exceeding only the city and county of Denver, its early history is credited with beginning the permanent establishment of Colorado. The mining district about 5 miles southeast of James Peak was first excavated in 1859 and was of such magnitude it began the establishment of Colorado and is known to this day as "the richest square mile on earth." Many camps were established in the area. Central City, so named for its central location, was a meeting place for miners from surrounding camps and was for a time more important than Denver. On May 21, 1874, a fire in Central City, started by Chinese laundrymen burning incense over coals in a religious ritual, destroyed nearly all of the dry frame structures. However, the town rebuilt under a new brick building code, including the famous Central City Opera House, which was described at the time as the most elegant between St. Louis and San Francisco. The county's economic base was revitalized in 1991 after Colorado voters approved limited-stakes gambling for Black Hawk and Central City. Gilpin County's chief industries are tourism and gambling, although gold, silver, lead, zinc, uranium, and tungsten mining activity continues.

Camping and services: There are no campgrounds in the vicinity of the trailhead, although primitive backpack camping is allowed along the route. The communities of St. Marys and Alice have no services, although a public phone is available at a building along the road, several hundred yards north of the trailhead. Full services are available along I-70 at Idaho Springs and Georgetown.

12 Grand County: Pettingell Peak

General description:	This day hike on trail and up scree slopes leads to an alpine peak on the Continental Divide.
Distance:	4 miles, one-way.
Difficulty:	Moderate.
Elevation gain:	3,253 feet.
Summit elevation:	13,553 feet.
Maps:	USGS Quads—Loveland Pass (required) and Grays Peak (optional), DeLorme p. 38, Trails Illustrated #104.
Access/permits:	Arapaho National Forest.
Best months:	July–September.

Location: North-central Colorado in the Front Range, about 15 miles west of Georgetown, and 3 miles east of the Loveland Basin Ski Area and the Eisenhower Tunnel.

Grand County: Pettingell Peak

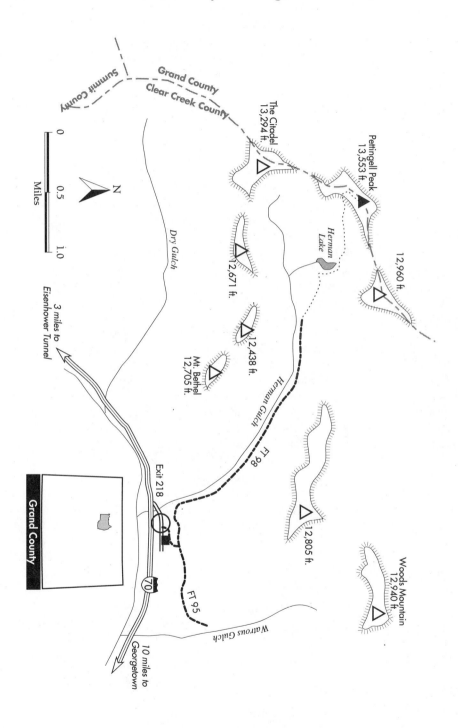

The Citadel
13,294 ft.

Pettingell Peak
13,553 ft.

12,960 ft.

Herman
Lake

12,671 ft.

12,438 ft.

Mt. Bethel
12,705 ft.

Dry Gulch

Herman Gulch

Summit County
Grand County
Clear Creek County

0
0.5
1.0
Miles

N

3 miles to
Eisenhower Tunnel

Exit 218

FT 98

Grand County

FT 95

Watrous Gulch

10 miles to
Georgetown

12,805 ft.

Woods Mountain
12,940 ft.

Finding the trailhead: From Denver, follow Interstate 70 west to exit 218, about 10 miles past Georgetown. From Summit County, take I-70 east through the Eisenhower Tunnel and continue about 4 miles from the east portal to exit 218. Exit 218 provides access to a highway maintenance storage area and to Herman Gulch. The trailhead is on the north side of the exit, about 100 yards east of the interstate on a good gravel road. Restrooms and a highway maintenance area are at the far east end of the ample parking lot.

Key points:
0.1   Junction of Herman Gulch and Watrous Gulch trails
3.0   Herman Lake
3.9   Ridge southwest of Pettingell Peak

The hike: The trailhead is located near the restrooms at the eastern end of the parking lot. Sign in at the trail register and stroll east along the wide trail for 500 feet until you reach a T-intersection. The right-hand trail (Forest Trail 95) goes east to the Watrous Gulch drainage, with access to Woods Mountain (12,940 feet) and Mount Parnassus (13,574 feet). The left-hand trail (FT 98) follows Herman Gulch for about 3 miles into the Upper Herman Gulch Basin and to Pettingell Peak. The first 2 miles or so are heavily wooded, and the last mile can be muddy. Snow lingers well into June each year and many hikers choose to ski or snowshoe this route. If you go during snowy conditions, inquire about the possibility of an avalanche since the gulch is very prone to these deadly snowslides.

The steep, rugged mountain directly to the west at the head of the basin is the Citadel (13,294 feet). At the point where you can see this peak, the basin begins to widen, and you soon reach timberline. Leave Herman Gulch Creek, and cross the tundra northwest up to Herman Lake. (From Herman Lake it is possible to climb north and hike west along the north edge of the valley, but this is slow going with no trail and substantial talus and rock scrambling.) Gain the ridge that extends southwest from Pettingell Peak by skirting the lake on either side and climbing into a gentle basin headed west. Follow a faint trail up a scree slope to a low point on Pettingell's southwest ridge. From this low point on the ridge it is an easy scramble on small boulders to the highpoint, marked by a cairn and register. This peak is exposed to weather that brews up quickly, so check the conditions of the sky periodically. Peer over the peak's impressive north face and then descend via the scree slope—and in June on the snow slope—all the way to Herman Lake. Return the way you came, down Herman Gulch.

The best time to visit is July through September. The trail is packed with deep snow until well into June each year. James Peak is visible to the northeast,

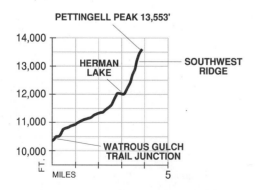

and the twin high peaks of Grays and Torreys are visible across I-70 to the southeast. Loveland Ski Area snuggles into the head of the Clear Creek valley to the south. You are likely to see bighorn sheep or mountain goats near the highway or on your hike. Traffic noise from I-70 can be heard faintly from the peak, and this is not one of the highpoints you would visit to escape civilization.

Pettingell Peak, originally named Ptarmigan Peak in honor of wildlife, was renamed to honor a judge and is one of six county highpoints in Colorado that lie directly astride the Continental Divide. For many years, the highest point of Grand County was thought to be North Arapaho Peak on the county's eastern border. You will pass by a marker inscribed "Carl Carlson, 10–14–92" just before Herman Lake. Perhaps he was a peakbagger.

County highlights: Hot Sulphur Springs is the county seat of Grand County, which was established in 1874. The county was named for the Grand River—later renamed the Colorado River—that flows from the largest natural lake in the state, Grand Lake. The county is bounded on the west by the Gore Range, on the north by the Rabbit Ears and Never Summer ranges, on the south by the Williams Fork Mountains, and on the east by the Arapaho Peaks, the Indian Peaks Wilderness, and Rocky Mountain National Park. A truly grand view can be had in any direction from the parklike interior of the county.

Kremmling is a classic Western working town, serving the area's ranchers and the miners who process the ore from the Henderson Mine near Empire, on the eastern side of the Continental Divide. The molybdenum-rich ore is sent via tunnel under miles of the Arapaho Mountains, near Jones Pass, to a mill where more room is available for processing and shipping. The small town of Heeney, about 25 miles north of Silverthorne, holds a summer festival to honor, of all things, ticks! Fall is hunting season in Grand County, and Kremmling and Hot Sulphur Springs are sportsmen's headquarters, with hunters spreading out in all directions, searching for elk and deer. The western edge of Rocky Mountain National Park lies in Grand County, and Trail Ridge Road funnels thousands of tourists from Estes Park over the Divide and into Grand Lake and Granby. Lake Granby was formed by human hands, as many lakes in Colorado were. Grand Lake, however, is one of the few lakes of any size in the state that is a natural lake. Also located in Grand County is Winter Park Ski Resort, just north of Berthoud Pass on U.S. Highway 40 and one of Colorado's fine ski areas.

Camping and services: There are no campsites in the vicinity of the Herman Gulch Trailhead, although there are spots about 2 miles up the trail at timberline that will do for the primitive backcountry camper. The trailhead has an emergency call box and restrooms. National forest campgrounds can be found south of Georgetown on Forest Road 381. Others can be found a bit farther away, north of Berthoud Pass on US 40 and south of Idaho Springs on Colorado 105. Full services are available in the towns of Georgetown and Silver Plume to the east and Dillon and Silverthorne to the west. Loveland Basin ski area, located directly south of Pettingell Peak across the head of Clear Creek valley, services only daytime skiers.

13 Jackson County: Clark Peak

General description: On trail and up grassy slopes, this day hike leads to the rocky summit of a lonely peak.

Distance: 3.7 miles, one-way.

Difficulty: Moderate.

Elevation gain: 3,351 feet.

Summit elevation: 12,951 feet.

Maps: USGS Quad—Clark Peak (recommended), DeLorme p.18, Trails Illustrated #112.

Access/permits: Rawah Wilderness in Roosevelt National Forest; Routt National Forest; Small fee required for daily pass in Colorado State Forest.

Best months: July–September.

Location: North-central Colorado in the Rawah Range of the Medicine Bow Mountains, about 30 miles southeast of Walden, and 8 miles east of Gould.

Finding the trailhead: The best approach to Clark Peak is from the west side of the Medicine Bow Mountains through Colorado State Forest. The east approach, via Chambers Lake, is usually plagued by deep snow well into summer and has no formal trail. From U.S. Highway 287 north of Fort Collins, drive about 79 miles on Colorado Highway 14 along the Cache la Poudre River up to Cameron Pass and down into Gould. Follow CO 14 west a couple miles more and turn right (north) onto County Road 41. At this point you will need to pay for a permit to proceed through an entry station into Colorado State Forest Park. Inquire about conditions, ask for a map, and continue on the dirt CR 41 to the lower (west) end of North Michigan Reservoir, a total of 2.2 miles from CO 14. Drive past the reservoir for about a mile and bear to the left (north) and continue north another mile or so to an unnumbered road on your right (east) at a sign for "Jewel Lake." Take this narrow road approximately a mile and a half to a parking area for two-wheel-drive vehicles. Beyond this point the road becomes muddy and steeper and a sign warns that four-wheel-drive is required. Vehicles so equipped can go another mile and a half to the official trailhead, only 1.5 miles from Ruby Jewel Lake. The road crosses the South Fork Canadian River to the trailhead but soon deteriorates.

Key points:
- 1.1 South Fork Canadian River
- 1.3 Four-wheel-drive parking area
- 2.5 Boulders at treeline
- 3.0 Ruby Jewel Lake
- 3.5 West ridge of summit

The hike: The hike from the passenger-car trailhead follows a rutted and occasionally steep road for a mile to the four-wheel-drive trailhead. The hike then follows a pleasant trail from the river crossing through an evergreen

Jackson County: Clark Peak

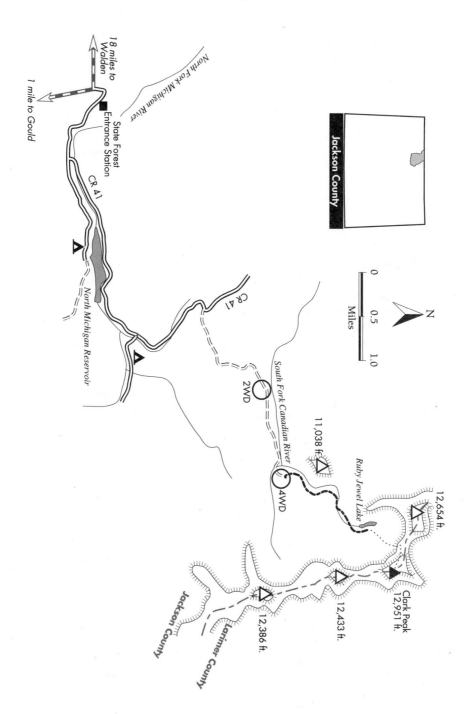

forest trail to timberline after almost 3 miles of hiking. The trail continues along an open boulder field, with an expansive view of the upper basin of the creek drainage, including Clark Peak itself. Ruby Jewel Lake lies just around the mountainside to the left. Once you reach the lake, you can decide to head for the saddle to the left (west) of Clark Peak at 12,250 feet or attack one of several gullies that offer a more direct approach to the peak. Use caution in the steep gullies if there is any snow present. If so, an ice axe will make your climb safer and allow for a good glissade back down if conditions are right. After exiting the gullies, continue your climb uphill on rocky outcrops and across steep, grassy tundra. The route consists of small talus and scree and will not be an obstacle if you have made it this far. The summit area has a few small boulders but is gently rounded and undistinguished. Look for a benchmark imbedded in a rock near a small summit cairn with a register. As with most alpine peaks, you may wish to descend off the peak a bit to enjoy lunch out of the wind. Return by the same route.

The best time to climb Clark Peak is July through September. This peak is in the Rawah Range of the Medicine Bow Mountains that extend south into Colorado from Wyoming. Once on the summit, you are treated to a seldom-seen view of the north side of Rocky Mountain National Park less than 10 miles to the south. North Park is directly to the west. Most of the hike is in Colorado State Forest, although the slopes above Ruby Jewel Lake are an isolated part of Routt National Forest. The east slopes of Clark Peak are part of the Rawah Wilderness in Roosevelt National Forest. The mileages are not well documented and little literature exists for this route. Colorado State Forest (70,768 acres) is Colorado's largest state park. Dogs must be kept on leashes.

County highlights: Walden is the county seat of Jackson County, which was established in 1909. The county was named for Andrew Jackson, the seventh president of the United States and hero of the Battle of New Orleans in 1815. Scenic Jackson County is dominated by North Park, a large open valley bordered to the west by the Park Range and to the east by the Medicine Bow Mountains. This area is relatively unvisited compared to the rest of Colorado's mountain country, yet it offers a wealth of outdoor recreational opportunities. It is one of the few areas in Colorado with a moose population.

The first visitors to this area were the Ute and Arapaho Indians, drawn by good buffalo, deer, and elk hunting. In the early 1820s, the first European traders and hunters explored the area. Silver was discovered in 1879 and the population grew, but transportation was so expensive that mining was not profitable. Today, hay farming

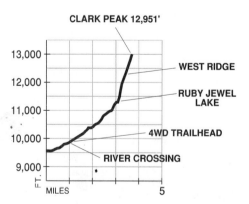

CLARK PEAK 12,951'

WEST RIDGE

RUBY JEWEL LAKE

4WD TRAILHEAD

RIVER CROSSING

13,000
12,000
11,000
10,000
9,000
FT.
MILES   5

A climbing party carefully scampers up soft snow in the couloirs just below Clark Peak.

as well as ranching form the backbone of the economy. Lumber is also important, with thousands of acres of timber cut annually in Routt and Arapaho national forests.

Camping and services: Camping is permitted in Colorado State Forest at several designated campgrounds, although a permit must be obtained in addition to a daily vehicle pass. Backpackers may consider primitive backcountry camping, which is allowed throughout the forest, including at Ruby Jewel Lake. Minimum-impact camping should be practiced to protect the fragile environment of the alpine lakes. For specific information, check with a ranger or at the state forest headquarters on CO 14 east of Gould. National forest campgrounds can be found along CO 14 east of Cameron Pass. Walden, about 21 miles northwest of the park, is a full-service town. Gould has limited services. Various services that cater to tourists and outdoor enthusiasts can be found along the route to Fort Collins.

For more information: Colorado State Forest State Park, 2746 Jackson CR 41, Walden, CO 80480, 970-723-8366.

14 Larimer County: Hagues Peak

General description: This very long day hike or backpack up an alpine peak in scenic Rocky Mountain National Park proceeds mostly on an excellent trail, with boulder scrambling at the summit.

Distance: 8.9 miles, one-way.

Difficulty: Strenuous.

Elevation gain: 4,940 feet.

Summit elevation: 13,560 feet.

Maps: USGS Quads—Trail Ridge and Estes Park (recommended), DeLorme p. 29, Trails Illustrated #200.

Access/permits: Rocky Mountain National Park, weekly admission fee.

Best months: July–September.

Location: North-central Colorado in the Mummy Range, at the north edge of the park, about 15 miles northwest of Estes Park.

Finding the trailhead: From Denver or Boulder take U.S. Highway 36 to Lyons and proceed about 19 miles to Estes Park. Follow the signs through town on US 36 to the Beaver Meadows entrance of Rocky Mountain National Park and pay a modest visitor toll. The park headquarters is just before the tollbooth. Continue on US 36 4.5 miles into the park, to the junction of US 34, also known as Trail Ridge Road. Turn right (north) on US 34 and go 2.0 miles down into the Fall River floodplain in Horseshoe Park. Turn left (west) onto Fall River Road (Endovalley Road) and go 0.1 mile to the Lawn Lake Trailhead.

You can also reach this trailhead by taking US 34 from the center of Estes Park to the Fall River entrance to the park, then following US 34 about 2 miles to the trailhead. Another approach is from Grand Lake on the west side of the park, following US 34 over the Continental Divide and down to the junction with US 36. Stay left on US 34 for 2 miles to the trailhead. Fall River Road, which joins US 34 near the Lawn Lake Trailhead, is the historic route over the Continental Divide but is now a recreational route with one-way traffic west, up the valley.

Key points:
1.3 Ypsilon Lake Trail junction
5.2 Black Canyon Trail junction
6.2 Lawn Lake
8.2 The Saddle

The hike: Follow the well-maintained Lawn Lake Trail northeast through the trees 6.2 miles to Lawn Lake, at timberline. The trail joins the banks of the Roaring River near Horseshoe Falls shortly after the trailhead and follows it all the way to a meadow just below Lawn Lake. Here at mile 5.2, the Lawn Lake Trail intersects the Black Canyon Trail and continues left (west)

Larimer County: Hagues Peak

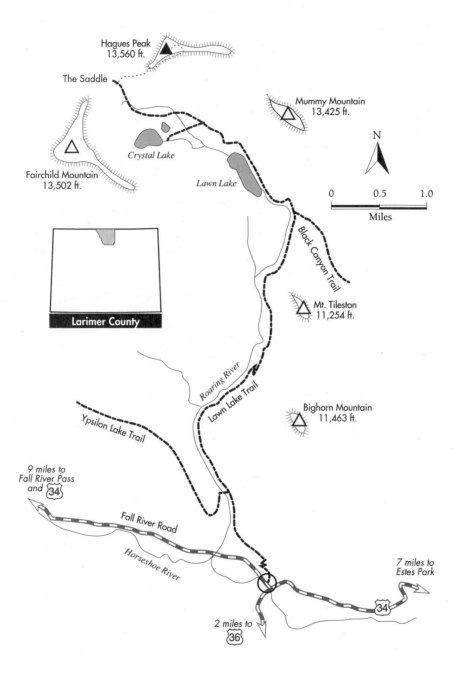

Hagues Peak
13,560 ft.

The Saddle

Mummy Mountain
13,425 ft.

Fairchild Mountain
13,502 ft.

Crystal Lake

Lawn Lake

N

0   0.5   1.0
Miles

Larimer County

Black Canyon Trail

Mt. Tileston
11,254 ft.

Roaring River

Lawn Lake Trail

Bighorn Mountain
11,463 ft.

Ypsilon Lake Trail

9 miles to
Fall River Pass
and (34)

Fall River Road

Horseshoe River

7 miles to
Estes Park

(34)

2 miles to
(36)

a short distance to Lawn Lake. The trail passes by the eastern edge of the lake, and then heads for The Saddle, a prominent pass between Hagues Peak and Fairchild Mountain to the southwest. The trail climbs above Crystal Lake and Little Crystal Lake and ends at The Saddle. Here you must choose whether you want to attain the summit by contouring northeast to the east ridge or by going directly up the southwest ridge. We climbed a direct route up easy tundra on the southwest ridge from The Saddle to serious boulder climbing at the summit. Alternatively, you can reach the east ridge via a long talus slope crossing northeastward under Hagues Peak's south face to gain the ridge just east of the peak. Try the former if you're up for it as there is no serious exposure and the distance is shorter, but exercise caution.

Return by either route. We recommend you backpack into the Lawn Lake area and then spend your days climbing Mummy Mountain, Fairchild Mountain, or other fine Thirteeners in the vicinity. Hagues Peak can be reached from the Chapin Pass Trailhead on Trail Ridge Road near 11,100 feet, but the up and down elevation gains you encounter on this route more than outweigh the benefits of a higher starting point, and the distance is almost as long. Hagues Peak receives a fraction of the attention that is given to the trophy peaks in the southern end of the park but is well worth the effort to reach it.

Although moderately strong hikers can successfully summit Hagues Peak in one day, it may be wise to reduce the stress and make this trip a backpack. The route to the summit from Lawn Lake is above timberline and exposed to the changing weather. The slopes leading to Hagues Peak have loose talus, and the summit blocks may require class-3 climbing moves that may become tricky in wet or frosty conditions. Be aware of the swift cold water in Roaring River.

County highlights: Fort Collins is the county seat of Larimer County, which was established in 1861. It is one of the original 17 counties established by the territorial legislature in 1861 and was named for General William Larimer, a pioneer whose name is intimately associated with the early history of Colorado. Arapaho Indians inhabited this area. In 1844, Antoine Janis established himself as the first permanent white settler to homestead in the Cache la Poudre Valley. Around 1860, disappointed gold seekers moved into the agricultural Cache la Poudre and Big Thompson river valleys. Increased attacks by Indians and bandits forced the establishment of 15 military posts along the trails in

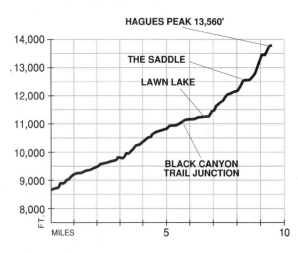

Hagues Peak over Lawn Lake in Rocky Mountain National Park.

Larimer County. Among these posts was Fort Collins, which also served as a major trading center for the region. As the need for military protection diminished and the post closed, settlers began to establish industries and businesses to support the existing agricultural economy. Colorado State University, located in Fort Collins, founded in 1870 as an agricultural college, is the largest employer in the county. Plan to visit the huge Anheuser-Busch Brewery for a free tour or the New Belgium Brewing Company, makers of Fat Tire Beer.

Rocky Mountain National Park, one of the premier gems of the national parks system, is pristine but heavily used. Buses move hordes of summer tourists in the most visited portions of the park, and traffic jams develop along US 34 and US 36 when elk come into view. Established in 1915, this 417-square-mile chunk of real estate attracts well over 2 million visits each year. Perhaps part of the attraction is the wildlife, the untouched landscape, or the 100 peaks that soar over 11,000 feet in elevation.

Plan to spend an afternoon or evening in visitor-friendly Estes Park visiting the shops and restaurants. You have a wide choice, from chuckwagon Western trips to sampling local honey ale at the Estes Park Brewery. Stop by the historic Stanley Hotel, which provided inspiration for the Stephen King novel *The Shining*.

On July 15, 1982, the Lawn Lake dam broke and sent a torrent of water and boulders rushing down the Roaring River and out over the Fall River floodplain, creating a delta of debris that can still be seen today. Unfortunately, this wall of mud and water flowed 8 miles or so down to Estes Park, where it flooded the main business district, left two dead, and caused millions of dollars in damage. As you hike up to Hagues Peak, notice that the

Roaring River's banks are devoid of trees and the water line of Lawn Lake is lower than the treeless shoreline, all evidence of the historic flood.

Camping and services: The National Park Service allows primitive backcountry camping at Lawn Lake as well as at several areas along Roaring Creek, one halfway up the trail. Permits, which can be obtained by mail or in person, are required for this regulated camping. Five automobile campgrounds are available throughout the park, the nearest being Aspenglen Campground on US 34, about a mile east of the trailhead. No reservations are required at this campground, although restrictions may apply to your length of stay. Additional campgrounds, as well as all forms of commercial enterprise, are outside the park in the tourist-oriented town of Estes Park. Only the daily park pass is needed to hike Hagues Peak, although a backcountry permit and fee are required to set camp along the Lawn Lake Trail.

For more information: Rocky Mountain National Park, Estes Park, CO 80517, 970-586-1206 general information, 970-586-1242 backcountry permits, website: www.nps.gov/romo.html.

Central Mountains

The Central Mountains are characterized by high and wide, massive mountains between major river valleys. This is classic Fourteener country, and the majority of Colorado's classic peaks are here. There are 15 Fourteeners in the Sawatch Range, 6 in the Elk Range near Aspen, and another 5 in the Ten Mile and Mosquito ranges near Breckenridge and Fairplay. While very high, it is interesting that none are on the Continental Divide. Each of these are full-day hikes and cannot be combined with one another, although several can be done in conjunction with another Fourteener. We suggest you consider doing Mount Lincoln with Mount Democrat, Mount Bross, and Mount Cameron, an unofficial Fourteener. Mount Harvard can be done in one day with Mount Columbia by a strong party, and Castle Peak hikers should be sure to visit nearby Conundrum Peak. Visitors to the state highpoint, Mount Elbert, can go about a mile out of their way and bag another unofficial Fourteener, South Elbert.

Central Mountains

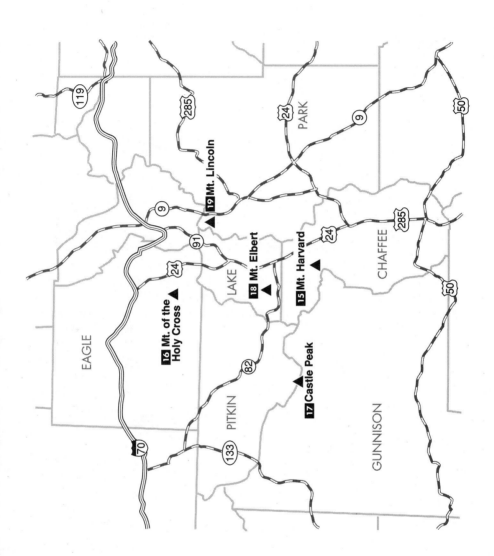

15 Chaffee County: Mount Harvard

General description:	A long day hike on trail leads to summit boulders on one of Colorado's highest Fourteeners.
Distance:	6.4 miles, one-way.
Difficulty:	Strenuous.
Elevation gain:	4,540 feet.
Summit elevation:	14,420 feet.
Maps:	USGS Quads—Mount Harvard (required) and Mount Yale (optional), DeLorme p. 59, Trails Illustrated #129.
Access/permits:	Collegiate Peaks Wilderness in San Isabel National Forest.
Best months:	July–September.

Location: Central Colorado in the Collegiate Peaks of the Sawatch Range, about 10 miles northwest of Buena Vista.

Finding the trailhead: From the junction of U.S. Highway 24 and County Road 350 at the north edge of Buena Vista, drive west out of town for about 2 miles on CR 350 and turn right (north) on CR 361. This will wind its way for about 1 mile and become a dirt road in the process. Make a hard left (south) at CR 365 and proceed about 5 miles to the North Cottonwood Trailhead. Note that the road becomes Forest Road 365 at the national forest boundary.

Key points:
- 1.5   Junction of FT 1448 and FT 1449
- 4.0   Horn Fork Creek
- 5.8   South ridge of Mount Harvard

The hike: Depart the wooded trailhead parking lot to the west on FT 1449, crossing North Cottonwood Creek twice before arriving at a trail junction at mile 1.5. Stay right (north) and continue into the Horn Fork Basin where you will eventually spot Mount Harvard ahead of you. At mile 4 the trail crosses Horn Fork Creek and goes to the head of the valley. The trail winds up around rock formations and boulders to gain the 13,400-foot south ridge of Mount Harvard at mile 5.8. From this point, head directly up the south ridge to the summit, following an indistinct trail until it reaches the rocky summit block. Sign the register, find a flat rock to eat lunch on, and return by the same route. Strong parties continue their trek southeast and visit Mount Columbia to nab two Fourteeners in a single trip.

The best time to attempt this peak is July through September to avoid snow. Take advantage of the drier days of late August and September. By late September or early October, snow will turn this into a technical route.

Mount Harvard was named in honor of the Ivy League university from which several members of the 1869 survey party graduated. Other nearby peaks were also named after graduates of eastern schools and the grouping became known as the Collegiate Peaks. The Sawatch Range has been, in the

Chaffee County: Mount Harvard

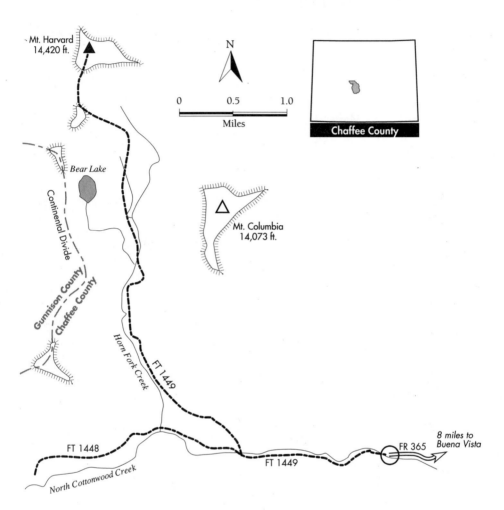

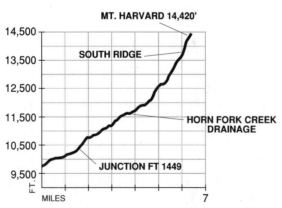

This distinctive boulder is a prominent landmark on the upper route to Mount Harvard.

past, referred to as Sierra Verde, White, Snow, Anahuac, and Sahwatch. The Indian word "Sawatch," which may also be the same as "Saguache," means "water of the blue earth." Nearby Mount Antero is known for its aquamarine crystals, pursued by those hardy enough to dig near its summit area.

County highlights: Chaffee County is considered a hiker's paradise, and a glance at the mountain ranges tells you why. More 14,000-foot peaks are located in this small area than in any other place in North America. The county is home to 12 Fourteeners, far more than runner-up Hinsdale County, with a mere 5, and larger Inyo County, California, with 10. The Upper Arkansas River runs swiftly through the canyons offering some of the best rafting in the country. A fun annual event held in the middle of June in Salida is FIBark (First-in-Boating-on-the-Arkansas), a 26-mile kayak race from Salida to Cotopaxi, said to be the longest kayak race in North America. Plan on making a weekend of it and enjoy the parade, the craft and food booths, and the music. Salida and neighboring Buena Vista have plenty of restaurants and accommodations for the weary hiker.

Salida is home to Il Vicino, a wood-oven pizzeria and microbrewery and great place to stop after your hike. Rumor has it that the majority of business comes from out-of-town guests, as the building was home to Salida's mortuary for over 100 years.

Salida is the county seat of Chaffee County, which was established in 1879. The county was named for Jerome Bunty Chaffee, who served as Colorado's speaker of the house in 1863. The gold discovery of 1860 was the first to draw large numbers of settlers to the Upper Arkansas River Basin. Farmers and ranchers settled the Arkansas River, and neighboring Buena

Vista grew as a supply town for miners and ranchers as well as a transportation center for those making their way upriver to Leadville. The railroad finally came to the Upper Arkansas Valley in the early 1880s, and both Salida and Buena Vista became rip-roaring towns. Today, most area residents make their living ranching, farming, or in tourism.

Camping and services: Backcountry camping is allowed in the Horn Fork Basin. The nearest national forest campgrounds are probably those found along Cottonwood Pass Road, west of Buena Vista. Full services are available in Buena Vista and Salida.

16 Eagle County: Mount of the Holy Cross

General description:	Often done as a backpack, this very long day hike on trail and boulders leads to one of America's most famous mountains.
Distance:	5.2 miles, one-way.
Difficulty:	Strenuous.
Elevation gain:	5,643 feet net.
Summit elevation:	14,005 feet.
Maps:	USGS Quad—Mount of the Holy Cross (required), DeLorme p. 47, Trails Illustrated #126.
Access/permits:	Holy Cross Wilderness in White River National Forest.
Best months:	July–September.

Location: North-central Colorado in the Sawatch Range, about 12 miles south of Vail, and 17 miles northwest of Leadville.

Finding the trailhead: From West Vail, take Interstate 70 west about 2 miles to exit 171 and head south on U.S. Highway 24 for about 4 miles to Forest Road 707, Tigiwon Road. Turn right (west) on this dirt road and climb about 6 miles to the Tigiwon Campground and 2 more miles to the Half Moon Campground. Park here.

Key points:
    1.7   Half Moon Pass
    2.9   East Cross Creek

The hike: This is one of the few Colorado county highpoints that requires a significant elevation gain on the return trip. This fact and the distance and elevation gain are enough to make many hikers don their backpacks and turn this trip into an overnighter.

From the Half Moon Trailhead, take the Half Moon Trail (Forest Trail 2009) to Half Moon Pass. This will take you up 1,300 feet in less than

Eagle County: Mount of the Holy Cross

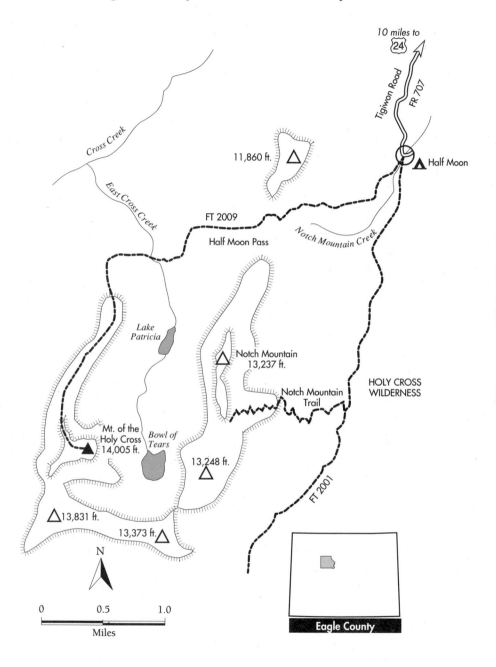

10 miles to
24

Tigiwon Road
FR 707

Cross Creek

East Cross Creek

11,860 ft.

Half Moon

FT 2009

Half Moon Pass

Notch Mountain Creek

Lake Patricia

Notch Mountain
13,237 ft.

HOLY CROSS
WILDERNESS

Notch Mountain
Trail

Mt. of the
Holy Cross
14,005 ft.

Bowl of
Tears

13,248 ft.

FT 2001

13,831 ft.

13,373 ft.

N

0   0.5   1.0
Miles

Eagle County

2 miles. From the grassy pass, follow the good dirt trail down 980 feet to East Cross Creek at mile 2.9. Ford Cross Creek and follow the trail west to gain the north ridge of the peak. The trail can be followed up this ridge for a short distance but is lost in the talus. Proceed up the crest of the ridge. In search of easy walking terrain, you may wish to exploit the snowfields that lie on the east edge of this ridge, but exercise caution to avoid the dangerous edge of the snow. At about mile 5 the route turns left (east) and begins the final climb over less steep terrain to a summit consisting of a jumble of boulders, 3,363 feet above Cross Creek. After signing the register and eating lunch, you may wish to wander over to the east face and peer down the vertical couloir that forms the upright of the cross. Return by the same route, saving enough energy to ascend the 980 feet from East Cross Creek to Half Moon Pass.

This route does not provide a good view of the cross, although the summit view of it, looking down, is rather unique. To best view the cross in all its glory, hike early in the summer when snow lingers in the cross couloir and bar to Notch Mountain via the Notch Mountain Trail. You can also access Notch Mountain from Half Moon Pass by bushwhacking south up the long ridge to the summit.

The name for this highpoint was attached to the peak in the early 1870s, and the peak has held celebrity status ever since. A painting of the Mount of the Holy Cross, by Thomas Moran, and a photograph, by William Henry Jackson, served to whet the appetite of a young nation eager to experience the mystique of the western frontier. Thousands made a pilgrimage here in the early twentieth century in hopes merely of viewing the cross. In 1929 President Hoover named the peak as a national monument. This area recently attained wilderness status after a lengthy battle over water rights. Fletcher Mountain near Hoosier Pass has a smaller cross formed by intersecting veins of quartz.

The best time to attempt this peak is July through September to avoid snow. Take advantage of the drier days of late August and September. By late September or early October, snows will come that turn this into a technical route.

County highlights: Eagle is the county seat of Eagle County, which was established in 1883 and named for the Eagle River. The first settlers were miners and prospectors searching for gold, silver, and coal. Eagle, with its prosperous mining fields and arable lands, grew in population. At first the county was thought unsuitable for agriculture, but persistence won out with the help of irrigation. Some vegetables, grains, and

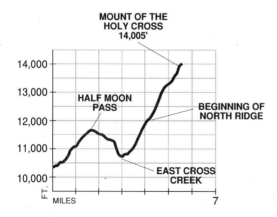

The goal of this county highpointer is achieved by standing on the distinct summit boulder of Mount of the Holy Cross.

hardier fruits produced satisfactory crops, and there also was ample room for horse and cattle ranching. The county has survived economic mishaps with the trifold ventures of farming, mining, and outdoor recreation. The county is 55 percent covered by the White River National Forest, which offers outstanding hunting and trout fishing. The world famous town of Vail is on I-70 in the eastern part of the county. Vail Mountain is annually voted the most popular ski resort in Colorado and perhaps the nation.

Camping and services: There has been talk of restricting backcountry camping due to overuse in prime areas. However, camping is currently allowed along the route as long as campsites are 100 feet from water sources and trails. The Forest Service campgrounds of Half Moon and Tigiwon are located on the approach road, FR 707. Services are available in the town of Minturn on US 24 and in West Vail and Avon on I-70.

17 Gunnison and Pitkin Counties: Castle Peak

General description:	This long day hike on trail and scree leads to a small, rocky Fourteener summit with the option of a nearby Fourteener subpeak.
Distance:	5.1 miles, one-way.
Difficulty:	Strenuous.
Elevation gain:	4,465 feet.
Summit elevation:	14,265 feet.
Maps:	USGS Quad—Hayden Peak (required), DeLorme p. 46, Trails Illustrated #127.
Access/permits:	Maroon Bells Snowmass Wilderness in White River National Forest.
Best months:	July–September.

Location: Central Colorado in the Elk Mountains, about 12 miles south of Aspen, and 4 miles east of East Maroon Pass.

Finding the trailhead: On Aspen's northwest end, look for the steeple of a brick church on the left (south) side of Colorado Highway 82 and turn at it onto Maroon Road. Immediately take a left onto paved Castle Creek Road, County Road 15, and proceed south toward the Elk Mountains. This road shortly becomes Forest Road 102. At about mile 5, pass FR 128 on the right (west); it leads to Conundrum Creek and an alternative approach to Castle Peak. Continue south on FR 102 and pass Ashcroft at about mile 11. Near mile 13 take dirt FR 102 to the right (west) as FR 121 bears to the left and crosses Castle Creek. Continue on FR 102 to mile 13.5 on the flats along Castle Creek. Two-wheel-drive vehicles park here. Four-wheel-drive vehicles may continue on the steeper and rougher road all the way to the Montezuma Mine at 12,500 feet or higher; however, snowdrifts and snowmelt may make this additional drive impossible.

Key points:
- 0.8 Castle Creek
- 3.8 Switchback to Montezuma Mine
- 4.9 Ridge between Castle Peak and Conundrum Peak

The hike: From the two-wheel-drive trailhead at 9,800 feet, hike the good road as it follows the Castle Creek drainage southwest. At mile 0.8 the road crosses the creek but we found it too deep to ford by vehicle in late June 1996. The creek may be shallow enough in August or September of most years. The road again crosses the creek at mile 2.1 and turns northwest to follow a major side drainage toward the Montezuma Mine. Note the road on the left (south) to Pearl Pass, a popular destination of four-wheel-drive enthusiasts. At mile 3.8 a side road begins a series of switchbacks north to the mine at 12,700 feet; however, turn left (west) and continue up the valley.

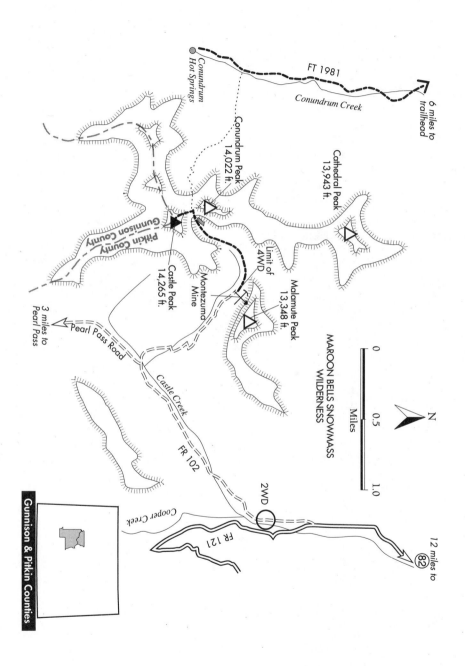

Conundrum Hot Springs

FT 1981

6 miles to trailhead

Conundrum Creek

Conundrum Peak
14,022 ft.

Cathedral Peak
13,943 ft.

Pitkin County
Gunnison County

Castle Peak
14,265 ft.

Montezuma Mine

Limit of 4WD

Malamute Peak
13,348 ft.

3 miles to Pearl Pass

Pearl Pass Road

Castle Creek

MAROON BELLS SNOWMASS WILDERNESS

N

Miles

0   0.5   1.0

FR 102

Cooper Creek

2WD

FR 121

12 miles to 82

The road curves broadly southwest toward a hanging valley bounded to the west by Conundrum Peak and to the south by Castle Peak. Follow a trail into the head of this valley and aim for the low point in the ridge connecting these two Fourteeners. The east face of this ridge holds snow throughout the year, so we recommend carrying an ice axe. Gain this rocky ridge and follow it south, staying to the right (west) around rock outcrops to the small, elongated summit of Castle Peak. Enjoy the fact that you've reached the highest point of two counties for your effort. The county line crosses over this summit, allowing both counties to share this high ground.

For extra credit, consider the relatively easy hike back across the ridge to the north and gain Conundrum Peak. Be sure to visit both the south and north peaks of this Fourteener that does not have sufficient geometric criteria to classify it as a peak in its own right. Contact the Colorado Mountain Club for additional information about the requirements for defining a Fourteener. Return by hiking back to the connecting ridge, drop down into the hanging valley, and follow the road back down to Castle Creek.

An alternative approach to Castle Peak takes you past Conundrum Hot Springs in Conundrum Valley to the west of the peak. Take FR 102 south for about 5 miles. Turn right (south) onto FR 128 and follow that narrow dirt road an additional mile through a residential area to the trailhead. Backpack about 8 miles up Conundrum Creek on Forest Trail 1981 to the hot springs at 11,200 feet. This narrow valley is subject to avalanches, so consider a later season attempt on this route. Campsites near the clothing-optional hot springs have been marked and are patrolled by rangers. Additional campsites can be found in the forest before you reach the springs. The route to Castle Peak begins about 0.5 mile north of the springs at 10,800 feet where you cross the creek to the east, push through willow thickets, and pick a route across talus into the basin west of the highpoint. Class-3 climbing allows you to gain the ridge between Castle Peak and Conundrum Peak, and from there the trail follows the ridge south to the peak.

The best time to attempt this peak is July through September to avoid snow, although we found June's blanket of snow in the upper basin to be a training ground for ice-axe use. Use caution against avalanche danger on

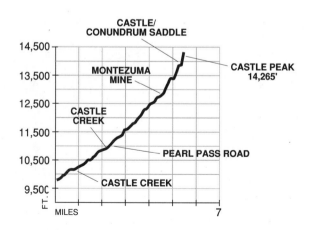

the steep cornice-crowned slopes. If you wish, take advantage of the drier days of late August and September. By late September or early October, snow will turn this into a technical route.

County highlights: Gunnison is the county seat of Gunnison County, which was established in 1877 and named for Captain John William Gunnison, a U.S. military academy graduate who participated in Indian campaigns in Florida in the 1830s. He was killed in 1853 by Indians while surveying a railroad route in Utah. The Gunnison area is quintessentially western, its character having been molded by Indians, miners, ranchers, and railroads. Gunnison National Forest encompasses 1.6 million acres of hiking, skiing, fishing, hunting, and the state's largest body of water, Blue Mesa Reservoir. Gunnison locals appear proud of the fact that chilling winter temperatures in the Gunnison Valley are often the coldest in the country.

Aspen is the county seat of Pitkin County, which was established in 1881 and named for Frederick Walker Pitkin, who traveled to Colorado to improve his health, yet found himself serving as the second governor. Once an active mining district that produced the world's largest silver nugget weighing over a ton, tourism has now become one of the largest industries in the county. The upscale town of Aspen is internationally known for its mountain beauty and challenging ski resorts, a dual attraction that lures celebrities from across the country. Aspen hosts the Mother Lode Volleyball Tournament each Labor Day weekend. This event draws hundreds of two-person teams and offers an interesting contrast to the usually upscale tourists. For potential celebrity sightings, try the Hotel Jerome for lunch.

Castle Peak, the highest point of two counties, is best viewed form nearby Conundrum Peak.

Camping and services: Camping is allowed along the road that leads into the Maroon Bells Snowmass Wilderness. Wilderness regulations apply west of the road's end, about 0.5 mile up the drainage from the Montezuma Mine. The Forest Service maintains several popular campgrounds on Maroon Creek Road that provide access to the world-famous scenery of the Maroon Bells. Aspen is a full-service town, although it may seem a bit crowded and pricey to those used to sleepy mountain towns.

18 Lake County: Mount Elbert

General description:	The highest point in Colorado, this Fourteener provides a popular day hike on a steep, loose trail.
Distance:	4.3 miles, one-way.
Difficulty:	Strenuous.
Elevation gain:	4,423 feet net.
Summit elevation:	14,433 feet.
Maps:	USGS Quads—Mount Elbert (required) and Mount Massive (recommended), DeLorme p. 47, Trails Illustrated #127.
Access/permits:	San Isabel National Forest.
Best months:	July–September.

Location: Central Colorado in the Sawatch Range, about 11 miles southwest of Leadville, and 4 miles northwest of Twin Lakes Reservoir.

Finding the trailhead: From Leadville, drive southwest on U.S. Highway 24 for about 3 miles to a point where the highway turns left (south) toward Buena Vista. At this curve, turn right (west) onto paved Colorado Highway 300, set your odometer, and drive 0.7 mile to County Road 11. Turn left (south) onto this all-weather road and proceed to San Isabel National Forest at mile 4 where the road becomes Forest Road 110. Continue south and pass Half Moon Campground at mile 5.5 and Elbert Creek Campground at mile 6.5 and arrive at the trailhead near mile 7. Park on the right (north) side of the road and walk across the road to the south to the trailhead. This trail is Forest Trail 1776, the Colorado Trail, which covers 469 miles from Denver to Durango and forms the major east-west trail across the state. The Continental Divide Trail forms the major north-south trail across the state.

Key points:
- 1.3 Unnamed trail to summit
- 3.7 Less steep summit area

The hike: From the trailhead on FR 110, take the Colorado Trail out of the Half Moon Creek drainage and hike south through woods for 1.3 miles, gaining little elevation along the way. Turn right (southwest) on a well-worn but unnamed trail. If you cross Box Creek you have traveled too far south;

Lake County: Mount Elbert

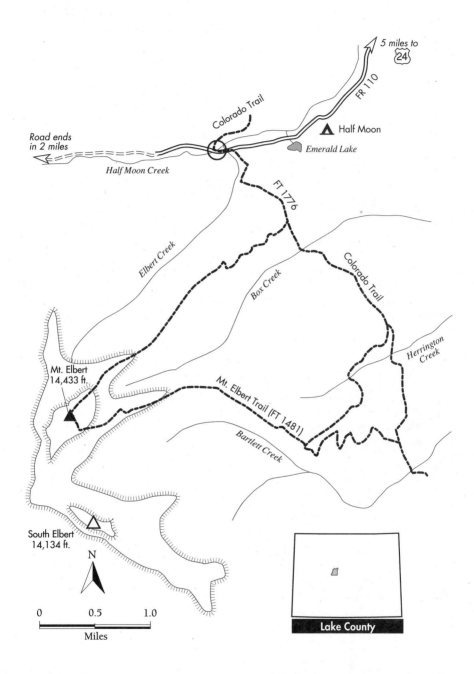

5 miles to
24

FR 110

Colorado Trail

Road ends
in 2 miles

Half Moon

Emerald Lake

Half Moon Creek

FT 1776

Elbert Creek

Box Creek

Colorado Trail

Herrington
Creek

Mt. Elbert
14,433 ft.

Mt. Elbert Trail (FT 1481)

Bartlett Creek

South Elbert
14,134 ft.

N

0   0.5   1.0

Miles

Lake County

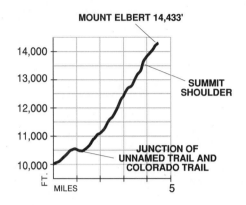

MOUNT ELBERT 14,433'

SUMMIT SHOULDER

JUNCTION OF UNNAMED TRAIL AND COLORADO TRAIL

14,000
13,000
12,000
11,000
10,000
FT.
MILES   5

the proper trail is signed for Mount Elbert. The unnamed trail makes up for the relatively flat initial mile and does so with a vengeance, gaining 3,900 feet in about 3 miles. This effort will take you out of the forest, past treeline, and up the northeast ridge of Mount Elbert to the summit. The trail is steep with loose rock, so pay attention and try not to slip too many times. The route becomes more blocky and less steep near the summit. Now that you've reached the highpoint of Colorado, it's time to consider the other 49 states! Sign the register and return by the same route.

Among the mountains visible from the summit are two Fourteeners, La Plata Peak to the south and Mount Massive to the north. There was a time when Mount Massive was considered the highest point in Colorado and old postcards proclaim this "fact." If you are in good condition and the weather allows it, consider a jaunt south along the ridge to another Fourteener, South Elbert. This 14,134-foot subpeak will cost you 2.3 round-trip miles.

The best time to attempt this peak is July through September to avoid snow. Take advantage of the drier days of late August and September. By late September or early October, snow will make this trip much more difficult. Take care when climbing Mount Elbert as much of the trail is above timberline and exposed to thunderstorms. You are likely to be in the midst of dozens of fellow peakbaggers on this hike. Some come to do a Fourteener, some want a state highpoint, and a handful know that it is a county highpoint.

County highlights: Leadville is the county seat of Lake County, which was one of the original 17 Colorado counties established in 1861. The county was named for Twin Lakes to the south of Mount Elbert. Mount Elbert is named for Samuel H. Elbert, who served as territorial governor and on Colorado's supreme court. Although it contains the second-highest peak in the 48 contiguous states, Lake County is the third smallest county in Colorado with only 379 square miles.

In 1880, Leadville was the second-largest city in Colorado, with a population of more than 24,000. Many miners made and lost fortunes mining gold, silver, zinc, molybdenum, and manganese. It may be one of the most highly mineralized areas in the world. Located high in the Arkansas Valley at an elevation of 10,152 feet, Leadville is said to have ten months of winter and two months of late fall. Despite the elevation, the town hosts a 100-mile foot race, a 23-mile pack burro race from Fairplay over Mosquito Pass into Leadville, and a February snowshoe race to the summit of Mount Elbert. The area is also a haven for winter sports enthusiasts, offering miles of cross-country ski and snowshoe trails. One of Colorado's best-kept secrets,

Stop along US 24 south of Leadville for this view fo Mount Elbert, Colorado's highest peak.

Ski Cooper, located at Tennessee Pass, has one run directly on the Continental Divide! Leadville holds many interesting historic sites, including the National Mining Hall of Fame and Baby Doe's Matchless Mine. The Leadville National Fish Hatchery located on CO 300 west of Leadville has impressive stone buildings to house its brood of young trout and provides an interesting tour for anglers and kids.

Camping and services: Camping is permitted throughout San Isabel National Forest. The Forest Service maintains two campgrounds within a couple miles of the trailhead on FR 110. Full services are available in Leadville, including a variety of accommodations such as the historic Delaware Hotel in the downtown district. Several miles south of Leadville on US 24, the Mount Elbert Motel offers an unobstructed view of your peak.

19 Park County: Mount Lincoln

General description:	This popular Fourteener is often hiked with three nearby Fourteeners from a very high trailhead as a modest day hike on trail through talus and across tundra to the rocky ridge summit.
Distance:	2.6 miles, one-way.
Difficulty:	Moderate.
Elevation gain:	2,300 feet.
Summit elevation:	14,286 feet.
Maps:	USGS Quads—Alma and Climax (recommended), DeLorme p. 48, Trails Illustrated #109.
Access/permits:	Pike National Forest.
Best months:	July–September.

Location: Central Colorado in the Mosquito Range, about 15 miles northwest of Fairplay, and 10 miles south of Breckenridge.

Finding the trailhead: From Breckenridge go south on Colorado Highway 9 for about 16 miles, over Hoosier Pass to the town of Alma, 5.6 miles south of the pass. If you are approaching from the South Park area, go about 6 miles north on CO 9 from Fairplay to Alma. In Alma turn west on Forest Route 416, which is directly across from the post office. This dirt road is signed Kite Lake, albeit 20 yards up the road by a building. Be sure to take the correct road, as County Road 10 also heads west from CO 9 at this point. The fork for the two roads is off the highway a few yards, past some buildings, and FR 416 goes to the right, staying on the north bank of Buckskin Creek. At 4.1 miles you will reach the Sweet Home Mine, which is the limit for county maintenance, including snowplowing. The road continues to mile 6 to the Kite Lake Trailhead. The last mile includes a switchback and a shallow stream crossing but is negotiable by most two-wheel-drive vehicles. Park on the east side of the lake. If you elect to stop short of Kite Lake, be sure to park off the road to allow more adventurous drivers to pass.

Key points:
- 1.2   Cameron/Democrat saddle
- 2.1   Mount Cameron
- 2.3   Cameron/Lincoln saddle

The hike: The primary approach to Mount Lincoln is the Kite Lake Trailhead, accessed from the south near Alma. Mount Lincoln can also be approached from the west, near the Climax Mine near Fremont Pass, and from the north, along Platte Gulch and Montgomery Reservoir, but these routes are addressed in other guidebooks more suitable to Fourteener enthusiasts. We have elected to describe the simplest and most commonly used approach.

The trail to Mount Lincoln follows the eastern edge of Kite Lake and winds north to the head of the valley, where it switchbacks to the saddle

Park County: Mount Lincoln

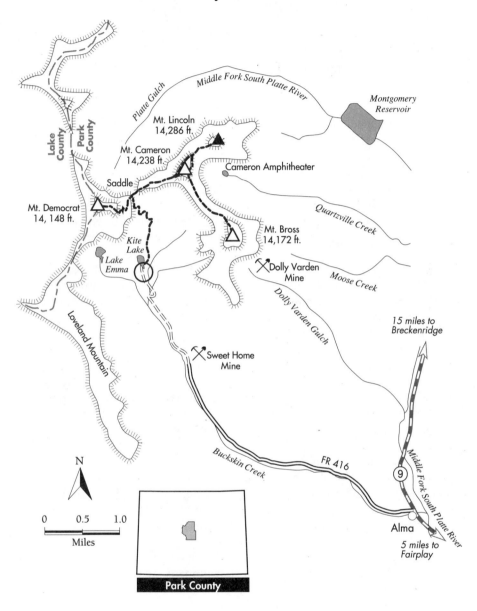

Montgomery Reservoir

Middle Fork South Platte River

Platte Gulch

Mt. Lincoln
14,286 ft.

Mt. Cameron
14,238 ft.

Cameron Amphitheater

Saddle

Quartzville Creek

Lake County
Park County

Mt. Democrat
14, 148 ft.

Kite Lake

Lake Emma

Mt. Bross
14,172 ft.

Dolly Varden Mine

Moose Creek

Dolly Varden Gulch

15 miles to Breckenridge

Loveland Mountain

Sweet Home Mine

Buckskin Creek

FR 416

Middle Fork South Platte River

9

Alma

5 miles to Fairplay

N

0   0.5   1.0
Miles

Park County

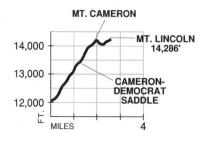

between Mount Cameron and Mount Democrat at 13,390 feet. Upon reaching the saddle at mile 1.2, your course will change to the right (northeast) as you hike up the southwest shoulder of Mount Cameron. The trail skirts Mount Cameron (14,238 feet) to the left (west), but you might as well go up and over to claim this unofficial Fourteener. There are at least a dozen similar "unofficial" Fourteeners in Colorado that carry names but are not recognized as official Fourteeners due to insufficient drop or distance between neighboring peaks.

Continue past Mount Cameron at mile 2.1, descending 90 feet to the saddle between Mount Cameron and Mount Lincoln at mile 2.3. This saddle is actually a half-mile-long sag in a gentle ridge that provides one of the easiest high-altitude traverses between Fourteeners in Colorado. The last few yards are through small boulders on an obvious cairned path. There is a peak register.

Follow the same route back to Kite Lake or visit Mount Bross, another Fourteener, by taking a trail south just before you reach Mount Cameron. We recommend that you return to the Cameron-Democrat saddle from Mount Bross, although some experienced hikers choose to descend to Kite Lake via any of several prominent gullies leading off the west slopes of Mount Bross and the Bross-Cameron saddle.

Many people actually drive up the east flanks of Mount Bross and Mount Lincoln in jeeps, so don't be surprised to see people four-wheeling in this area. Talk about a drive-up! Strong parties can start their day with an ascent of Mount Democrat, retrace their path down the saddle between Mount Cameron and Mount Democrat, and continue as above, collecting four Fourteeners in one outing.

The best time to visit is July through September, although access is dependent upon seasonal snowfall. The gravel road is usually passable to the Sweet Home Mine, the end of county plowing. You can still make the summit in a timely fashion by leaving your vehicle at the last snowdrift. The majority of the route is visible from the approach on FR 416; take an ice axe with you if you see substantial snow on the upper slopes. The Mosquito Range is notorious for summer thunderstorms, so plan on an early departure. Kite Lake is one of the highest trailheads in Colorado, and many peakbaggers are seduced by the easy access and multiple peaks. A great number are stymied by their lack of acclimatization while spending several hours above the 14,000-foot level. Few other trails in Colorado present as much sustained elevation. Be careful, drink plenty of fluids, go slowly if needed, and descend to the trailhead if you are experiencing difficulties.

The amount of mining on the slopes, especially on the east side of the massif, is staggering. The most famed mines are the Dolly Varden and Moose mines on the east flank of Mount Bross and the Buckskin Joe Mine to the south, where thousands once lived and searched for silver and gold. The entire area is premier ghost-town country, with remnants of many thriving late-1800s towns now mere piles of timbers and memories. The Climax Mine at Fremont Pass, about 3 miles west of Mount Lincoln, is the site of one of the world's largest molybdenum operations.

Ancient bristlecone pines deserve a visit. Contemplate these inspiring relics by turning right (northeast) off FR 416, about 3 miles from Alma, and driving north on FR 415 to Windy Ridge.

It is interesting to note that in the 1860s Mount Lincoln, a truly outstanding peak, was measured to be over 17,000 feet. The local folks considered several famous presidents for the name of this peak and settled on Abraham Lincoln. Mount Democrat was once known by the name Buckskin, and Mount Bross was named after an Illinois politician who owned nearby mining claims. These peaks are part of the Mosquito Range that separates the Arkansas River Valley from South Park. North of the Continental Divide, this range is known as the Ten-Mile Range.

County highlights: Fairplay is the county seat of Park County, which was established in 1861. The county name refers to the South Park Basin, the dominant geographic feature that extends for miles to the east from Fairplay. The town of Alma, on CO 9 north of Fairplay, is regarded as the highest incorporated town in North America, although Leadville, across the mountains to the west, challenges that assertion. Be sure to visit Alma and visit the highest bar on the continent!

Vast game reserves provided easy hunting grounds for the Ute Indians in this area. European trappers were attracted to the park, primarily for beaver.

It is easy to stroll the ridge between rounded Mount Cameron (left) and rocky Mount Lincoln (right).

During the gold rush in 1859 the settlement of towns began and by 1879 the railroad finally had completed the route from Denver to Como. Although the railroad was abandoned in 1938, you can still identify its trace along US 285. The South Park area remains a quiet place in the center of Colorado.

Camping and services: The USDA Forest Service maintains a rugged, treeless campground at Kite Lake. High-altitude hikers in training for mountains such as Mount McKinley (Denali) in Alaska may actually camp on the summit of these Fourteeners—in winter! The mountain community of Alma offers basic services, as does Fairplay farther to the south.

Southern Mountains

This region is dominated by the mighty Sangre de Cristo Range and includes two peaks in other nearby ranges. The mountains are hot and dry and conducive to spring and fall hiking. While Greenhorn Mountain is relatively easy, all the others require a full-day hike. There is a great deal of southwestern influence in the towns and cities in this area, and hikers are rewarded with wonderful opportunities for shopping or experiencing a different cuisine after a hard day's climb. Blanca Peak and Crestone Peak are each surrounded by two or three other Fourteeners that can be combined with the county highpoint for a challenging excursion. We suggest camping after hiking into these two highpoints and setting up a base camp for extended exploration of the high alpine valleys. Blanca Peak is the only "three-fer," or three-county highpoint, in the United States.

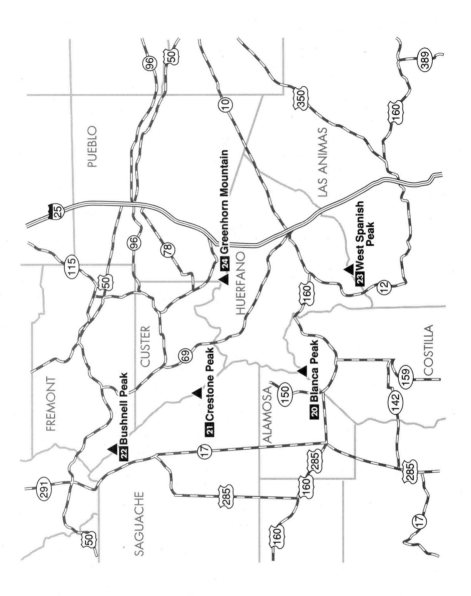

20 Alamosa, Costilla, and Huerfano Counties: Blanca Peak

General description:	This classic backpack into legendary Fourteener country requires a strenuous hike on a long trail and up a boulder field and summit ridge.
Distance:	7.0 miles, one-way, depending on where you park.
Difficulty:	Strenuous.
Elevation gain:	5,615 feet.
Summit elevation:	14,345 feet.
Maps:	USGS quads—Blanca Peak and Twin Peaks (required), DeLorme p. 81.
Access/permits:	Rio Grande and San Isabel national forests.
Best months:	July–September.

Location: South-central Colorado in the Sangre de Cristo Range, about 35 miles west of Walsenburg, and 25 miles northeast of Alamosa.

Finding the trailhead: The unestablished trailhead for Blanca Peak is on the southwest flanks of the mountain. There are three ways to get there. (1) From Walsenburg, take U.S. Highway 160 over La Veta Pass to Fort Garland. From Fort Garland, continue west on US 160 for about 10 miles to Colorado Highway 150, passing through the small town of Blanca. Turn right (north) and go approximately 3 miles to an unmarked dirt road. Turn right (east) onto this road and continue up the lower slopes of Blanca Peak until you feel you should stop for the well-being of your automobile. Most folks who respect their cars park at about the 8,000- to 8,700-foot level. The road becomes cluttered with cobbles and begins to steepen considerably beyond 8,000 feet. Hardy adventurers with high-clearance four-wheel-drive trucks and jeeps can make it a mile beyond the Chokecherry Canyon switchbacks at 9,000 feet to the stream crossing at Holbrook Creek. Those

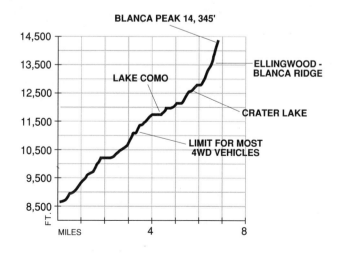

113

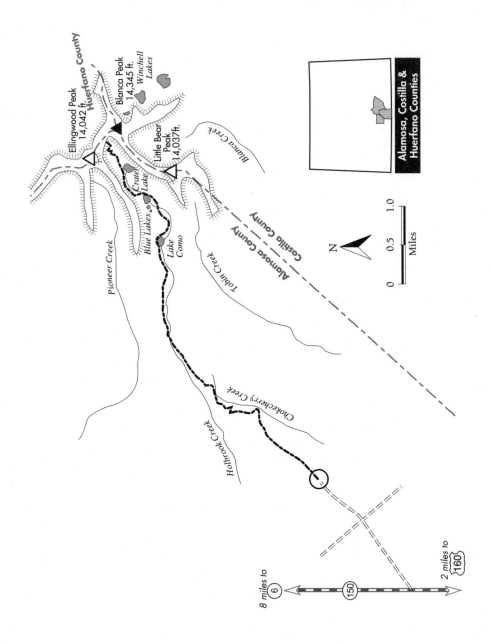

Alamosa, Costilla & Huerfano Counties

N

0   0.5   1.0
Miles

Ellingwood Peak
14,042 ft.

Huerfano County

Blanca Peak
14,345 ft.

Winchell Lakes

Little Bear Peak
14,037ft.

Blanca Creek

Crater Lake

Blue Lakes

Lake Como

Tobin Creek

Pioneer Creek

Alamosa County
Costilla County

Chokecherry Creek

Holbrook Creek

8 miles to
6

150

2 miles to
160

highpointers with an extreme propensity for VDL (vehicle damage likely) approach roads opt to try for Como Lake itself, about 6 brutal miles from CO 150. Few succeed.

(2) From Alamosa take US 160 about 16 miles east to CO 150, and follow north as above.

(3) From near Salida to the north, take US 285 south over Poncha Pass about 4 miles south of Villa Grove, stay left, straight south onto CO 17. Continue south for 37 miles, past Hooper, to County Road 6N Lane (Six Mile Lane), just north of Mosca. Turn left (east) and go about 16 miles to CO 150. Turn right (south) and go about 10 miles to the unmarked dirt road on your left.

Key points:
   0.1   Forest edge, road deteriorates rapidly to four-wheel-drive
   0.9   Switchbacks from Chokecherry Canyon
   2.9   Cross Holbrook Creek
   4.2   Lake Como
   5.2   Blue Lakes
   5.9   Crater Lake
   6.7   Blanca/Ellingwood ridge

The hike: From wherever you leave your vehicle, don your backpack and follow the road to Como Lake. The initial stretch up Chokecherry Canyon is steep and hot, especially up to the ridge that descends to Holbrook Creek. Here the trail is shaded and offers a brief but welcome respite from the sun. The trail crosses Holbrook Creek, and the road crawls across large granite outcrops, creating a sense of bushwhacking in the middle of a 6-mile-long road. After about 4 miles of steady uphill climbing you will reach Como Lake. Be aware that some of the property surrounding Como Lake is private. Continue on the trail through this basin, avoiding the old cabins on the southwest side of the lake. The pine trees on the east side of the lake offer a good spot to camp for the night. You may also camp at Blue Lakes, uptrail from Como Lake at mile 5.2. Get a good rest. The trail climbs steeply up to Crater Lake and across the basin formed by the headwall of the Blanca-Ellingwood ridge. Ascend directly up this headwall on a faint trail, looking for cairns as you go. Avoid the temptation to get off trail and head directly for the peak, as you will end up scrambling on loose talus. You will attain the ridge just south of the saddle at about 13,800 feet. Lean over the edge of this cirque to the east, and peer into the remote headwaters of the Huerfano River. This view has been indelibly etched into the memories of thousands of peakbaggers. Follow the ridge up to the summit plateau, scrambling occasionally over and around boulders. The summit itself is well marked by a large stone windbreak of talus-sized boulders and is the highest point of Alamosa and Costilla counties. Apparently the highest point of Huerfano County is 150 feet northeast at the junction of the north and east ridges leading up to the summit of Blanca Peak. If county boundaries follow the high ridgelines, then Huerfano County's summit is at this junction. Look for a summit register. Blanca Peak is the highest point of three counties and as such is the only "three-fer" peak in the nation.

For the typical backpacker, the best time to attempt this peak is July through September to avoid high-country snow. The summer heat will be oppressive at lower elevations.

Blanca Peak was once believed to be the highest point in the state, in part because of a local publicity campaign. Old postcards have been found proclaiming this fact. "Blanca" is the Spanish word for "white" and probably describes the snowy summit rather than the presence of lighter colored rock. The four-wheel-drive road up Blanca Peak's southwest flank to Lake Como is one of the most difficult in the state and should only be attempted by groups of experienced drivers. There is some controversy about allowing vehicles beyond Lake Como to Blue Lakes.

County highlights: Alamosa is the county seat of Alamosa County, which was established in 1913 and is the most recently created county in Colorado. The county name is the Spanish word for a cottonwood grove. San Luis is the county seat of Costilla County, which was established in 1861. "Costilla" is the Spanish word for "rib" and "furring timber." Walsenburg is the county seat of Huerfano County, which was established in 1861. Its name is the Spanish word for "orphan" and refers to Huerfano Butte, a small volcanic plug that sits alone on rangeland along the Huerfano River, about 6 miles north of Walsenburg on Interstate 25.

If you have extra time, don't miss the Great Sand Dunes National Monument, located about 15 miles north of the Blanca Peak Trailhead. Proclaimed

A backpacker inspects the ruined cabins near Lake Como en route to Blanca Peak, seen in the background.

a national monument by President Herbert Hoover in 1932, 50 square miles of dunes rise as high as 700 feet in one of the places in the state most visited during summer. A local hot spring provides water for a thriving alligator farm southeast of Hooper on CO 17. Also in the area is a bison ranch with accommodations.

Camping and services: Hikers camp at their cars along the unmarked dirt and cobble road on Blanca's southwest flank. Backpackers typically camp east of Como Lake and at Blue Lakes. Campgrounds are located throughout the San Luis Valley and at Great Sand Dunes National Monument. Full services are available in Alamosa and Walsenburg, and limited services are available in Fort Garland. Blanca, a small town on US 160 west of Fort Garland, was named for the peak and is the site of unobstructed views of this giant mountain.

21 Custer and Saguache Counties: East Crestone and Crestone Peaks

East Crestone Peak

General description:	An overlooked Fourteener subpeak in the shadow of its slightly higher neighbor requires a strenuous climb up steep class-3 couloirs and exposed rock ledges, usually after an overnight camp.
Distance:	5.7 miles, one-way.
Difficulty:	Strenuous.
Elevation gain:	5,800 feet from west, 4,740 feet from east.
Summit elevation:	14,260 feet.

Crestone Peak

General description:	The higher of twin 14,000-foot towers demands a strenuous climb up steep couloirs and exposed rock ledges, usually after an overnight camp.
Distance:	5.7 miles, one-way.
Difficulty:	Strenuous.
Elevation gain:	5,854 feet from west, 4,794 feet from east.
Summit elevation:	14,294 feet.

Maps: USGS Quads—Crestone Peak (required), Crestone (optional for Cottonwood Trailhead), and Beck Mountain (optional for Colony Lakes Trailhead), DeLorme p. 81.

Access/permits: San Isabel and Rio Grande national forests.

Best months: August–September.

Location: South-central Colorado in the Sangre de Cristo Mountains, about 50 miles northeast of Alamosa, 20 miles southwest of Westcliffe, and 10 miles north of Great Sand Dunes National Monument.

Finding the trailhead: Leave Colorado Highway 17 at the south edge of Moffat in the San Luis Valley and head east on paved County Road T for about 12 miles to the foothills community of Crestone. Turn right (south) on paved Baca Grande Chalet Road, which services, amazingly, a subdivision. Drive south for about 5 miles, crossing South Crestone Creek, Willow Creek, and Spanish Creek before coming to Cottonwood Creek. Look for a water tank on your left (east) on the north side of the creek. Park in this area and exploit the scrub trees for shade.

Key points:
- 3.1 Exposed rock slabs
- 3.3 Junction with FT 861
- 4.3 Cottonwood Lake
- 4.9 Base of south couloir at 13,500 feet
- 5.2 Red saddle at top of south couloir
- 5.5 Crestone Peak
- 5.6 Red saddle at top of south couloir

The hike: Before attempting these peaks, you should have experience in rock scrambling with exposure and route finding on rock faces. Both of these gems are climbed in a single outing as they share the same summit saddle; however, you must decide which approach to use. The popular east approach is through the scenic South Colony Lakes Valley but is not the safest approach because of the northwest couloir that is steep, loose, and often hides ice through the summer. The west approach requires more elevation gain but places you in the safer south couloir. We used the west approach to reach these highpoints and have chosen to describe only that hike. Consult other references if you wish to hike from the east.

From the Cottonwood Trailhead, begin the long journey by hiking eastward along the north edge of the creek on an old road that becomes less and less distinguishable. At mile 3.1 the trail crosses exposed sheets of rock that provide poor footing. At mile 3.3, look to the left (north) for a side canyon and the trail (Forest Trail 861) that leads to Cottonwood Lake. Hike up FT 861 to isolated Cottonwood Lake at mile 4.3. This area is scenic with a collection of Crestone behemoths towering overhead. To gain the highpoints, hike back west from the lake 0.2 mile to pick up a worn trail that leads north into the small basin formed by Crestone Peak and Crestone Needle. Identify the south couloir, which has a distinctive red saddle at its top.

Custer and Saguache Counties: East Crestone and Crestone Peaks

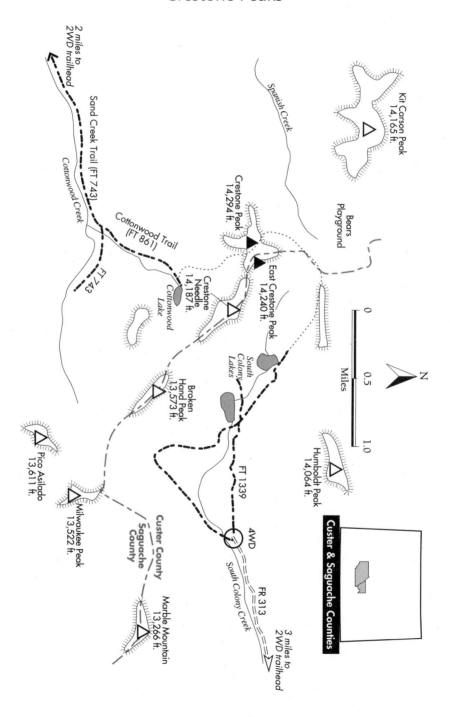

Kit Carson Peak
14,165 ft.

Spanish Creek

Bears
Playground

Crestone Peak
14,294 ft.

East Crestone Peak
14,240 ft.

Crestone
Needle
14,187 ft.

Cottonwood
Lake

Cottonwood Trail
(FT 861)

Sand Creek Trail (FT 743)

Cottonwood Creek

FT 743

2 miles to
2WD trailhead

South
Colony
Lakes

Broken
Hand Peak
13,573 ft.

Pico Asilado
13,611 ft.

Milwaukee Peak
13,522 ft.

Custer County
Saguache
County

Marble Mountain
13,266 ft.

FT 1339

4WD

South Colony Creek

FR 313

3 miles to
2WD trailhead

Humboldt Peak
14,064 ft.

N

0   0.5   1.0
Miles

Custer & Saguache Counties

Approach the base of the couloir from the right (east) via a series of ledges and outcrops, but do not commit to any climbing more difficult than class 3. Enter the couloir at 13,500 feet to avoid the steep, smooth rock at its base and begin your ascent by traveling up the couloir itself or negotiating the ledges along its right side. The couloir is wide and open and consists of ledges and blocks in its lower half and loose scree in its upper section. The rock type is unlike any other seen on Colorado's Fourteeners: a coarse, knobby conglomerate that affords numerous handholds and visual interest as you hike away the miles.

From the reddish saddle at the top of the couloir, you can peer down the northwest edge into the couloir accessed from South Colony Lakes. Turn left (west) and climb the class-3 narrow ledges and rock to the summit, staying on the left (south) side of the summit block.

The summit is a small place, rocky and airy, from which it may be possible to shout to those on Crestone Needle and the other Fourteeners in the area. The view is outstanding and surreal. East Crestone Peak is a short distance east, Crestone Needle stands isolated to the southeast, broad Humboldt Peak stretches off to the northeast, and Kit Carson Mountain lies to the northwest. Due east lies a great profile of Greenhorn Mountain, the highpoint of Pueblo County. Also visible are the Spanish Peaks to the southeast, Pikes Peak to the northeast, and Blanca Peak to the south. If you can pick out Bushnell Peak on the ridgeline extending to the north and Bennett Peak to the southwest, you can claim to have seen the highest point of at least 11 Colorado counties from one perch!

Fourteener guidebooks may describe Crestone Peak's east peak as "extra credit," but to county highpointers it is a crucial goal. If the weather and your physical condition are in fine shape, drop back down to the red saddle off Crestone Peak and ascend 300 feet up the southwest ridge of East Crestone Peak. This scrambling is on looser rock and requires a bit more exertion than its twin. Bear right (southeast) as you near the summit. Field observation with a handlevel suggests the middle of the three rises is the highest

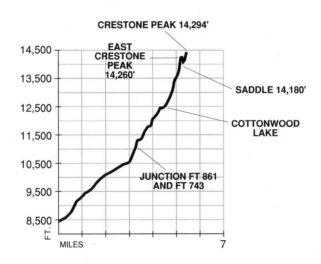

View north from Crestone Peak of Kit Carson Peak beyond the Bear's Playground.

and therefore the highpoint of Custer County. Early climbers of these peaks, unable to discern the 30-foot difference in elevation, thought that East Crestone Peak might be higher than Crestone Peak. Return by the same route.

The best time to attempt these peaks is August and September to avoid any snow or ice hiding in the couloirs and to take advantage of drier days. By late September or early October, snow will turn this into a technical route. Strong parties often combine these peaks with other nearby Fourteeners.

County highlights: Westcliffe is the county seat of Custer County, which was established in 1877 and named for General George Armstrong Custer, who led the U.S. cavalry into its disastrous defeat at the Battle of the Little Bighorn in Montana in 1876. Saguache is the county seat of Saguache County, which was established in 1866. The county namesake is the Ute Indian word "Sawatch." The Crestone Fourteeners have been referred to as "the Three Tetons" and "the Spanish Crags." The current term, "Crestone," is a Spanish word for "cock's comb" or "helmet crest," which would certainly describe this section of ridgeline in the Sangre de Cristo Mountains. The mountain-range name is the Spanish phrase for "blood of Christ."

Westcliffe lies in the Wet Mountain Valley and hosts Jazz in the Sangres, held the second week of August. If you pass through Saguache in the San Luis Valley, visit the old town jail museum that houses what is said to be the largest Indian artifact collection in the country. The jail includes the Alferd Packer display, in honor of the notorious cannibal held briefly in Saguache in 1874 before his escape from the jail.

Camping and services: Primitive backcountry camping is allowed along the route to these peaks; however, the approach drive and trailhead from the west is on private property and as such should be avoided when camping. The USDA Forest Service maintains North Crestone Creek Campground a couple miles north of Crestone on Forest Road 950. The town of Crestone offers a general store, art and gift galleries, and several places to get a well-deserved meal after your successful highpointing trip. This community attracts a spiritual kind of population, perhaps because Ute Indians had used this place to train their shamans. In fact, the San Luis Valley was called "Bloodless Valley" by the Utes in recognition of its sacred nature and prohibition against warfare. The town of Moffat also offers limited services. Great Sand Dunes National Monument attracts many tourists, and as a result various services can be found in addition to campgrounds.

22 Fremont County: Bushnell Peak

General description:	An unrelenting uphill climb on an old jeep road to a seldom visited alpine peak that finishes on very steep scree and a rocky ridge.
Distance:	4.2 miles, one-way.
Difficulty:	Strenuous.
Elevation gain:	4,735 feet.
Summit elevation:	13,105 feet.
Maps:	USGS Quad—Bushnell Peak (required), DeLorme p. 70.
Access/permits:	Sangre de Cristo Wilderness in Rio Grande and San Isabel national forests.
Best months:	July–October.

Location: South-central Colorado in the Sangre de Cristo Mountains, about 25 miles south of Salida, and 7 miles northeast of Villa Grove.

Finding the trailhead: You reach Bushnell Peak from the San Luis Valley to the west and from the Wet Mountain Valley to the east, approaching this peak directly up its slopes or along the ridges from Red Mountain to the north and Hayden Pass to the south. The direct route from the east requires a 5,305-foot elevation gain in approximately 6 miles, and the direct route from the west requires a 4,735-foot elevation gain in about 4.2 miles. In addition to less elevation gain, the west approach is recommended for its more even, albeit steep, terrain, and its exposure to the afternoon sun.

The west approach to Bushnell Peak, the highpoint of Fremont County, lies entirely within Saguache County. From Villa Grove near milepost 105 on U.S. Highway 285, head northwest for about 0.7 mile to the junction with County Road 57. Veer right (north) and travel CR 57 for 4.4 miles to a T-intersection. At mile 1, CR 57 passes over an old railroad bed used for

Fremont County: Bushnell Peak

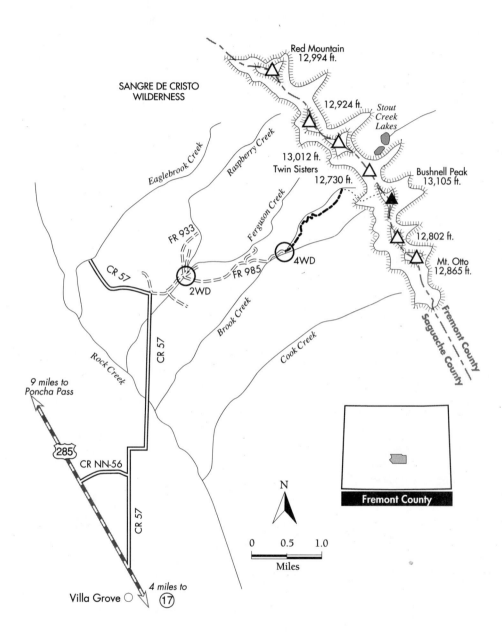

Red Mountain
12,994 ft.

SANGRE DE CRISTO
WILDERNESS

12,924 ft.

Stout
Creek
Lakes

Eaglebrook Creek

Raspberry Creek

13,012 ft.
Twin Sisters

12,730 ft.

Bushnell Peak
13,105 ft.

Ferguson Creek

FR 933

FR 985

4WD

12,802 ft.

2WD

Mt. Otto
12,865 ft.

CR 57

Brook Creek

Cook Creek

Fremont County

Saguache County

Rock Creek

CR 57

9 miles to
Poncha Pass

285

CR NN-56

CR 57

N

Fremont County

0   0.5   1.0
Miles

Villa Grove ○

4 miles to
17

hauling iron ore from the Orient Mine area to the south. At mile 1.5, pass CR NN 56. There is a jog to the right after about 2 miles. At the T-intersection, turn right (east) on a dirt range road and immediately veer right (east) at a Y-intersection. Continue generally northeast, gaining elevation, and after 0.6 mile take a faint range road to the right (east) at an intersection with a phone junction box. If you pass this turnoff at 0.6 mile, you will see a small house at 0.7 mile. Take the faint range road to the right, cross Raspberry Creek, bear right, and go through a wire gate. Park your low-clearance vehicle here as the road is very rocky in spots for the next 1.7 miles.

Hike or take a high-clearance vehicle east on this range road toward Bushnell Peak. Begin your hike by taking the right (south and east) fork immediately after crossing Raspberry Creek and continue on the dirt road to the Rio Grande National Forest boundary. Follow Forest Road 985 as it crosses from the Ferguson Creek drainage south to the Brook Creek drainage. The road ends at approximately 9,300 feet.

Key points:
- 0.9   Dogleg to the left
- 1.1   Faint road to the left
- 1.5   Brook Creek drainage
- 1.9   Abandoned cabins along Brook Creek
- 2.3   Road switchbacks
- 3.2   End of old road
- 3.6   Southwest ridge to the summit

The hike: This is a remote peak, seldom visited by hikers. It requires steep hiking with some rock scrambling near the top. The summit and ridge crests are exposed to weather, and during two visits to the peak we experienced strong winds created by the afternoon warming of the valley. Downed trees are a warning that avalanches do occur on the north slope of Bushnell's southwest ridge. Hunting is allowed in the forest, so use caution during the fall hunting season and wear orange. The approach to the wilderness boundary is in open range. The Sangre de Cristo Wilderness, established in 1993, is one of Colorado's most recently preserved areas.

Before setting out to find the trailhead, it is a very good idea to identify which of the mountain peaks along the Sangre de Cristo ridge crest is Bushnell Peak. From US 285, immediately north of Villa Grove in the San Luis Valley, use your topo map to generally locate Bushnell Peak. It is the fourth prominent peak north of Hayden Pass and bears a flatter summit block instead of a pyramidal shape. Bushnell Peak is

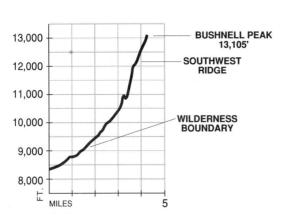

unique with its light and dark banding; other peaks are solid gray in appearance. Immediately north of Bushnell Peak is a wide saddle in the middle of which is a small but prominent peak, the southern peak of the Twin Sisters. Finally, the north flank of the ridge to the summit has no trees due to a forest fire; the other peaks have ridges that are uniformly covered with trees up to timberline.

The route to Bushnell Peak follows an old jeep trail along the south side of North Fork Brook Creek. From the gated fence near Raspberry Creek, hike east on the range road as it climbs the foothills toward Bushnell Peak. After 0.9 mile the road takes a significant dogleg turn to the left (north). After the dogleg, you might note a faint road (FR 955) to the left (northeast), but stay right and enter scrub oak forest. At mile 1.5, the road levels off as it enters the Brook Creek drainage, and at mile 1.7 the road ends at the boundary of the Sangre de Cristo Wilderness into which no motorized vehicles are allowed. High-clearance vehicles can reach the clearing at the wilderness boundary without much difficulty, although the rocky road gains 930 feet of elevation from the gated fence near Raspberry Creek.

The next portion of the hike is in steep forest along an old jeep trail that breaks through timberline at approximately 10,900 feet. At this point, note the avalanche-flattened trees. The old road eventually ends after a final set of switchbacks, and you are left staring at the headwall formed by the saddle between Bushnell Peak and Twin Sisters. To your right (south) is the southwest ridge of Bushnell Peak. The grassy slope of this ridge has only a few dead pine trees, remnants of a historic forest fire. Choose your poison and either hike directly up the southwest ridge of Bushnell or continue east on rocky talus and gain the southwest ridge farther uphill.

Once on the southwest ridge, proceed directly uphill to where the southwest ridge joins the main spine of the Sangre de Cristo Range. If you are not afraid of heights, stay to the left on the ridge crest and enjoy the views from the precipitous drop to the northeast. The summit can be accessed with a small amount of scrambling around blocks, but overall this is not a difficult stretch. Enjoy the pink and white granite near the top as you appreciate your successful arrival on top of Bushnell Peak. There is a register and remnants of a benchmark. Return by the southwest ridge, dropping off to the right (north) at whatever terrain you feel comfortable. The farther downhill you descend on the ridge, the more grassy the slope; however, it is steep and covered with small rocks on which you may slide. Watch for the old road as you near the bottom of the drainage and follow this down to your vehicle.

Bushnell Peak can be attained from the east side of the mountain range as well, although the hike is greater in distance and elevation gain. Begin this hike from Hayden Creek Campground (7,800 feet) about 4 miles southwest of Coaldale on FR 6. From the campground proceed north on Forest Trail 1336 (Rainbow Trail) and take FT 1402 left (west) to Bushnell Lakes. The peak is about 0.5 mile from Bushnell Lakes and 6 miles total from the campground.

A steep, unrelenting slope defines your hike of Bushnell Peak.

The best time to visit is July through October, when the snowpack is not prone to avalanches. The summit of Bushnell Peak reveals many peaks to the north and south following the long spinelike trace of the Sangre de Cristo Range. The west side of the range has steep, smooth slopes, but the east side is characterized by glacial gorges, cliffs, and lakes. To the south, Cottonwood Peak is the first large, pointed peak. To the north Twin Sisters and Red Mountain are nearby, and to the east you look directly down on Bushnell Lakes. To the west is the San Luis Valley, the size of Connecticut, which is bounded on the east by a fault whose recent activity has left fresh facets at the foot of the mountains; try to identify these smooth triangular shapes as you drive through the valley. The geologic processes that created the San Luis Valley cause mountain water runoff to be transported through porous layers deep underground, creating pressure that is released on the surface by farmers and ranchers as artesian wells.

County highlights: Canon City is the county seat of Fremont County, which was established in 1861 and named for John Charles Fremont, the unsuccessful 1856 presidential candidate, who led numerous western expeditions in the mid-1800s. Canon City was a favorite camping area for the Ute Indians, and it served as a war line between the mountainous domain of the Utes and the territory of the eastern plains Indians. Sporadic tribal fighting kept permanent settlers away in the early 1800s. The gold rush of 1859 eventually brought settlers to Canon City. The town grew quickly, and within two years there were 900 residents. Canon City hit the skids by 1863 as men rode wagons east to join either the Union or the Confederate side in fighting the Civil War. A territorial prison was built in 1871.

The steady growth of the prison system has provided residents with jobs over the years, without depriving them of small-town status. In the early 1900s, Canon City was a prime location for movie making. Spectacular scenery provided the backdrop for local cowboy Tom Mix, a hero of many silent Westerns.

Camping and services: Primitive camping is permissible once the national forest boundary has been crossed. Though remote, Bushnell Peak has a motel practically at its doorstep, the Inn at Villa Grove, which we found to be quite accommodating. The town of Villa Grove has full services. Valley View Hot Springs, about 15 miles southeast of Villa Grove at the base of Cottonwood Peak, offers weekday cabins and tent sites to nonmembers in a clothing-optional environment.

23 Las Animas County: West Spanish Peak

General description:	The higher of twin isolated mountains offers a day hike through woods and up steep talus to its airy alpine summit.
Distance:	3 miles, one-way.
Difficulty:	Moderate.
Elevation gain:	2,378 feet.
Summit elevation:	13,626 feet.
Maps:	USGS Quads—Cucharas Pass (required), Spanish Peaks (recommended), and Herlick Canyon (optional), DeLorme p. 92.
Access/permits:	Proposed Spanish Peaks Wilderness in San Isabel National Forest.
Best months:	June–October.

Location: South-central Colorado, about 30 miles northwest of Trinidad, and 20 miles west of Interstate 25.

Finding the trailhead: From I-25 at Walsenburg, drive about 11 miles west on U.S. Highway 160 to the La Veta exit. Go left (south) on Colorado Highway 12 for 4.5 miles to La Veta. From La Veta, continue on CO 12 for about 17 miles to Cucharas Pass, passing the Devils Staircase igneous dike after approximately 6 miles and Cuchara ski area after approximately 12 miles. At the pass, turn off the paved road left (east) onto County

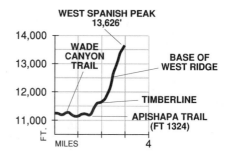

Las Animas County: West Spanish Peak

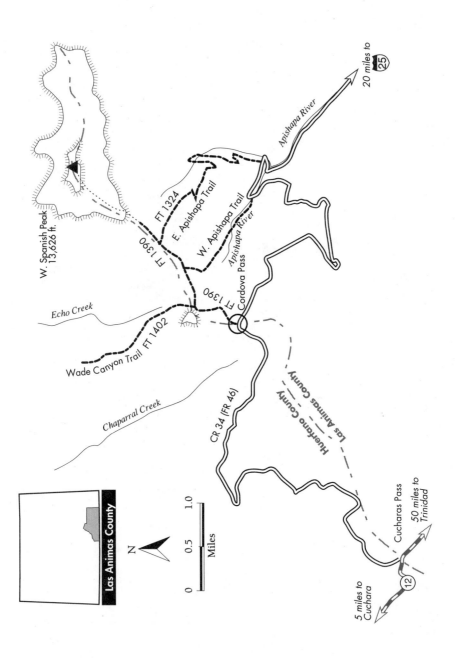

W. Spanish Peak 13,626 ft.

Echo Creek

FT 1390

FT 1324

E. Apishapa Trail

W. Apishapa Trail

Apishapa River

Cordova Pass

FT 1390

Wade Canyon Trail FT 1402

Chaparral Creek

CR 34 (FR 46)

Apishapa River

20 miles to 25

Huerfano County

Las Animas County

Cucharas Pass

50 miles to Trinidad

5 miles to Cuchara

12

Las Animas County

N

0   0.5   1.0

Miles

Road 34 (Forest Road 46) which is shown as FR 415 on some maps. Wind about 6 miles to Cordova Pass, known as Apishapa Pass until 1978. Park at the pass at a signed trailhead. For an excellent alternative return route, drive down off Cordova Pass on CR 34 to the east for approximately 25 miles to the hamlet of Aguilar near I-25. You may also approach Cucharas Pass from the south on CO 12, approximately 50 miles east and north from I-25 in Trinidad.

Key points:
- 0.3   Open meadow
- 0.5   Junction with Forest Trail 1402 and Wade Canyon Trail
- 1.1   Junction with Apishapa Trail, west branch
- 1.5   Junction with FT 1324, Apishapa Trail, east branch
- 2.0   Timberline

The hike: From Cordova Pass, follow the prominent West Peak Trail (FT 1390) east through the horse-fence gate near the roadside. At 0.3 mile pass through an open meadow that affords an unobstructed view of West Spanish Peak. Do not be intimidated by the apparent steepness of this peak. At mile 0.5, pass Wade Canyon Trail (FT 1402) to the left (north) and at mile 1.1 pass the west branch of the Apishapa Trail, which leads right (south) to FR 46. Continue on the distinct but poorly signed trail to an intersection with Apishapa Trail's east branch (FT 1324), which was once part of the Figure 8 Trail. (The Figure 8 Trail formed a figure eight around both peaks by circling around West Spanish Peak in both directions, meeting at the saddle between the peaks, and looping around East Spanish Peak. Many years ago guided tours were available for this popular hiking destination.) Keep to the left and go uphill at this intersection. Continue on FT 1390 up the west ridge toward the summit, passing several easy switchbacks until you reach timberline at mile 2. The trail basically dies here but picks up intermittently along the steep west ridge in front of you. Boulder hop steeply for about a mile near the crest of the ridge to the summit area. You will see a few cairns along the way. Stay just to the right (southeast) side of the crest if the wind is blowing. Once the ridge flattens out onto the summit block, follow the cairns and a better trail to the left (north) for 200 yards to the actual summit. The true summit is the westernmost of three gentle knobs on the crest of West Spanish Peak. A summit register was not found in the fall of 1996 but was present a year earlier.

A much less used north approach from the hamlet of Wahatoya uses FT 1304 to access the 10,300-foot saddle between West Spanish Peak and East Spanish Peak. The Figure 8 Trail can be followed around the mountain to the right (west) to reach the west ridge trail described above. The peak can also be climbed from this saddle by scrambling up the steep trail-less east ridge.

Early fall is the best season to hike in the Spanish Peaks area. Summer is very hot and dry. Winter snow may make the Cordova Pass road inaccessible. In spring, snow in this area melts sooner than in most major ranges in Colorado, and you should be able to do a spring hike by May, though the

The twin mountains of Wahatoya have long served a landmarks in southern Colorado.

snow will still be melting. Unlike most Colorado peaks, this isolated mountain sits apart from the nearest mountain ridge, and the 360-degree view of the lower countryside reflects this. The horizon is dominated by East Spanish Peak, 943 feet lower and about 3 miles to the east. There is a full view of the Sangre de Cristo Range, including Culebra Peak to the southwest and the cluster of summits in the Blanca Peak area to the northwest. The Crestones area can be seen to the distant northwest, and Greenhorn Mountain is clearly visible directly north. The plains sweep away to the east. West Spanish Peak is on the Huerfano–Las Animas county line. Because of their isolated prominence and unique double peaks, the Spanish Peaks served as critical landmarks to early inhabitants and explorers. The 18,000 acres encompassing these peaks is being considered for official wilderness status. Less than 5 percent of Colorado is currently designated wilderness.

The eroded igneous stocks of the Spanish Peaks rise over 7,000 feet from the high plains. This is a classic area for studying igneous dikes, and a sign at the trailhead denotes that this is a national natural landmark. Over 500 dikes spoke out in a radial pattern from West Spanish Peak and reach 50 feet in height and several thousand feet in length. A close view of one such dike is provided where CO 12 passes by the Devils Staircase dike, approximately 6 miles south of La Veta. Another good viewing spot is at the Apishapa Picnic Area, about 2 miles off Cordova Pass to the southeast.

The flanks of the mountain are covered with scrub brush, mostly oak, which turns a brilliant red in the fall and is a startling contrast to the golden glow of aspens in the Sangre de Cristos across the valley to the west. Numerous deer live in these thickets, and several species of birds can be seen here that do not travel farther north into Colorado, due to the dry, hot microclimate of the peaks. The area is popular during hunting season from October through November, and you are encouraged not to be in the area then; however, it should be safer than most due to the relatively short hiking distance in the forest before reaching treeline. Wear orange!

County highlights: Trinidad is the county seat of Las Animas County, which was established in 1866. The county was named for "the souls" from "El Rio de Las Animas Perdidas en Purgatoria," which is Spanish for "the River of the Lost Souls in Purgatory." The Indian term for the Spanish Peaks is "Wahatoya," meaning "Breasts of Mother Earth." T-shirts are available at Echo Canyon Ranch that promote the Figure 8 Trail with the imprinted exclamation, "Hike the Cleavage!"

Indians drove away the earliest settlers, but by the early 1860s the influx of white settlers was too strong to overcome. Agriculture that used irrigation ditches was the earliest occupation, later augmented by raising livestock. By 1890, the livestock industry had decreased by 75 percent, and the major industry had become coal mining. During World War I, more than 5 million tons of coal were mined annually; however, as other fuels became available and unionization took over, coal production started a downward trend.

Camping and services: Camping is permitted at the Cordova Pass Trailhead, although the USDA Forest Service maintains campgrounds on FR 413 north of Cuchara Pass and just south of the town of Cuchara. La Veta is an interesting little town with shops on the main street, while Cuchara is home to a low-key ski area and manages to have a nightlife at the local establishment. This is a good spot to stop after your hike. The first weekend in October in La Veta is Octoberfest, a great festival with Southwestern shopping booths, live music, food, and beer. You can be back to town by late afternoon, a reward for your successful endeavors. La Veta has a motel, and many motels are available in Walsenburg and Trinidad.

24 Pueblo County: Greenhorn Mountain

General description:	A seldom-visited tundra ridge crest is enjoyed during this half-day loop hike to the highest point in the Wet Mountains.
Distance:	2.4 miles, one-way.
Difficulty:	Easy.
Elevation gain:	1,527 feet.
Summit elevation:	12,347 feet.
Maps:	USGS Quad—San Isabel (recommended), DeLorme p. 82.
Access/permits:	Greenhorn Mountain Wilderness in the San Isabel National Forest.
Best months:	June–October.

Location: South-central Colorado in the Wet Mountains, about 20 miles east of the Sangre de Cristo Range, and 25 miles southwest of Pueblo.

Finding the trailhead: From Canon City on U.S. Highway 50 go east approximately 5 miles and turn left (south) on Colorado Highway 67 and proceed south across the Arkansas River and through Florence. Continue until you reach the hamlet of Wetmore, about 14 miles from US 50. Keep right (south) on CO 96 and follow about 10 miles along Hardscrabble Creek to MacKenzie Junction at CO 165. Go left (south) on CO 165, Greenhorn Highway, and drive 9 miles, going over Bigelow Divide to a sharp U-turn on Middle Creek where a dirt road (FR 360, shown on older maps as FR 400) leads west to the right.

The Forest Service has renamed the forest roads in this area during the past several years, so it is a good idea to purchase the latest map, dated 1998. A sign indicates the way to Ophir Campground. Do not take FR 361 left (south) to the camp but follow FR 360 for another mile, past a house with no-trespassing signs and coyote pelts strung along the fence, to the junction with FR 364 (shown on older maps as FR 401). Bear left and remain on FR 360 as the gravel road begins to climb the long ridge that forms the backbone of the Wet Mountains. At mile 3 you'll enter Burris Meadow and at mile 8 you'll come to the Custer-Huerfano saddle, Promontory Divide, at which point FR 634 (old FR 400) goes right (west) and FR 369 (old FR 403) continues straight (south).

Stay left on FR 369, Greenhorn Mountain Road. At mile 17 watch for hikers on the Cisneros Trail and Pole Creek Trail. During our visit, a sign labeled this road as FR 401 and stated that Blue Lakes were 5.9 miles ahead. Proceed southeast through islands of fir and pine in an impressive timberline meadow setting. At mile 22 you reach Blue Lakes. The road ends about 1 mile past these three lakes. All but the final 2 miles or so are excellent

Pueblo County: Greenhorn Mountain

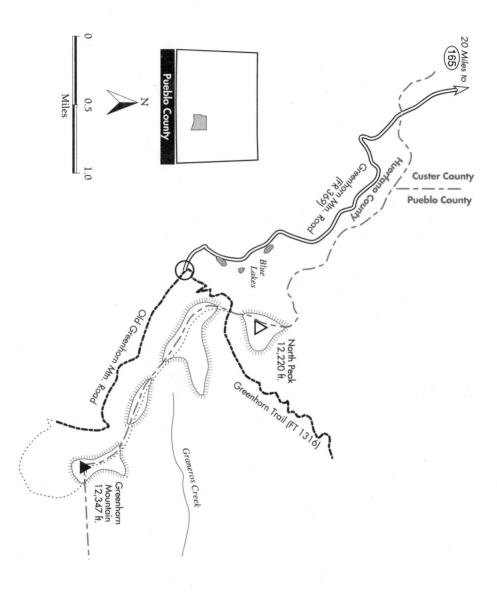

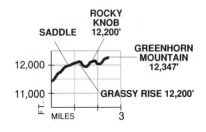

gravel roads, and the last portion is passable, albeit bumpy, and four-wheel-drive is not needed. Many years ago, Greenhorn Mountain Road continued to the very end of the ridge to the Bartlett Trail, but now it is barricaded less than 2 miles short of being even with the summit. You cannot see Greenhorn Mountain itself from this trailhead. The mountain was named for an eighteenth-century Comanche chief, Cuerno Verde, who wore a bison headdress with the horns painted green.

The junction of FR 360 and CO 165 at Ophir Campground can also be reached by taking exit 74 on Interstate 25 at Colorado City. Proceed west and northwest on CO 165 through the town of Rye and past Lake Isabel for approximately 24 miles to the junction. Continue to the trailhead as described above.

A completely different approach is possible up the Bartlett Trail (FT 1310) from FR 427 at the south edge of Rye. This is a major hike, involving 5,000 feet of gain, although many hiking enthusiasts prefer this over the relatively easy stroll from Blue Lakes.

Key points:

    0.1   Junction of Greenhorn Mountain Road and Greenhorn Trail (Forest Trail 1316)
    0.7   Saddle between North Peak and Greenhorn Mountain's high ridge
    1.3   Grassy rise at 12,200 feet
    1.8   Rocky knob at 12,200 feet

The hike: The route to the summit can be made even more interesting by following a loop hike. From the trailhead just past Blue Lakes, walk along the barricaded road to the prominent Greenhorn Trail (FT 1316) and take this trail east a short distance through the trees. This path will follow several switchbacks as it gains 600 feet to the saddle formed by North Peak to the north and the high ridgeline to the south. Upon reaching the saddle, turn right (south) and follow the ridge southeast along grassy meadows for 1.5 miles. There are several false summits, and the last one has a drop of 200 feet. Watch for a faint path on the last section as the ridge steepens. The summit has a small windbreak and a register. The ridge forms the boundary of Huerfano County to the right (southwest) and Pueblo County to the left (northeast). An unobstructed view opens to the south of the nearby Spanish Peaks and the length of the Sangre de Cristo Range to the west. This seldom-seen view of these magnificent mountains includes a peek up the narrow valley to the Colony Lakes and Crestone Peak.

If weather conditions permit, return by the same route or, to complete a loop hike, drop off the summit to the south and follow a road back to the trailhead. To do this, scramble 600 feet down the fairly steep southeast slope to the meadows and locate an old fence line, now just gnarled remnants of posts. The fence leads west a few hundred feet to an old road. Avoid dropping off the summit to the south or west as it is unpleasant rocky talus. The

An alternative to hiking the road is to take this grassy tundra ridge south to Greenhorn Mountain.

southeast slope is preferable for its grassy surface. Follow the old road around the southern terminus of Greenhorn Mountain's ridge and stroll northeast for about 2 miles on old Greenhorn Mountain Road to the trailhead.

The best season to hike in the Wet Mountains is from snowmelt in June to first snowfall in October. Phone the Forest Service and ask for current conditions if you aren't certain. The road from Ophir Campground to Blue Lakes traditionally opens in April and closes in November; however, snowfall may block the route much later in the spring and earlier in the fall. The trailhead is relatively remote due to the long approach on Forest Service roads. Take care when descending off the steep rock-strewn south slopes of the peak. As you travel the ridge crest, you will be above timberline and exposed to the elements.

The area is popular during hunting season from October through November. Numerous elk and deer inhabit the valley to the west of the Wet Mountains. The town of Westcliffe is a major staging area for hunting expeditions. Field checkers observed bighorn sheep in this area. Hikers are discouraged from being in any hunting area during this time of year, but this highpoint should be safer than most due to the very short hiking distance in the trees and the high trailhead elevation. Wear orange!

The Wet Mountains were formed when Precambrian granite pushed up through the sediments to form a long ridge. Faults mark the northeast edge of this mountain ridge. In unusual contrast, the highest point of the granite core of the mountain is at the southern terminus, where sedimentary rocks form the valley to the south.

County highlights: Pueblo is the county seat of Pueblo County, which was established in 1861. The county name is the Spanish word for "village," probably for the city of Pueblo itself, which was inhabited prior to 1800 and once an important trading post at the edge of the plains and mountains.

Rye is an interesting little town with shops on the main street, while Pueblo is a larger city dominated by a once-thriving steel mill. Canon City and Florence are home to Colorado's maximum-security prisons. Nearby, just west of Canon City, is famous Royal Gorge with its high suspension bridge, a must-see attraction. On CO 165, 24 miles north of Colorado City, is Bishop Castle. This unique and bizarre stone edifice is being constructed by Jim Bishop on donated land. Carefully park your vehicle along CO 165 and, with some additional care, walk up to the castle site and take a self-guided tour of the place. Be very careful when climbing the towers and turrets.

Camping and services: Scenic but primitive camping is permitted next to the trailhead at Blue Lakes and along FR 369 in the national forest. Ophir Campground is an established forest service camping area. Locally, Rye and Canon City offer several motels and hotels, some historic and some modern. San Isabel, located about 20 miles northwest of Colorado City, is home to the Pine Lodge, which offers rustic cabins. The purist in you may prefer to stay at the namesake Greenhorn Inn Motel in Colorado City.

Northwestern Mountains

The remote peaks of northwestern Colorado are very diverse, with mesas, high plateaus, and rugged mountains. Most approaches involve long drives on dirt or gravel roads. Be prepared for an emergency! None of the highpoints exceeds 13,000 feet in elevation, but most are plagued by snow that stays well into early summer each year. The good news is that snow doesn't generally fall until late October or November, a month later than Colorado's very high peaks. We suggest combining Flat Top Mountain and the northwest ridge of Orno Peak into a weekend outing; they are too far apart to be done in a single day but share a common trailhead area and can be done in a single trip.

Northwestern Mountains

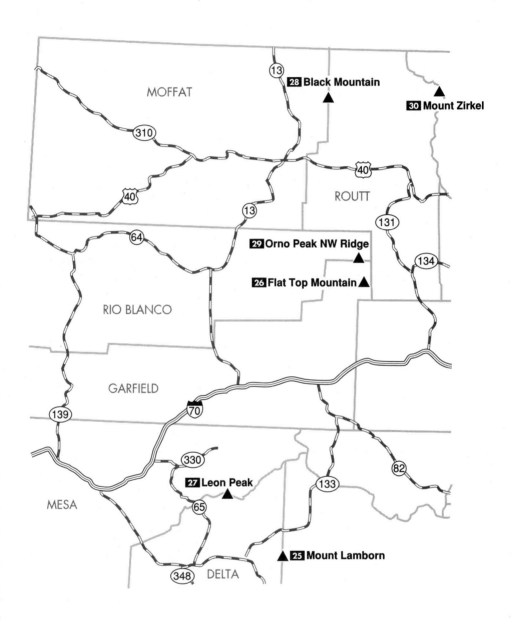

MOFFAT

⑬

28 Black Mountain ▲

30 Mount Zirkel ▲

310

40

ROUTT

⑬

131

64

29 Orno Peak NW Ridge ▲

RIO BLANCO

26 Flat Top Mountain ▲

134

GARFIELD

139

70

330

27 Leon Peak ▲

82

133

MESA

65

▲ 25 Mount Lamborn

348 DELTA

25 Delta County: Mount Lamborn

General description:	This subalpine peak requires a moderate full-day hike on trail and then a bushwhack to a bouldered summit.
Distance:	4.9 miles, one-way.
Difficulty:	Moderate.
Elevation gain:	3,446 feet.
Summit elevation:	11,396 feet.
Maps:	USGS Quad—Paonia (required), DeLorme p. 57.
Access/permits:	West Elk Wilderness of the Gunnison National Forest.
Best months:	July–October.

Location: West-central Colorado in the West Elk Mountains, about 30 miles east of Delta, and 5 miles southeast of Paonia.

Finding the trailhead: This peak can be approached from the north, west, or south sides. We recommend the approach from the south to minimize the elevation gain. In the small town of Crawford, on Colorado Highway 92 between Hotchkiss and Curecanti National Recreation Area, find Dogwood Avenue just north of the town post office. Proceed east on Dogwood Avenue, which will become E 50 Drive at the edge of town. Continue east along Smith Fork for 2.2 miles from CO 92 to County Road 42.00 just west of a prominent rock monolith. This awesome igneous plug is a local landmark, known as Needle Rock. The road turns north, and you continue straight (north) on CR 42.00 and proceed 0.5 mile to a T-intersection. Turn right (east) onto CR F.00. Proceed 0.9 mile to another T-intersection. Turn left (north) and remain on CR F.00 past Needle Rock and proceed 2.3 miles from the turn to the Gunnison National Forest boundary. At this point the county road becomes Forest Road 835 and follows Little Coal Creek as a dirt road. About 0.5 mile into the national forest, the road splits and a fork to the left goes toward Landsend Peak. Stay to the right and continue 1.3 miles on FR 835 to the end of the road. The trailhead for Forest Trail 890 is at the end of a turnaround. Park here, being careful not to prevent vehicles with trailers from using the turnaround.

There are two alternate approaches. The west approach to Mount Lamborn is south of the town of Paonia and uses FR 834 to reach Bell Creek Springs. From there FT 894 leads east to Inter-Ocean Pass after breaching the broad saddle between Mount Lamborn and Landsend Peak. An approach from the north requires you to follow Minnesota Creek east out of Paonia to Lone Cabin Reservoir. The trailhead for FT 890, about 0.5 mile east of the reservoir, will set you on a path due south to Inter-Ocean Pass.

Key points:
0.9   Junction FT 892
2.7   Junction FT 894
3.4   Inter-Ocean Pass
4.3   Saddle near 10,627-foot subpeak on Mount Lamborn's southeast ridge

Delta County: Mount Lamborn

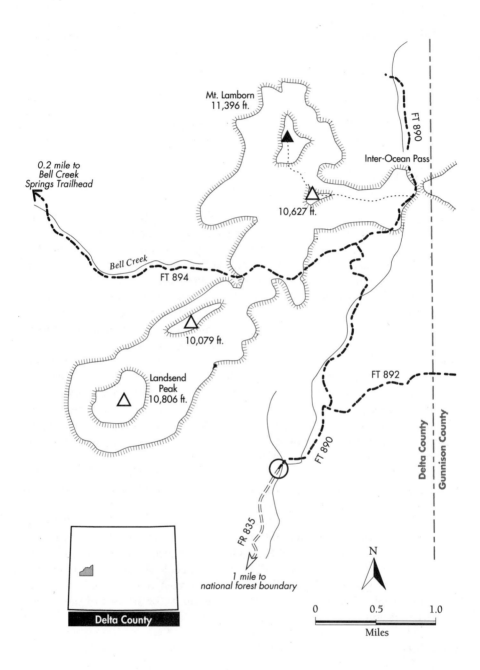

Mt. Lamborn
11,396 ft.

0.2 mile to
Bell Creek
Springs Trailhead

Inter-Ocean Pass

FT 890

10,627 ft.

Bell Creek

FT 894

10,079 ft.

FT 892

Landsend
Peak
10,806 ft.

FT 890

Delta County

Gunnison County

FR 835

1 mile to
national forest boundary

N

Delta County

0   0.5   1.0

Miles

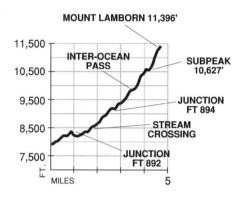

MOUNT LAMBORN 11,396'

INTER-OCEAN PASS

SUBPEAK 10,627'

JUNCTION FT 894

STREAM CROSSING

JUNCTION FT 892

11,500
10,500
9,500
8,500
7,500
FT.
MILES   5

The hike: The route to Mount Lamborn begins as FT 835 along Little Coal Creek through pine and aspen forest. Watch for evidence of beavers. During our hike of Mount Lamborn, we were shocked by the sharp slap of a startled beaver's tail on the pond water. The well-worn but wide trail, apparently an old road, climbs 1,800 feet out of the creek drainage and switches back up to Inter-Ocean Pass. Stay on FT 890, passing FT 892, which goes east into the heart of the West Elk Wilderness to Little Elk Basin. Just beyond this junction, FT 890 becomes a single-track path. Cross the creek several times and climb to a level aspen grove to another junction where FT 894 forks to the left at mile 2.7. (FT 894 is the west access from Paonia to Mount Lamborn and Landsend Peak.) Just before reaching Inter-Ocean Pass on FT 890, you will note on the topo map a Y-intersection that allows you to use the east side or west side of the pass, skirting a 9,880-foot hill that bisects the pass. On two separate occasions we failed to find this cutoff to the west saddle. Hike to Inter-Ocean Pass and contour west at the 9,760-foot level for 800 feet across grassy slopes to the west saddle. This pass is a gentle, forested saddle between Mount Lamborn and Coal Mountain. Watch for cattle that range the area, and leave them a wide berth.

Upon reaching the west saddle, hike an east-trending ridge to Mount Lamborn's 10,627-foot southeastern shoulder. This ridge is narrow, which helps you stay on course, and you travel through an aspen grove for the first 0.4 mile from the pass. Gain 800 total feet of elevation to the prominent but small rocky ridge that is the southeast shoulder of Mount Lamborn's summit. Bushwhack an additional 1,000 feet through patchy aspen and then evergreen forest up the mountain's grassy shoulder. Look for a faint path slightly west of the ridgeline, leading to the summit. Once on the flatter summit area, stroll north along a path to the boulders that mark the actual highpoint. A canister just below two huge summit boulders contains the summit register. Sign in and carefully climb up onto the summit boulders to locate the benchmark. Return by the same route, taking care not to wander off the ridge to the north side of Inter-Ocean Pass.

The best time to visit is July through October. The dirt roads may be passable earlier, but there is a high likelihood of getting stuck in mud or stopped short of the trailhead by snowdrifts. Consider another approach to Mount Lamborn during the wet season, into June. There is private property along the county roads, so please respect the rights of property owners by not attempting to access the peak through private land. The local Boy Scout troop in Paonia has maintained a trail to the peak over the years and has compiled the summit register since the 1940s, transcribing every entry into a notebook. A copy of this log remains in the large metal canister cemented into the summit boulders. Mount Lamborn seems to get a surprising number of visitors for a peak only 11,396 feet in elevation and surrounded by many peaks of greater stature in the West Elks.

The peak offers an unobstructed view to the south of Landsend Peak and a panoramic view of the West Elk Mountains to the east. The Grand Mesa can be seen to the northwest, and Leon Peak is discernible to the expert county highpointer. The San Juan Mountains are far to the south; try to identify Uncompahgre Peak or Mount Sneffels. Inter-Ocean Pass is visible far below to the east. Hunting is allowed in this area in the fall, so be cautious and wear orange.

On your way back into Crawford, stop by Needle Rock. There is public access to this monolith, and an interesting sign at the base explains the geology and local lore.

County highlights: Delta is the county seat of Delta County, which was established in 1883 and named for the town's location on the delta of the Uncompahgre River at the point where it enters the Gunnison River. Into the 1880s, Ute Indians hunted plentiful game and foraged into the area around the Black Canyon and the North Fork Valley. A Ute trail that came down out of the Uncompahgre Plateau to the west went through present-day Delta and up to Grand Mesa to the north. The Ute council tree, an ancient cottonwood that still stands in north Delta, was a famous meeting place for the Indians. Crawford serves the cattle industry in the North Fork area, and you might see a herd of cattle being driven through town on the way to market or pasture.

The route to Mount Lamborn is straightforward until you reach the final summit blocks.

Camping and services: There is primitive camping at the trailhead and along the trail. There are no nearby national forest campgrounds. Camping is allowed at Crawford State Park just south of Crawford. Services are available in Paonia to the northwest and Crawford to the southwest. Crawford boasts a nice restaurant, the Crystal Gardens, and a country store at the center of town, Crawford Enterprise & Motel. Another interesting spot is the Mad Dog Ranch Fountain Cafe, right at Dogwood Avenue and CO 92. This establishment, run by Pam and Joe Cocker, has a terrific, reasonably priced lunch and dinner menu and an ice cream and soda fountain; it opens at 7 A.M. for breakfast and has patio seating and entertainment.

For more information: Crawford State Park, Box 147, Crawford, CO 81415, 970-921-5721. Website: www.parks.state.co.us.

26 Garfield County: Flat Top Mountain

General description:	A subalpine plateau requires a half-day hike up to and on a high, flat mesa with expansive views of the Flat Tops Wilderness.
Distance:	4.3 miles, one-way.
Difficulty:	Easy.
Elevation gain:	2,064 feet.
Summit elevation:	12,354 feet.
Maps:	USGS Quads—Orno Peak (required) and Devils Causeway (recommended), DeLorme p. 26, Trails Illustrated #122.
Access/permits:	Flat Tops Wilderness in White River National Forest.
Best months:	July–September.

Location: Northwest Colorado on the Flat Tops, about 15 miles west of Yampa, and 40 miles southwest of Steamboat Springs.

Finding the trailhead: From Interstate 70 about 14 miles west of Vail, take Wolcott exit 157 north on Colorado Highway 131 for 45 miles, crossing the Colorado River at State Bridge and passing the unusual Finger Rock outcrop shortly before Yampa. Take paved County Road 7 left (west) at the convenience station and follow CR 7 along the edge of the village of Yampa and south out of town. Check out those ornate street lamps on the dirt Main Street! The road turns to gravel after a few miles and becomes Forest Road 900. Drive 17 miles total from CO 131, past Upper Stillwater Reservoir (Yampa Reservoir), to the road's end at the Stillwater Reservoir dam parking lot. When we encountered the "upper" reservoir before we came to the "main" reservoir, we were just as confused as you may be.

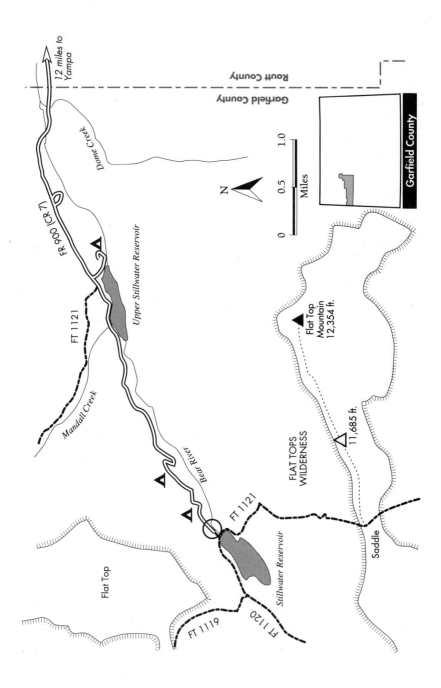

Key points:
- 0.3 Forest Trail 1122 at dam
- 1.8 Base of steep north face of the Flat Tops
- 2.0 Saddle
- 3.2 11,685-foot knob

The hike: Leave from the parking lot by the dam and proceed on a gravel road south along the crest of the dam to the far side. Drop off the dam to your left once you are across it and pick up FT 1122 south into the woods. A small sign at the south side of the dam marks this trail. Follow this trail about 2 miles up switchbacks and through a pleasant pine forest on the north slopes of the Flat Tops.

At mile 1.8, the trail steepens as it climbs up to the timberline saddle at 11,190 feet. The trail continues down off the saddle to the south; however, you turn left (east) and follow a use trail up a steep section to gain the ridge on the northern rim edge of the Flat Tops. At mile 3.2 the trail rises up over an 11,685-foot knob along the ridge only to dip down to a shallow saddle. Continue northeast on the mostly nonexistent trail through open alpine tundra meadows to the rocky summit. Watch for ptarmigans and cairns and stay left along the northern edge of the Flat Tops. The summit has an enormous 8-foot cairn on top. The flat volcanic rocks are very conducive to cairn building—add a rock; it's tradition! For lunch, duck out of the wind behind the cairn or just east of the summit near a permanent snowfield. Sign the register and return by the same route. One interesting aspect of this highpoint is that you can see the entire route from the trailhead. Bring sufficient water, since none is available on top. This route is seldom used, so be sure to notify friends of your intentions to do this highpoint.

The best time to explore the Flat Tops is after snowmelt in July and through first snow in mid-September. Flat Top Mountain could be an excellent, if remote, snowshoe or cross-country ski in deep snow. The terrain is relatively gentle for most of the hike, with a few steeper switchbacks near the saddle. There are magnificent views northeast to the Steamboat area, northwest to the Elkhead Mountains, southeast to the Gore and Sawatch ranges, and southwest to the Grand Mesa. The highpoint of Rio Blanco County, on the northwest ridge of Orno Peak, is easily distinguished about 6 miles to the northwest of Flat Top Mountain. These two county highpoints can be combined into a long two-day trek with camping and hiking above 11,000 feet for most of the distance.

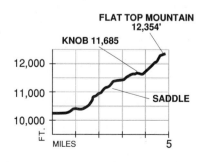

The Flat Tops are volcanic flows from the Tertiary age. They are fairly flat and rise gently to the east, culminating in Flat Top Mountain itself. The western portion of the wilderness, about 40 miles distant, is actually wooded on top. The eastern half is above timberline as much as 500 feet in places. One can access the mesa top from only a few key saddle areas. Elk and coyotes can be seen and

The route to Flat Top Mountain begins in forest (left) and finishes on the high Flat Tops.
PHOTO BY KURT MITCHLER

heard in the summer and fall and the wildflowers on top are spectacular, rivaling the San Juan and Aspen areas.

The major danger at the Flat Tops is the proximity of many hiking trails to the cliff edges. Perhaps 90 percent of the edge of the Flat Tops follows sheer 600-foot drop-offs. As you hike, be sure to keep an eye on children. Dogs are not permitted in wilderness areas. Also the Flat Tops Wilderness is a major elk hunting area, though there is little hunting in the area between the dam and the saddle, and none on top.

County highlights: Glenwood Springs is the county seat of Garfield County, established in 1883 and named for James Garfield, the twentieth U.S. president, who was assassinated two years before the county was established. In 1879, several prospectors found surface evidence of carbonate, indicating silver deposits, near what is now Glenwood Springs. Cabins and a small fort were constructed (the fort later came to be known as Fort Defiance). That spring, some men moved farther north and established another small settlement, Carbonate City. In 1882, Isaac Cooper bought the present site of Glenwood Springs for $1,500, surveyed a townsite, and named it Defiance. He renamed it Glenwood Springs in 1885 after his hometown of Glenwood, Iowa.

Coal mining and agriculture became the basis of Garfield County's economy. In 1982, Garfield County withstood a severe blow when Exxon Corporation pulled out of its Colony oil shale project and 5,000 people lost

146

their jobs. Three years later, Battlement Mesa, the company town built by Exxon for an anticipated 25,000 employees, was on its way to becoming a flourishing retirement haven.

Camping and services: Three national forest campgrounds are established along FR 900 near the Stillwater reservoirs. No reservations are required. Primitive camping is allowed in the wilderness area. Yampa, a former stage stop, is now a small farming community with a few shops and one convenience store. Historic cabins are found in Yampa. Steamboat is a 45-minute drive north and a great place to visit year-round.

27 Mesa County: Leon Peak

General description:	Bushwhacking dominates a rough half-day hike across a jumble of volcanic boulders to a ridge crest topped by an abandoned lookout.
Distance:	1.5 miles, one-way.
Difficulty:	Moderate.
Elevation gain:	830 feet.
Summit elevation:	11,236 feet.
Maps:	USGS Quad—Leon Peak (required), DeLorme p. 44.
Access/permits:	Grand Mesa National Forest.
Best months:	July–October.

Location: West-central Colorado on the Grand Mesa, about 40 miles east of Grand Junction and 30 miles northeast of Delta.

Finding the trailhead: The Leon Peak Trailhead can be approached from all directions. From the west, leave Interstate 70 at exit 49, and head east on Colorado Highway 65, and approach the mesa's northwest face. After about 18 miles you will reach Powderhorn Ski Resort and begin the climb to the mesa's top. Continue east on CO 65. At mile 34 you will reach the junction of CO 65 and Forest Road 121. From this junction go east on FR 121 for 8 miles to FR 126 and turn right (east). Leon Peak will be visible from FR 121 after about 7 miles. Proceed east on FR 126 for 3 miles to the trailhead at Weir and Johnson Reservoir Campground.

Key points:
- 0.3   Saddle
- 0.7   Swampy flat ground
- 0.9   Leon Peak Reservoir
- 1.0   Treeline at boulder field

The hike: This peak offers some of the most brutal boulder scrambling of any Colorado county highpoint. Please use extreme caution when negotiat-

Mesa County: Leon Peak

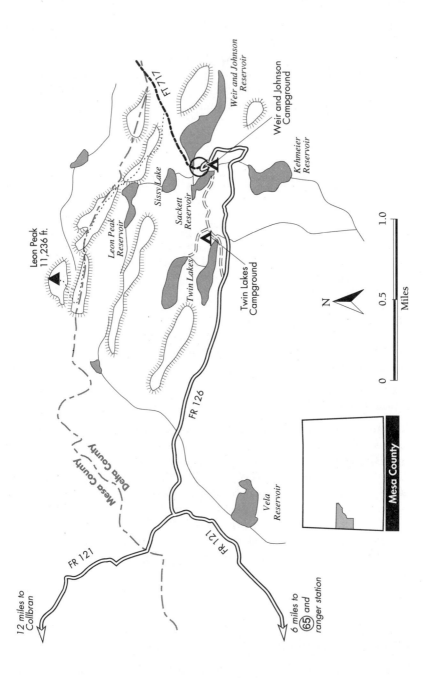

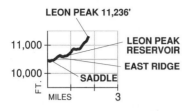

LEON PEAK 11,236'

11,000
10,000
FT.
MILES   3

LEON PEAK
RESERVOIR
EAST RIDGE
SADDLE

ing the rocks, taking care not to catch a leg between them. Once you leave the fishing lakes, you will be in remote wilderness, seldom used by hikers. The topography of the landscape can be confusing, so be very aware of local landmarks, plot your route on a topographic map as you hike, and use a compass to orient yourself. The approach roads to the trailhead are steep in places and can be snowpacked. This is a good one for practicing your compass skills.

With compass in hand, leave the wooded parking lot at the west end of Weir and Johnson Reservoir. Take the distinct Leon Lake Trail (Forest Trail 717) across the spillway and northeast along the north edge of the reservoir to a gentle saddle; take care not to take the faint trail at the spillway that goes left to Sissy Lake. (A sign indicates a trail to Sissy Lake, although most maps do not show this body of water.) After about 0.3 mile you reach a broad saddle where you depart from the trail to your left (northwest) and bushwhack through pine trees along the ridge, being careful to stay on the high ground of the wooded ridge top. At 0.7 mile the ridge flattens and becomes swampy. The ridge resumes in a hundred yards—just maintain a compass bearing of 315 degrees. Regain the ridge, even more pronounced than before, and follow it uphill until it becomes a mass of jumbled volcanic boulders. The trees will give way to these boulders, and although technically treeline is not reached, the volcanic rock makes it difficult for plant life to thrive above this level. Once you have passed the trees and skirted the small rocky knob along the ridge above treeline, you can see Leon Peak for the first time, rising from the lunar landscape.

At this point you must decide on which approach to Leon Peak you want to take. There is no easy (boulder-free) route, and we recommend you let your bushwhacking instincts take over. We have approached the peak from the south ridge, the central southeast gully, and the north slope. All are tough scrambles up very rough, loose boulders, many the size of a refrigerator. The north slope is steep, with fewer boulders down near treeline, but it is difficult to access from the ridge. The central gully is straightforward but requires the most boulder scrambling. The south ridge leads from the edge of the boulder field west to the southwest flank of Leon Peak and is easy hiking, but you must lose a bit of elevation down into the central gully at its western end before beginning a steep scramble up the south slopes of the peak.

Utmost care is required when walking and hopping across the boulders that make up most of Leon Peak. The relatively flat summit is a welcome relief from the uneven ground you have just been hiking. An old wooden structure is in its final stage of decay on the summit although the Forest Service is considering saving it. Return by your approach route, taking care not to drift left (northeast) off the ridge on the way back to FT 717.

The USGS quad for Leon Peak is extremely confusing due to the scale. The contours lead in all directions, with drainages disappearing into porous boulder fields, flowing under ridges, and reappearing on the other side.

Leon Peak rises above the lakes and dense forest of the Grand Mesa.

Significant rises are not represented, leading you into a feeling of bewilderment. Use caution and note trees for landmarks to aid in your return.

The best time to visit Grand Mesa is July through first snowfall in October. The gravel roads on top of Grand Mesa may be passable earlier, but snow tends to linger where it has accumulated in large drifts until well past Memorial Day. If there is any snow at all blocking the roads, it may be many miles to the trailhead on foot or by snowshoe, so this is a peak best left until complete snowmelt. The top of the mesa is relatively flat, with rolling hills, some rising above timberline. There are numerous lakes on top of the mesa, and the fishing is reported to be very good. With an absence of large streams, the mesa is not known for trout or other large gamefish that inhabit the rivers of Colorado. Grand Mesa is reported to be the highest flat-topped mountain in the world and is bordered to the north by the Colorado River and the south by the Gunnison River. Most of the height of Grand Mesa is formed by the Green River and Wasatch formations of the Tertiary age, whose shales and sandstones are protected from erosion by the thick basalt flows that form the surface of the mesa. The entire area is part of Grand Mesa National Forest. The only paved road that crosses the mesa is CO 65, which connects Delta, south of the mesa, to I-70, northwest of the mesa. Powderhorn Ski Area lies on the north edge of the mesa, just off CO 65.

County highlights: Grand Junction is the county seat of Mesa County, which was established in 1883. The county name is Spanish for "table," in recognition of the enormous flat mountain to the east of Grand Junction that offers cool respite from the hot summers in the river valleys below. Over 70 percent of Mesa County is owned by the federal government. Leon

Peak joins several other geographic features in the area that bear the name Leon in honor of an early settler to the region.

In 1881 settlers were initially drawn to the valley for the semiarid land, which was perfect for pasturing cattle. By the end of that year, however, irrigation of the valley caused the rich red soil to spring to life. With new emphasis placed on agriculture, cattle ranchers were soon relegated to the high mesas. The young town of Grand Junction, named for the convergence of the Colorado and Gunnison rivers, began carving a niche as a trade center for western Colorado when the Denver & Rio Grande Railroad's main line started service in 1887. Over the years, apricots, cherries, grapes, and peaches have provided an economic mainstay for the town. A growing wine industry is centered in the town of Palisade, just east of Grand Junction at the entrance to an impressive canyon through which I-70 and the Colorado River extend.

Camping and services: There are many campgrounds, including Weir and Johnson Campground near the trailhead and Twin Lake Campground about a mile west on FR 126. The small hamlet of Grand Mesa is the only sizable town on the mesa, with limited services available. Sonny's Country Store is about a mile east of CO 65 on FR 121, with food, bait, and other amenities. Be sure to stop at the visitor center at the junction of CO 65 and FR 121. The nearest full-service facilities are in Cedaredge to the south, Collbran to the north, and Palisade to the west.

28 Moffat County: Black Mountain

General description:	A pleasant half-day hike leads to a wooded mesa top.
Distance:	3.1 miles, one-way.
Difficulty:	Easy.
Elevation gain:	980 feet.
Summit elevation:	10,840 feet.
Maps:	USGS Quad—Buck Point (required), DeLorme p. 15.
Access/permits:	Routt National Forest.
Best months:	June–October.

Location: Northwest Colorado in the Elkhead Mountains, about 20 miles north of Craig, and 15 miles south of the Wyoming border.

Finding the trailhead: From U.S. Highway 40 in Craig go north 12 miles on Colorado Highway 13 and turn right (east) at the lumber mill onto County Road 27. Proceed through private land about 10 miles to the boundary of Routt National Forest where the dirt road becomes Forest Road 110. Pass through an open wooden fence and continue approximately 7 miles, past Sawmill Campground, to a gentle ridge and a sign for a trail to Black Mountain. In the national forest you will notice many primitive, unofficial camping

Moffat County: Black Mountain

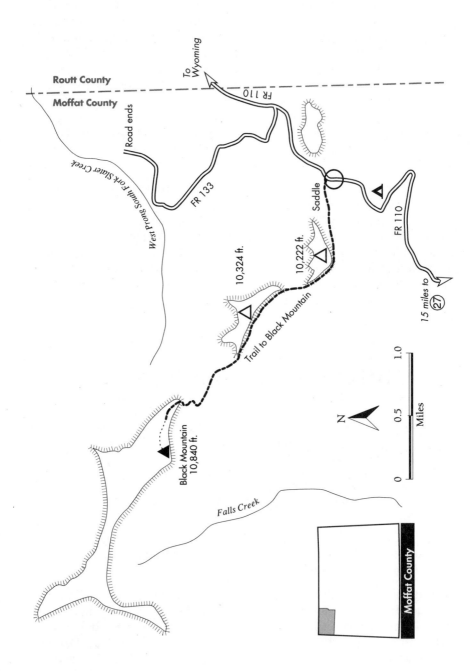

To Wyoming

Routt County

Moffat County

FR 110

Road ends

West Prong South Fork Slater Creek

FR 133

Saddle

FR 110

10,324 ft.

10,222 ft.

Trail to Black Mountain

15 miles to 27

N

Miles

0   0.5   1.0

Black Mountain
10,840 ft.

Falls Creek

Moffat County

areas where hundreds of hunters congregate in October each year, hoping to bag the big one. We county highpointers prefer to think that Mount Elbert is the big one, but that's a different hobby. Park at the small trailhead on the right (south) side of the forest road.

Access is also possible via CR 11 off CO 13, a short distance north of the turnoff to the CR 27 turnoff, about 12 miles north of US 40 in Craig. Take CR 11 (FR 112) to Freeman Reservoir and start your hike from the campground there. This route requires you to bushwhack northeast to gain Black Mountain's flat summit. From there you will stroll through pine forest north and east to the far eastern end of the mesa. This route requires good map and compass skills.

Key points:
- 1.1 Saddle
- 2.2 Base of switchbacks
- 2.8 Mesa top

The hike: Follow the signed trail northwest from the road for 2.8 miles to the relatively level summit area on top of Black Mountain. The trail is fairly well maintained through most of its length, although it gets steep as you approach the top and there are several short switchbacks. It gains the southeast ridge of the mountain soon after leaving the road and follows this all the way up. The summit area is approximately 0.5 mile long, over 100 yards wide, and crested by pine and fir trees. The actual highest point is approximately 100 yards west of the east edge of the platform where the trail breaks out on top, close to the nearly indistinguishable trail. We handleveled to determine the location of the highest point at a small rock cairn, although the surrounding acres are within a foot or two of the same elevation.

The best season to hike in the Elkhead Mountains is from snowmelt in very late spring to the first major snowfall in fall because snowdrifts will make the forest roads impassable. Contact the Forest Service in Craig to determine conditions. One of us visited this area during Memorial Day and found the route blocked several miles short of the trailhead, yet could reach the peak with snowshoes. Snowmobiling on Black Mountain is a favorite pastime for outdoor enthusiasts.

Numerous elk and deer inhabit the flanks of the Elkhead Mountains, and the town of Craig is a major staging area for hunting expeditions. Hikers are discouraged from being in the area during hunting season. If you choose to satisfy your highpoint craving during the month of October, do it somewhere other than Black Mountain! It may be the most dangerous highpoint to be on during hunting season. The entire mountain is wooded; visibility is poor due to the density of the forest growth, even on top. There were over 300 hunters on the flanks of the mountain during opening weekend in 1997.

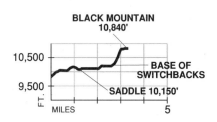

Consider an early season snowshoe trek to Black Mountain.

County highlights: Craig is the county seat of Moffat County, which was established in 1911 and named for David Halliday Moffat, president of the Rio Grande Railroad from 1884 to 1891. This young county is a land of open grazing. Moffat County ranchers raise cattle and sheep and grow wheat. Much of this region is remote, rugged, and wild. The Bureau of Land Management (BLM) manages over a million and a half acres in Moffat County that are open to hiking and exploring. Craig serves as the service center for this vast outdoor playground. In addition to recreation and hunting, ranching is a key economic activity in the county. A large coal mine operates south of Craig and feeds a power plant that produces electricity for the valley. Perhaps the least traveled paved public road in Colorado is CR 318, which leaves US 40 in Maybell and heads northwest to the Flaming Gorge Recreation Area in Utah and Wyoming. Dinosaur National Monument in western Moffat County is a terrific place to visit if you have budding young paleontologists with you. Access is from US 40 just east of the Colorado-Utah state line. The Yampa River provides some of the state's best float trips, especially if you're not into whitewater rafting.

Camping and services: Camping is permitted throughout the national forest, and formal campgrounds can be found at the trailheads. Craig has full services.

29 Rio Blanco County: Northwest Ridge of Orno Peak

General description: A full-day hike up and onto a flat mesa leads to a flower-covered ridge providing an extraordinary subalpine experience.
Distance: 5.7 miles, one-way.
Difficulty: Moderate.
Elevation gain: 1,827 feet.
Summit elevation: 12,027 feet.
Maps: USGS Quads—Devils Causeway and Orno Peak (required), DeLorme p. 26, Trails Illustrated #122.
Access/permits: Flat Tops Wilderness in Routt National Forest.
Best months: July–September

Location: Northwest Colorado on the Flat Tops, about 40 miles southwest of Steamboat Springs, and 15 miles west of Yampa.

Finding the trailhead: From Interstate 70 about 14 miles west of Vail take Wolcott exit 157 north on Colorado Highway 131 for about 45 miles to Yampa, crossing the Colorado River at the small center called State Bridge and passing the unusual Finger Rock outcrop shortly before Yampa. Take paved County Road 7 left (west) at the convenience station and follow CR 7 along the edge of the village of Yampa and south out of town. The road turns to gravel after a few miles and becomes Forest Road 900. Follow a total of about 14 miles from CO 131 to Upper Stillwater Reservoir to a parking lot on the left (south) side of the road, just beyond the Stillwater Campground. A marked trail on the right (north) side of the road heads north to Mandall Lakes and Mandall Pass.

Key points:
3.6   Side trail to Black Mandall Lake
4.4   Base of Mandall Pass
4.9   Mandall Pass

The hike: Begin to hike to Orno Peak's northwest ridge by signing the trailhead register and then following FT 1121 to the north along the Mandall Creek drainage. Negotiate four tricky stream crossings and follow the well-marked trail north for 3.5 miles past Slide Mandall Lake to a trail that heads off to the right (east) to Black Mandall Lake. Stay on the main trail and head for the saddle between the north–south trending Flat Top cliff to

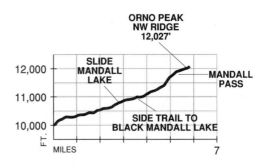

155

Rio Blanco County: Northwest Ridge of Orno Peak

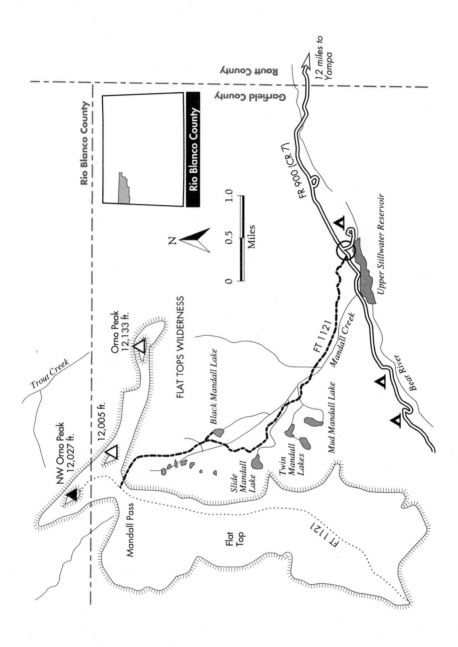

Routt County

Garfield County

12 miles to Yampa

Rio Blanco County

Rio Blanco County

Rio Blanco County

N

0   0.5   1.0
Miles

FR 900 (CR 7)

Upper Stillwater Reservoir

FT 1121

Mandall Creek

Bear River

Orno Peak
12,133 ft.

FLAT TOPS WILDERNESS

Black Mandall Lake

Trout Creek

NW Orno Peak
12,027 ft.

12,005 ft.

Slide Mandall Lake

Twin Mandall Lakes

Mud Mandall Lake

Mandall Pass

Flat Top

FT 1121

the left (west) and the east–west trending Flat Top cliff straight ahead (north). Orno Peak tops the cliffs in front of you a few miles to the right (east) of the saddle. Orno Peak is in Garfield County but the Garfield–Rio Blanco county line crosses the northwest ridge of Orno Peak so that the highpoint is just north of the county line. The trail becomes less discernible as it leaves the trees and crosses swampy grassland to mile 4.4 at the foot of the steep hike up to Mandall Pass. Watch for mosquitoes in the summer; a vicious horde carried off the author's favorite bandana. As you approach the pass, stay right (east) of the spine of rock that extends south from the pass. Pass these cliffs to the right and do not get involved in much rock scrambling. Mandall Pass, with a profusion of low-growing wildflowers at mile 4.9, is a beautiful spot to camp. From here the highpoint is a relatively flat 0.5-walk on grassy tundra to the north, up 375 feet. The highpoint is located near the northern cliff edge of the Flat Tops. Watch for a small cairn and a glass jar register. Return by the same route.

If you have an extra day and can camp on top, your party can continue its trek by walking south on top of the Flat Tops for 3.5 miles, all on grassy tundra, to the Devils Causeway, a prominent neck between two broad, flat sections of the Flat Tops just northwest of Stillwater Reservoir. The narrows are only 4 feet wide for 200 feet or so with a drop-off on either side of several hundred feet—definitely not for the faint of heart! Explore this narrow sidewalk if you can deal with heights and return to Stillwater Reservoir via the switchbacks on Forest Trail 1119 to your left (south). By returning to the reservoir, you will be in a position to hike to Flat Top Mountain to the south. You will not be able to stay high on the Flat Tops and walk to Flat Top Mountain because steep cliffs inhibit all but the most serious rock climbers.

The best time to explore the Flat Tops is well after snowmelt in July through first snow in mid-September. The terrain is relatively gentle for most of the hike, with a few steeper switchbacks near Mandall Pass. The stream crossings are tricky during snowmelt due to high water. From the highpoint you will have a magnificent view northeast to the Steamboat area, northwest to the Elkhead Mountains, southeast to the Gore and Sawatch ranges, and southwest to Grand Mesa. The highpoint of Garfield County, Flat Top Mountain, is easily distinguished about 6 miles to the south. These two county highpoints could be combined into a long two-day trek with camping and hiking above 11,000 feet for most of the time.

The Flat Tops are volcanic flows from the Tertiary age with an undulating surface that rises to the east. The western portion of the wilderness, about 40 miles distant, is actually wooded on top. The eastern half is above timberline, by as much as 500 feet in places. We saw and heard elk and coyotes, and the wildflowers on top are spectacular, rivaling the San Juan and Aspen areas. Many active beaver ponds can be seen throughout the approaches to the Flat Tops.

The major danger on the Flat Tops is the proximity of many hiking trails to the sheer 600-foot cliffs. One can access the tops at only a few key passes. As you hike by the cliffs, be sure to keep an eye on children. The Flat Tops

A group of highpointers share wildflowers and the view from the summit of Rio Blanco County.
PHOTO BY KIM GALBRAITH

Wilderness is a major elk hunting area, but on the route described in this chapter there is little hunting.

County highlights: Meeker is the county seat of Rio Blanco County, established in 1889. The county name is Spanish for "white river," a reference to the main drainage in the area. Rangely is the center of one of the largest oil fields in Colorado, with substantial production today, a half century since the initial discovery.

Camping and services: Because of the proximity of the trailheads to the highpoints of Garfield and Rio Blanco counties, see the "County highlights" and "Camping" sections in Garfield County (chapter 26). You may camp on top of the Flat Tops, and we highly recommend this. The grass is soft and you actually feel guilty as you settle onto a multitude of wildflowers for the night. Practice minimum-impact camping (see "Introduction"). The 360-degree view of the night sky may be the best you will find in Colorado. There is little light pollution, and you're above a significant portion of the atmosphere at 11,000 feet or higher. Try to use an existing fire ring if you're crazy enough to lug in wood; better yet, use your cookstove.

30 Routt County: Mount Zirkel

General description: This relatively low-elevation backpack travels through forest and across tundra to rocky, exposed crags.

Distance: 8.7 miles, one-way.

Difficulty: Strenuous.

Elevation gain: 3,180 feet from traditional trailhead.

Summit elevation: 12,180 feet.

Maps: USGS Quads—Mount Zirkel (required) and Farwell Mountain (recommended for west approach), Boettcher Lake and Pearl (recommended for east approach), DeLorme p. 17, Trails Illustrated #116.

Access/permits: Mount Zirkel Wilderness in Routt National Forest.

Best months: July–September.

Location: Northwest Colorado in the Park Range, about 30 miles north of Steamboat Springs, and 10 miles south of the Wyoming state line.

Finding the trailhead: Until 1997, the primary approach to the highest point in Routt County and the Park Range was from the Slavonia Trailhead, accessed west of Steamboat Springs by County Road 129 and Forest Road 400. A freak windstorm late in the year felled 20,000 acres of timber, forcing the USDA Forest Service to move the trailhead 2.5 miles farther west, at least for the next few years. You should now consider an approach from the North Platte River valley east of Mount Zirkel to avoid additional mileage. We describe both routes in the following pages.

For the traditional approach, head northwest on U.S. Highway 40 through Steamboat Springs until you reach the turnoff for CR 129 at the west edge of town. Turn right (north) and continue about 18 miles on CR 129, 1 mile past the hamlet of Clark, until you reach CR 64, Seed House Road. Turn right (east) on this good gravel road, which becomes FR 400 upon entering Routt National Forest in 1 mile. Proceed on FR 400 for 9.5 miles to the Seed House Campground, which has been closed under a pile of a hundred or so fallen trees. Continue 0.5 mile beyond the campground to the temporary gate.

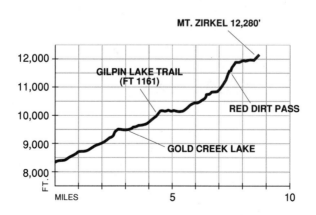

Routt County: Mount Zirkel

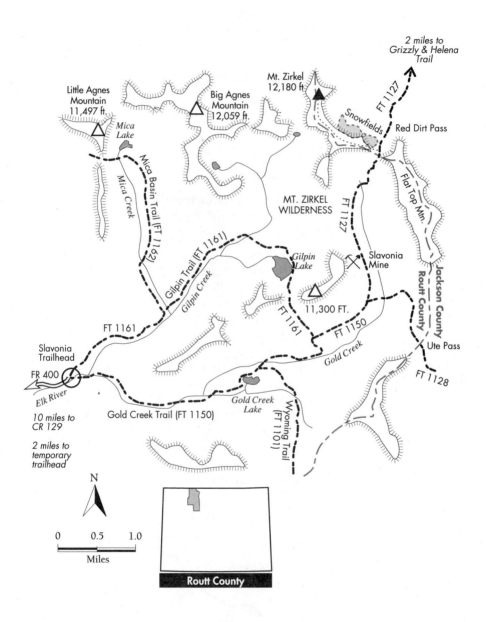

Little Agnes
Mountain
11,497 ft.

Mica
Lake

Big Agnes
Mountain
12,059 ft.

Mt. Zirkel
12,180 ft

2 miles to
Grizzly & Helena
Trail

Snowfields

FT 1127

Red Dirt Pass

Mica Creek

Mica Basin Trail (FT 1162)

MT. ZIRKEL
WILDERNESS

FT 1127

Flat Top Mtn.

Jackson County

Routt County

Gilpin Trail (FT 1161)

Gilpin Creek

Gilpin Creek

Gilpin
Lake

Slavonia
Mine

FT 1161

11,300 FT.

FT 1150

FT 1161

Slavonia
Trailhead

FR 400

Elk River

Gold Creek

Ute Pass

FT 1128

10 miles to
CR 129

2 miles to
temporary
trailhead

Gold Creek Trail (FT 1150)

Gold Creek
Lake

Wyoming Trail (FT 1101)

N

0   0.5   1.0
Miles

Routt County

Venturing farther in your vehicle risks your being trapped if unstable trees topple across the road.

To avoid the longer western approach, forest rangers suggest you go to the Grizzly-Helena Trailhead at Big Creek Lakes. From Walden, take Colorado Highway 125 north for about 9 miles and turn left (west) onto CR 6W for about 17 miles as it winds west and north to CR 6A. Turn left (southwest) and proceed on CR 6A, which becomes FR 600 for approximately 6 miles to Big Creek Lakes Campground and the Grizzly-Helena Trailhead.

Key points:
0.0   Slavonia Trailhead
1.8   Gold Creek crossing
2.3   Gold Creek crossing
2.8   Gold Lake
3.1   Junction with Wyoming Trail (Forest Trail 1101)
4.4   Junction of Gold Creek Trail (FT 1150) and Gilpin Trail (FT 1161)
5.3   Three-way junction of Gold Creek Trail (FT 1150), Ute Pass Trail (FT 1128), and Frying Pan Basin Trail (FT 1127)
7.5   Red Dirt Pass
8.6   Base of summit block

The hike: If you select the traditional western approach, hike along FR 400 for 2.5 miles to the Slavonia Trailhead at an abandoned mining camp. From the east end of the parking lot, follow a dirt trail a short distance before coming to a fork in the trail. The Gilpin Lake Trail (FT 1161) goes left and the Gold Creek Trail (FT 1150) goes right.

Go right on well-worn Gold Creek Trail, which has been cleared of the recent downfall. The trail crosses the stream twice. The first crossing at mile 1.8 is on an obvious log, and the second at mile 2.3 is best accomplished by walking to the right 100 feet, on the south side of the stream, to a fallen log, and then regaining the trail back where the stream crosses. Pass by serene Gold Lake at mile 2.8, a nice rest spot if the mosquitoes aren't hungry. At mile 3.1, pass the Wyoming Trail (FT 1101), which leads south. Stay on FT 1150 as it continues along Gold Creek Trail. At mile 4.4, watch for the junction of the Gold Creek Trail with the Gilpin Lake Trail (FT 1161), which leads left (north) to Gilpin Lake. Stay on FT 1150. At mile 5.3 you'll notice Ute Pass Trail (FT 1128), which drops off to the right as it heads across the valley to gain the far ridge. Gold Creek Trail heads right (south) to Ute Pass. Bear left (north) on the Frying Pan Basin Trail (FT 1127) and follow it all the way to timberline where Red Dirt Pass becomes visible for the first time. On some maps this trail is labeled as Red Dirt Pass Trail (FT 1142).

The trail switchbacks gently up to the pass at mile 7.5, which is approximately 500 feet above timberline. An alpine tundra environment dominates here at an altitude of 11,540 feet, quite a bit lower than you may be used to experiencing in the southern part of the state. At the pass, turn left (northwest) and proceed up a grassy slope a few hundred feet to a high plateau, and cross the level expanse to the base of the Mount Zirkel promontory at mile 8.6 from the Slavonia Trailhead. As you approach the peak, you'll notice three separate subpeaks a few hundred feet apart. Very large boulders must be crossed to reach the first of these. A trail develops near the top of the first and leads along a narrow exposed ridge to the third and highest peak, Mount Zirkel. At the summit are a register and a few nooks in which you can duck out of the wind. Take care when walking near the awesome west cliffs near the summit. Although modest in height, this peak requires a long hike on the exposed summit plateau, where lightning storms present a very real danger. Plan to summit early in the day to avoid the storms. Return by the same route. This peak is visited by relatively few people annually, and you may have it to yourself if you go on a weekday.

To reach Red Dirt Pass from the east, hike south from the Grizzly-Helena Trailhead along what used to be a road until it was closed in the 1970s. This trail (FT 1126) is still open to off-road motorized vehicles and follows the trace of the old road south along the eastern edge of the Mount Zirkel Wilderness. After about 5 miles on FT 1126, turn right (west) on FT 1127 and hike about 3 additional miles to gain elevation into the Frying Pan Basin before bushwhacking up to Red Dirt Pass.

The best time to visit Mount Zirkel is July through September. The Park Range can be snowy and windy early in the fall, and the long hike will lead you into remote country.

The area was brought to national attention late in 1997 when a freak "blowdown" toppled thousands of acres of pine and fir along the western approaches to Mount Zirkel. The trail has been cleared of most debris, but

The rocky peaks of Mount Zirkel provide a fun finish to a long hike. The summit knob is third from the left.

the devastating effects are quite visible, especially from above. All of the timber appears to have been "combed" and laid down flat, pointing to the east. There is a debate between the local timber industry and environmental groups about the impact of retrieving the downed timber, with the core issues being resource use versus natural policies in a primitive wilderness. This area may serve as a model for future forests, whatever the outcome.

Mount Zirkel is one of six county highpoints in Colorado that lie directly astride the Continental Divide. This rock garden of a mountain was named in honor of Ferdinand Zirkel, a German scientist who assisted in the early surveys of the region by studying and describing rocks and minerals. The area is not noted for mining activity.

County highlights: Steamboat Springs is the county seat of Routt County, which was established in 1877 and named for John Long Routt, who came from Illinois and served as the mayor of Denver and the first and seventh governor of Colorado. Steamboat is famous for its world-class ski resort, but there is year-round recreation to be found in this area. Major statewide softball tournaments are held here throughout the summer, and the range is noted for elk and deer herds, with massive hunting expeditions forming in the fall.

Stop at the A. L. Lamp outfitter store in Steamboat. Several generations of the family have been selling Western wear since the turn of the century. If you have a chance, park at the crest of Rabbit Ears Pass and hike northeast to the famous twin rock outcrops. According to Ute Indian legend, the valley casts a spell over those who enter it, compelling them to return year after year.

Camping and services: A national forest campground, Hinman, is along FR 400 on the approach to the Slavonia Trailhead. On the east side of the divide, the Forest Service maintains a campground at Big Creek Lakes. Primitive backcountry camping is allowed along the hiking trails but not within 100 feet of creeks and lakes and not in the vicinity of the trailheads. Full services are available in Steamboat Springs to the south and Walden to the east. On the way back out from the traditional trailhead, we highly recommend a stop at the Clark Trading Post on CR 129. Stop in for a cold beverage or, if you feel like celebrating, try one of the post's famous ice cream cones. A small cone will do, as the large is way too big for anyone short of Paul Bunyan.

San Juan Mountains

The San Juan Mountains are rugged and remote and must not be taken lightly. This area of Colorado has the highest concentration of county highpoints, in part due to the small size of several of the counties. With the exception of Castle Rock in Montrose County, a prominent ridge extending north from the San Juans, all the peaks are well over 13,000 feet in elevation. The area has been dominated for a century by mining, resulting in good access in otherwise remote areas. The mining roads provide a good challenge for those who own four-wheel-drive vehicles. Several of these peaks require class-3 or class-4 climbing near the summit, and we recommend obtaining experience elsewhere before attempting the more difficult ones. Mount Wilson and Wilson Peak can be done in a day by a strong party, although you could make a weekend of it and try for El Diente, another Fourteener, in tandem with Mount Wilson. The three summits in the eastern San Juans near Del Norte can be combined into an enjoyable weekend, since Bennett Peak can be done with either Summit Peak or Conejos Peak in a single day.

San Juan Mountains

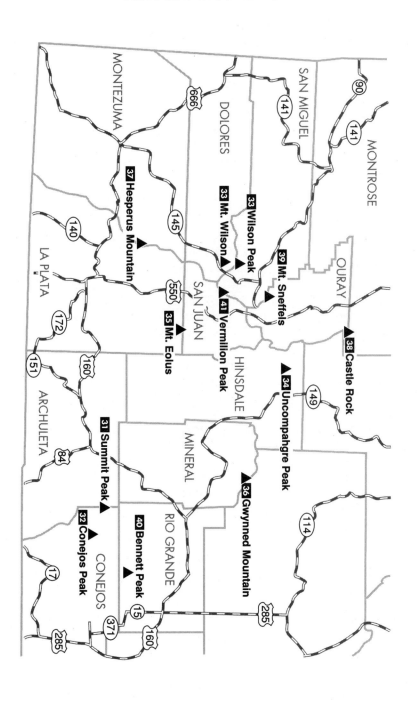

31 Archuleta County: Summit Peak

General description: A moderate day hike on trail crosses grassy tundra to a subalpine peak.

Distance: 3.6 miles, one-way.

Difficulty: Moderate.

Elevation gain: 2,300 feet.

Summit elevation: 13,300 feet.

Maps: USGS Quad—Summit Peak (required), DeLorme p. 89.

Access/permits: South San Juan Wilderness in Rio Grande and San Juan national forests.

Best months: June–October.

Location: South-central Colorado in the eastern San Juan Mountains, about 30 miles west of Alamosa, and 10 miles southwest of Summitville.

Finding the trailhead: The trailhead is located northwest of the town of Platoro. From the junction of U.S. Highway 160 and US 285 in Alamosa, go south on US 285 for about 3 miles to Colorado Highway 370, and turn right (west) on CO 370. Proceed about 13 miles to CO 15. Turn left (south) and go 2 miles to County Road 250. Turn right (west) and head into the South San Juan Mountains. CR 250 becomes Forest Road 250 at the Alamosa Campground just west of the Terrace Reservoir. After about 30 miles you reach Stunner Campground. Continue straight past the campground to the right (west) on FR 380 for 6 miles to the junction with FR 243 at Lake De Nolda, a private lake. Signs at this junction announce "Stunner 6, Platoro 12, Summitville 8," and "US 160 22." Stay left (west) on the road signed "Dead End." Cross Prospect Creek after 0.7 mile and stay right at the bridge after 1.2 miles, following Treasure Creek for 2.9 miles. The end of the road is the trailhead.

To approach from the south via an easier but longer route, leave US 285 at the south edge of Antonito and go west on CO 17 for about 23 miles. Turn right (west) onto FR 250 and continue for about 22 miles to Platoro. Continue up and over Stunner Pass about 6 miles to Stunner Campground. Turn left (west) past the campground on FR 380 and continue for aboout 6 miles to the junction with FR 243. Turn left (west) on the road signed "Dead End" and follow Treasure Creek for 2.9 miles to the end of the road and the trailhead.

If you are approaching from Del Norte, take CR 14 south off US 160 at the west edge of Del Norte, immediately west of the hill by the highway. At mile 11.1, the pavement ends and the road becomes FR 14, although some maps show it as FR 330. FR 14 is a good gravel road that enters the Rio Grande National Forest at mile 11.6. Continue south, climbing 2,600 feet to mile 17.6 at the junction of FR 14 (from the north), FR 329 (to the east), and FR 330 (to the west). Turn right (west) on FR 330 and proceed about 10 miles to Summitville on a fair gravel road. Pass around the large open pit

Archuleta County: Summit Peak

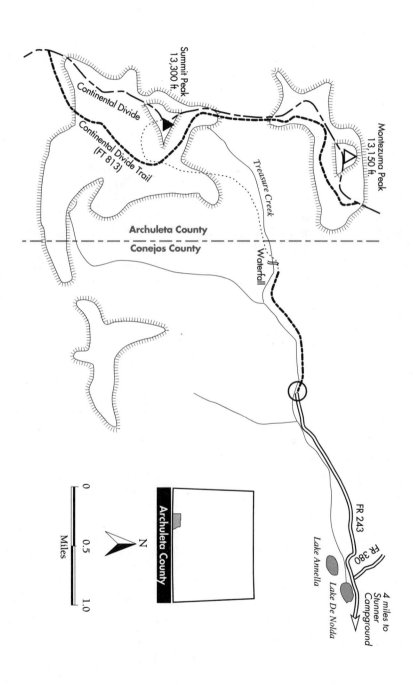

Summit Peak
13,300 ft.

Montezuma Peak
13,150 ft.

Continental Divide

Continental Divide Trail
(FT 813)

Treasure Creek

Waterfall

Archuleta County

Conejos County

Lake Annella

Lake De Nolda

FR 243

FR 380

4 miles to
Stunner
Campground

N

Archuleta County

0   0.5   1.0

Miles

mining operation that forms Summitville, and continue about 3 miles to an intersection with FR 380. Turn left (south) on FR 380 and proceed about 8 miles to an intersection with FR 243 at Lake De Nolda, about 4 miles south of Elwood Pass. Make a hard right (west) on the road signed "Dead End" and follow Treasure Creek for 2.9 miles to the end of the road and the trailhead.

Key points:
- 1.0   Base of waterfall
- 1.7   Timberline
- 2.9   Intersect the Continental Divide Trail
- 3.1   Talus at base of east ridge

The hike: From the road's end, follow a faint trail west along the north side of Treasure Creek as it climbs toward the Continental Divide. Watch for a significant series of cascades and waterfalls after 1 mile. After the first set of waterfalls, choose a safe spot to cross this small stream. The stream can be swift during spring runoff, although it is only a few feet wide in many spots, and there are numerous logs that have fallen across it. The trail is indistinct in this area, so be careful to parallel the creek through the evergreen forest until you reach timberline at mile 1.7. As you enter the upper basin bounded by Montezuma Peak to the north and Summit Peak to the south, you will leave the drainage and head south up to the gentle east shoulder of Summit Peak. Notice for the first time Summit Peak, with its prominent eastern subpeak rising above you. You will join the Continental Divide Trail as you approach the shoulder. Use this trail to swing south of the sharp eastern ridge and approach Summit Peak from its gentle south slopes. Resist the temptation to cut west too soon and instead skirt the small talus field at the bottom of the east ridge. Continue southwest until there is nothing between you and the summit but grassy slopes. Go northwest up the slopes, heading for the low point between Summit Peak and its 13,200-foot eastern subpeak. Gain the ridge and go west along the high ground to the highpoint. The north face of Summit Peak is very steep, so exercise caution when approaching the edge. There is a small register and a large mammal skull at the summit. Return via the same route.

An alternate route begins at Elwood Pass on FR 380 several miles west of Summitville. Follow a trail west to the junction of Forest Trail 707 and FT 813, the Continental Divide Trail, and continue south on FT 813 past Montezuma Peak to the east shoulder of Summit Peak. Stay high at the junction of the two trails and do not descend west to Crater Lake. This route is longer and carries you at more exposed elevations but offers better views along the route.

The best time to visit is June through September. The gravel roads may be passable earlier, but the bushwhack

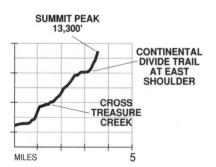

SUMMIT PEAK
13,300'

CONTINENTAL
DIVIDE TRAIL
AT EAST
SHOULDER

CROSS
TREASURE
CREEK

MILES   5

The waterfall on Treasure Creek is a landmark on the hike to Summit Peak. PHOTO BY BECKIE COVILL

through the woods will involve deep snowdrifts until June. The view of the southeastern San Juan Mountains spreads around you in a 360-degree panorama, with Conejos Peak visible to the southeast and Bennett Peak far to the northeast. Just to the north rises Montezuma Peak, which provides a fine secondary target for strong hikers to attain on their way back to the trailhead. Summit Peak is one of six county highpoints in Colorado that lie directly astride the Continental Divide.

County highlights: Pagosa Springs is the county seat of Archuleta County, which was established in 1885 and named in honor of Antonio D. Archuleta, the state senator from Conejos County who introduced the bill in the legislature to create a new county from Conejos County.

Following a devastating flood of the San Juan River in 1911, it was determined that a new road to the northeast was needed. After several years of research, work on the road was started. Opening ceremonies for the west side of Wolf Creek Pass Road took place on August 21, 1916. The road was hard-packed dirt, steep, and narrow. It was the beginning of the change that would alter the face of the county. Automobile and truck routes created a vast and complicated supply system that would nearly kill the railroads and end the self-sufficiency of communities like Pagosa Springs.

The San Juan Mountains surround the town of Pagosa Springs on three sides. It was once called "Shangri-La." Pagosa Springs is named for the Ute word meaning "healing waters," which recognizes the hot mineral springs that the residents use to heat many buildings. There are several interesting outdoor hot pools, and several motels have small concrete pools and indoor bathhouses open to the public.

Camping and services: The nearest services are in the hamlet of Platoro, which serves the South San Juan Mountains; however, when visiting this area be sure to bring plenty of fuel and supplies. Stunner Campground is located on FR 380, about 7 miles east of the trailhead. Other national forest campgrounds in the area include Mix Lake Campground on the north side of Platoro and Lake Fork Campground about 5 miles south of Platoro.

32 Conejos County: Conejos Peak

General description:	This remote subalpine peak provides a moderate but pleasant day hike across a grassy tundra ridge deep within the interesting eastern San Juan Mountains.
Distance:	3.5 miles, one-way.
Difficulty:	Moderate.
Elevation gain:	1,800 feet.
Summit elevation:	13,172 feet.
Maps:	USGS Quad—Platoro (required), DeLorme p. 89.
Access/permits:	South San Juan Wilderness in Rio Grande National Forest.
Best months:	June–September.

Location: South-central Colorado in the eastern San Jun Mountains, about 40 miles west of Alamosa, and 4 miles southwest of Platoro.

Finding the trailhead: The trailhead is located south of the town of Platoro, which can be most easily reached from the east and south. From the junction of U.S. Highway 160 and US 285 in Alamosa, go south on US 285 for 3 miles to Colorado Highway 370. Turn right (west) on CO 370 and proceed about 13 miles to CO 15. Turn left (south) and go 2 miles on CO 15. Turn right (west) on CR 250 and head into the South San Juan Mountains. After about 30 miles you will reach Stunner Campground. CR 250 becomes Forest Road 250 at the Alamosa Campground just west of the Terrace Reservoir. Continue south up and over Stunner Pass on FR 250 for about 6 more miles to Platoro. Continue 5.2 miles south from Platoro to Lake Fork Campground. About 1 mile south of the campground turn right (west) on FR 105 and follow this good gravel road as it winds along Saddle Creek. After 4 miles and several switchbacks, the road intersects with FR 100. Stay left on FR 105 and continue 1.8 miles to a major switchback where FR 105 turns sharply back to the right (east) at 11,300 feet. This is an unofficial trailhead and provides a shorter, albeit more confusing, route into the Conejos Peak area. Continue 2 more miles to the intersection of Forest Trail 719 to a better trailhead. This old road was constructed for logging and continues a bit farther west and downhill but dead-ends.

To approach from the south via an easier but longer route, leave US 285 at the south edge of Antonito and go west on CO 17 for about 23 miles. Turn right (west) onto FR 250 and continue for about 16 miles to FR 105. If you encounter Lake Fork Campground you have gone about a mile too far to the north. Continue as described above.

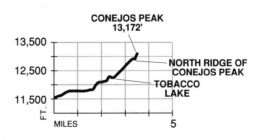

Conejos County: Conejos Peak

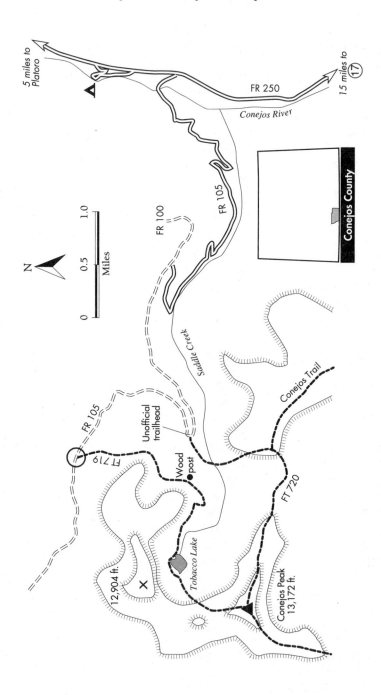

Key points:

1.4   Wooden post at trail junction
2.6   Tobacco Lake
3.3   North ridge of Conejos Peak

The hike: From the intersection of FR 105 and FT 719, hike south for 1.4 miles as the trail hugs the base of the ridge to a wooden post marking a possible trail descending to the unofficial trailhead at the switchback in FR 105. Continue along this good trail as it sweeps right (west) into the Tobacco Lake Basin. The trail skirts the north side of the lake at mile 2.6 and sweeps southwest again to gain the north ridge of Conejos Peak at mile 3.3. Once on the ridge, you have an easy stroll to the summit, but be alert for changing weather that may bring lightning. The actual summit is small and rocky with a wooden tripod and glass-jar register. Return by the same route.

If you are confident of your route-finding abilities, you may choose to use the unofficial trailhead at the hairpin curve on FR 105, but be aware that we and other field checkers encountered a muddy and confusing maze of pack trails west of this trailhead. Thankfully the Forest Service is employing summer youth brigades to improve this trail, especially the steep section gaining the south ridge of Conejos Peak, and may assign a trail number to it in the future. From the trailhead, boldly enter into the woods due west on a muddy pack trail. Follow this trail as it curves to the south, crosses Saddle Creek at mile 0.3, leaves timberline, and works its way up the steep slopes of the eastern ridge of Conejos Peak. Once you gain the saddle on the ridge at mile 1.1, turn right (west) on FT 720, being careful not to continue east on the Conejos Peak Trail. Enjoy the pleasant tundra walk along the faint trail all the way to Conejos Peak at mile 2.8. Return by the same route or complete a loop hike by following the north ridge off Conejos Peak and dropping down to Tobacco Lake at mile 3.8. Pick up a trail along the north side of the lake and follow it around the prominent buttress that juts eastward into the Saddle Creek drainage to mile 4.8. Carefully watch for a wooden post along this trail that marks the spot you should descend toward the trailhead.

The best time to visit is June through September, although this area is treasured by outfitters as prime hunting ground. If you must hike this peak in the fall, be very careful and wear orange! In early spring, deep in the forest the gravel USDA Forest Service roads may be hidden by snowdrifts that may make the going rough. Wildflowers abound in the Tobacco Lake Basin, so take along an identification book. The summit offers a nice view of the less-promoted eastern San Juan Mountains. This is a remote region, so take precautions when traveling and hiking here.

County highlights: Conejos is the county seat of Conejos County, which was established in 1861 as Guadalupe County. The county name was soon changed to Conejos, the Spanish word for "rabbits." Some say the Spaniards of New Mexico first applied the name to the swiftly flowing river, which seemed to run as quickly as a jackrabbit. Others say the name comes from the fact that the area was once overrun by rabbits that found shelter in the profuse undergrowth covering the land. Geographically, this county is marked by diverse landforms, including many rivers and various mountain ranges. In fact, the San Juan Mountains presented a formidable barrier to settlement of the area. Splendid outdoor recreation is undoubtedly the pride of this county's western residents, while the San Luis Valley's agriculture dominates the eastern half of the county. The South San Juan Wilderness provides protected mountains for hikers south of Conejos Peak, while nearby Platoro Reservoir offers a mountain fishing experience. Take a moment to study the Potosi Vista Volcanic Site, 1.6 miles south of Stunner Campground on FR 250. Farther south, along the New Mexico border, you may wish to take an 8-hour ride on the historic Cumbres and Toltec narrow gauge-railroad and pass over 10,015-foot Cumbres Pass, the highest point on any scheduled passenger rail route in the country.

Camping and services: The nearest services are in the community of Platoro, which serves the South San Juan Mountains; however, when visiting this area be sure to take plenty of fuel and supplies. Lake Fork Campground is located on FR 250, about 7 miles east of the trailhead. Other national forest campgrounds in the area include Conejos and Spectacle Lake, about 9 miles south of Lake Fork Campground, Mix Lake Campground on the north side of Platoro, and Stunner Campground about 6 miles north of Platoro.

33   San Miguel County: Wilson Peak Dolores County: Mount Wilson

Wilson Peak

General description:	A day hike up this Fourteener begins with a mine road on talus and ends with tricky rock scrambling over class-3 ledges and blocks.
Distance:	3 miles, one-way.
Difficulty:	Strenuous.
Elevation gain:	3,367 feet.
Summit elevation:	14,017 feet.

Mount Wilson

General description:	This challenging Fourteener requires a long day hike or overnight trip on trail and talus slopes to exposed class-4 rock climbing near the summit.
Distance:	4 miles, one-way.

Location: Southwest Colorado in the San Miguel Mountains, about 20 miles southwest of Telluride, and 5 miles west of Lizard Head Pass.

Finding the trailhead: From the junction of Colorado Highway 62 and CO 145, about 23 miles west of Ridgway, take CO 145 east toward Telluride. Drive 6.5 miles and turn right (south) on dirt County Road 60.M, which follows Big Bear Creek. Go about 6 miles to the Uncompahgre National Forest, where the road becomes Forest Road 622. After an additional mile a gate blocks the road. Park about half a mile before reaching this gate at a flat wooded area.

Key points:

0.0	Gate, start of Forest Trail 1108
0.6	Silver Pick Mill
1.6	Ruins at 12,140 feet
2.4	Saddle, junction of FT 408, FT 635, and FT 505
2.6	Gladstone Peak, Wilson Peak ridge
3.0	Wilson Peak
3.6	Saddle
4.4	Bottom Navajo Basin
5.2	Notch on ridge north of Mount Wilson

The hike: Before attempting these peaks, you should have experience in rock scrambling with exposure and route finding on rock faces. Both peaks can be accessed from either the north or the south and are usually climbed in a single overnight outing. We used the north approach and describe that route. Leave your parked vehicle at the wooded camp area and hike the road a half mile to the gate. Continue beyond to the Silver Pick Mine, after which you encounter a fork in the road. Be easy on yourself and take the longer but less steep road to the right (west), which eventually cuts back left (east) and leads into the upper Silver Pick Basin. At mile 1.6 (12,140 feet), this road (FT 408) passes some interesting old mine buildings set on a gentle ridge extending into the basin. This road, which slumping talus covers in places, switchbacks up the slopes and eventually angles upslope to the east to access the saddle at mile 2.4. We "experimented" with crossing the loose scree slopes in this basin and don't recommend it. Follow the old road.

Upon reaching the saddle, stroll east on FT 505 along the saddle on the south slopes of the southwest ridge of Wilson Peak and gain the ridge between Wilson Peak and Gladstone Peak. Stay low enough to arrive at the

San Miguel County: Wilson Peak
Dolores County: Mount Wilson

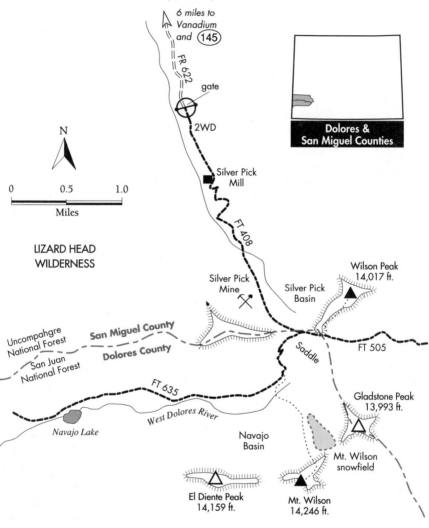

6 miles to
Vanadium
and (145)

FR 622

gate

2WD

Silver Pick
Mill

FT 408

N

0   0.5   1.0

Miles

LIZARD HEAD
WILDERNESS

Silver Pick
Mine

Silver Pick
Basin

Wilson Peak
14,017 ft.

Dolores &
San Miguel Counties

Uncompahgre
National Forest

San Miguel County

Dolores County

San Juan
National Forest

Saddle

FT 505

FT 635

West Dolores River

Navajo Lake

Navajo
Basin

Gladstone Peak
13,993 ft.

Mt. Wilson
snowfield

El Diente Peak
14,159 ft.

Mt. Wilson
14,246 ft.

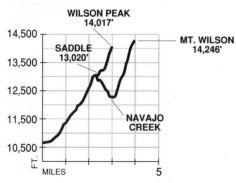

WILSON PEAK
14,017'

SADDLE
13,020'

MT. WILSON
14,246'

NAVAJO
CREEK

14,500

13,500

12,500

11,500

10,500

FT.

MILES   5

ridge at a saddle. We chose to strike northeast, staying at the same height of the saddle and crossed class-3 ledges. You may wish to descend due east from the saddle and immediately strike northeast on easier terrain. Either choice will lead you northeast as you traverse up the ridge on weak trail traces to gain the southwest ridge of Wilson Peak. Hike along the ridge crest to an airy false summit at 13,900 feet and pause a moment to study the cliffs ahead of you. The route descends a modest height directly off the false summit and then ascends the rock cliffs on the left (northwest) side of the ridge until you climb high enough to reach the summit flats, about 3 miles from the trailhead. The climbing from the false summit to the true summit is class 3, although the handholds are numerous. This summit offers unobstructed views of spirelike Lizard Head Peak to the southeast. Return by the same route to the saddle on the north ridge of Navajo Basin.

To reach Mount Wilson from the saddle on the north ridge of Navajo Basin, descend into the basin on FT 635 and reach the creek flowing at the bottom at mile 4.4. Do not follow the trail (FT 635) west downstream, but instead continue straight across the creek at an elevation of 12,300 feet and ascend the south ridge of Navajo Basin. Use the gentle ridge that borders the right (west) side of a large permanent snowfield that lies just left of Gladstone Peak. Climb up the slopes but do not attempt to reach the ridge crest as you did on Wilson Peak. Instead, stay well under the ridge and traverse right (southwest) across talus and a snow-filled chute toward a notch in the ridge at mile 5.2. This notch may be difficult to pick out until you have traveled 1,000 feet or so to the southwest. From the notch, summon your courage and rock-climbing skills to climb 150 feet along the rock spine south to the small flat summit. Some attack this ridge by climbing directly on top of its crest and others choose to monkey cling along the left (east) side of the ridge. Handholds are scarce but good. Many teams handle the exposure by electing to rope up across this class 4 section.

From the summit you will probably spend most of your time fascinated by the ridge that connects El Diente Peak and Mount Wilson, especially if climbers are working their way across it. A direct view of Wilson Peak to the north allows you to study the route you just completed. Return by the same route. Regain the saddle on the north ridge of Navajo Basin and descend to the Silver Pick Trailhead.

The best time to attempt this peak is July through September to avoid snow. Take advantage of the drier days of late August and September. By late September or early October, snows will turn this into a technical route.

Mount Wilson was originally named Glacier Peak. Both Wilsons were named for A. D. Wilson, a prominent member of the Hayden Survey.

County highlights: Rico is the county seat of Dolores County, which was established in 1881 and named after the Dolores River, an abbreviated form of the Spanish name "Rio de Nuestra Señora de los Dolores" or "River of Our Lady of Sorrow." Telluride is the county seat of San Miguel County, which was established in 1883. The county is named for Saint Michael, the archangel who smote the rebel Lucifer.

The rock summit ridge of Mount Wilson in Dolores County may be the toughest challenge on any Colorado county highpoint.

White settlers and prospectors were first drawn to this region by rumors of abundant gold and silver, as well as a treaty that ceded the Ute Indian mineral rights. The recent emphasis on the tourism industry in San Miguel County has proven to be as stimulating for the economy as the discovery of gold more than a century ago. Tourism has overtaken both agriculture and mining to become the primary source of income for the county.

Telluride is as famous and storied a western town as Colorado has to offer. Telluride Ski Area opened in the early 1970s and is one of the most beautiful ski resorts in Colorado. There are many things to do in Telluride, but music lovers will not want to miss the Telluride Bluegrass Festival held in late June or the annual Telluride Jazz Festival held in mid-July each year. Telluride also hosts a film festival on Labor Day weekend.

Camping and services: Primitive trailhead camping is allowed in the woods near the Silver Pick Trail, as well as throughout the Silver Pick and Navajo basins. National forest campgrounds are located north and south of Lizard Head Pass on CO 145 just west of the wilderness area in which the Wilsons are located. Full services are available and then some in Telluride.

34 Hinsdale County: Uncompahgre Peak

General description:	With the most distinctive profile of any Colorado Fourteener, this highpoint is reached by a day hike across tundra with a short stretch of steep, loose talus near the summit.
Distance:	7.8 miles, one-way.
Difficulty:	Moderate.
Elevation gain:	4,989 feet.
Summit elevation:	14,309 feet.
Maps:	USGS Quad—Uncompahgre Peak (required), DeLorme p. 67, Trails Illustrated #141.
Access/permits:	Uncompahgre Wilderness in Uncompahgre National Forest.
Best months:	July–September.

Location: Southwest Colorado in the San Juan Mountains, about 40 miles southwest of Gunnison, and 7 miles northwest of Lake City.

Finding the trailhead: From Gunnison, drive about 19 miles west on U.S. Highway 50 to the junction with Colorado Highway 149. If coming from Montrose, drive about 66 miles east on US 50 to this intersection. Turn south onto CO 149 and immediately cross the Gunnison River. Follow its shores for several miles before heading south and west about 46 miles to Lake City. In Lake City, turn left (west) on Second Avenue in the residential

Hinsdale County: Uncompahgre Peak

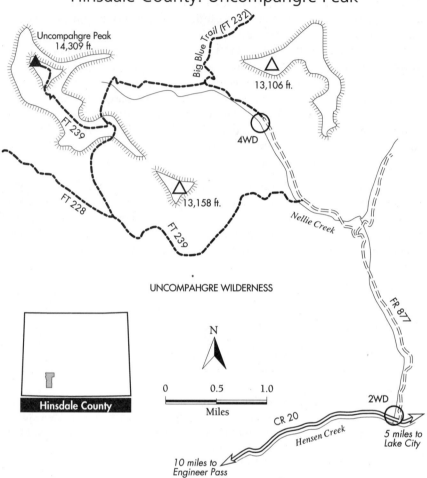

Uncompahgre Peak
14,309 ft.

Big Blue Trail (FT 232)

13,106 ft.

FT 239

4WD

13,158 ft.

FT 228

FT 239

Nellie Creek

UNCOMPAHGRE WILDERNESS

Hinsdale County

N

0   0.5   1.0
Miles

FR 87

2WD

CR 20

Hensen Creek

5 miles to
Lake City

10 miles to
Engineer Pass

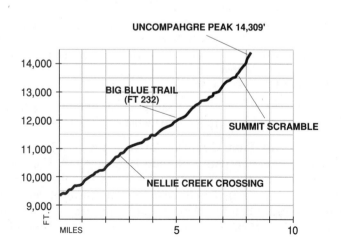

UNCOMPAHGRE PEAK 14,309'

14,000

13,000   BIG BLUE TRAIL
                (FT 232)

12,000   SUMMIT SCRAMBLE

11,000

10,000   NELLIE CREEK CROSSING

9,000

FT.

MILES   5   10

section of this small town and drive 2 blocks to Bluff Street, which leads you to County Road 20. Turn left (south) and head out of town and into the small gorge of Henson Creek. After about 5 miles, turn right (north) onto Forest Road 877 and park your two-wheel-drive vehicle at the forest boundary. The dirt road continues up Nellie Creek for 3.9 miles to a parking area for four-wheel-drive vehicles, but it is rough and steep enough in spots that many elect to begin hiking near CR 20.

Key points:
  3.9 Four-wheel-drive trailhead
  4.8 Junction with Big Blue Trail (Forest Trail 232)
  6.5 FT 239
  7.5 Base of summit mass at 13,920 feet

The hike: From the two-wheel-drive parking area just off CR 20, hike 3.9 miles north with a gain of 2,210 feet on FR 877 along Nellie Creek to the four-wheel-drive parking area at the Uncompahgre Wilderness boundary. Note that the 1993 USDA Forest Service map shows the original wilderness name of "Big Blue." From this upper trailhead, hike northwest along a well-worn trail following Nellie Creek. At a point where the creek turns west, the trail steeply exits the drainage and gains the flatter ground 160 feet above the creek. At the top of this embankment is a junction with the Big Blue Trail (FT 232). Stay left and continue west on the well-worn trail as it aims for the peak. The trail curves broadly south around the head of the Nellie Creek drainage and ends at FT 239 at mile 6.5. (Staying left on FT 239 would lead you to FT 228 which provides access to nearby Wetterhorn Peak.) Continue gaining the high ground south of Uncompahgre Peak. Throughout this section, the trail is not too steep and is in good shape and easily discernible, that is, unless a sudden snowstorm blankets the land as happened to us on our first attempt of this peak. Once on higher ground, the trail flattens and leads you northwest to the base of the summit mass. Follow the trail to the left (west) of the cliffs and then cut right to climb through cliffs with loose scree to the upper summit flats, where the trail heads north to the huge summit. Lie on your stomach and peer over the north cliff face that gives Uncompahgre Peak its unique appearance. Return by the same route.

The best time to attempt this peak is July through September to avoid snow, although the grade is not too steep and the route finding is relatively easy. By late September or early October, snows will turn the upper section into a technical route. To the west, Wetterhorn Peak is often considered a companion Fourteener that is hiked on the same weekend as Uncompahgre Peak. There are three other Fourteeners about 10 miles to the south that Colorado peakbaggers consider when in this area.

County highlights: Lake City is the county seat of Hinsdale County, which was established in 1874 and named for Colorado Lieutenant Governor George A. Hinsdale. The county has quite a complicated geographic setting. The San Juan Mountains cross the southern part of the county and form a portion of its western boundary. The Continental Divide crosses the diminutive

The highpoint of Hinsdale County, Uncompahgre Peak, is also the highest peak in the San Juan Mountains. PHOTO BY DAWN HOWARD

county twice, cutting it into thirds. The northern and southern thirds drain into the Pacific Ocean, and the central third drains into the Rio Grande and ultimately the Gulf of Mexico. Lake City is the only community in this least populated of all Colorado counties.

Although dominated by a rich mining history, Hinsdale County will always be remembered for Colorado's most sensational crime. Drive a couple miles south on CO 149 to visit the Alferd Packer Victim Memorial, which memorializes five miners who died in 1874 and, through cannibalism, may have allowed Packer to survive a winter trip. Several miles farther south on CO 149 a pullout allows you to view one of the world's largest slumps, the Slumgullion Earth Flow. The county road that takes you to the Nellie Creek Trailhead continues west to some of the most popular high-altitude four-wheel-drive routes in the state, including Engineer Pass, Cinnamon Pass, and the ghost town of Animas Forks. Reward yourself by stopping in Gunnison at the A&W for a chili dog and a root beer float.

In the nineteenth century, a great variety of minerals were mined in Hinsdale County, including iron, manganese, sand and gravel, and zinc. The early mines also produced silver, gold, and lead. Millions of dollars worth of ore were extracted and mining remained fairly steady until 1900. Chief agricultural crops today are hay, grain sorghum, and forage. Approximately 80 percent of the land in Hinsdale County is devoted to national forest, and the cattle and sheep ranchers take advantage of the extensive federal land open to grazing. The county is especially known for the quality of Hereford cattle raised on high-mountain ranches.

Camping and services: Car camping is common at the Nellie Creek Trailhead at CR 20. Pitching your tent is permitted all along the route as long as you select a site 100 feet from the trail and water; inside the wilderness area this is not a recommendation but a rule that can bring a fine if violated. The Bureau of Land Management and USDA Forest Service both maintain campgrounds some 10 miles south of Lake City on CR 30. Lake City has full services, including a lively mountain nightlife on Saturday evenings.

35 La Plata County: Mount Eolus

General description: A climb on class-3 ledges and along an exposed catwalk climaxes this overnight backpack trip that begins with a train ride into the San Juan Mountains.
Distance: 9 miles, one-way.
Difficulty: Strenuous.
Elevation gain: 5,871 feet.
Summit elevation: 14,083 feet.
Maps: USGS Quads—Columbine Pass (required) and Mountain View Crest (recommended), DeLorme p. 77, Trails Illustrated #140.
Access/permits: Weminuche Wilderness in San Juan National Forest; fare for narrow-gauge railroad.
Best months: July–September.

Location: Southwest Colorado in the Needle Mountains, about 13 miles south of Silverton, and 25 miles northeast of Durango.

Finding the trailhead: A charming and practical way to access Chicago Basin and Mount Eolus is via the Durango and Silverton Narrow Gauge Railroad. The train leaves Durango up to six times a day from May through September and is operated as a tourist attraction. The round-trip fare as of this writing is $40. For this highpoint, your trailhead actually begins at the Durango Depot at 479 Main Avenue. Contact the rail service in advance to secure your tickets and, on departure day arrive early to beat the crowds (see railroad information below). Be there early: Passengers not in their seats a half hour before departure are considered "no shows." Because backpackers are on board, the train will stop at Needleton, an abandoned site along the river. Disembark there. The conductor will retrieve your backpack from a boxcar.

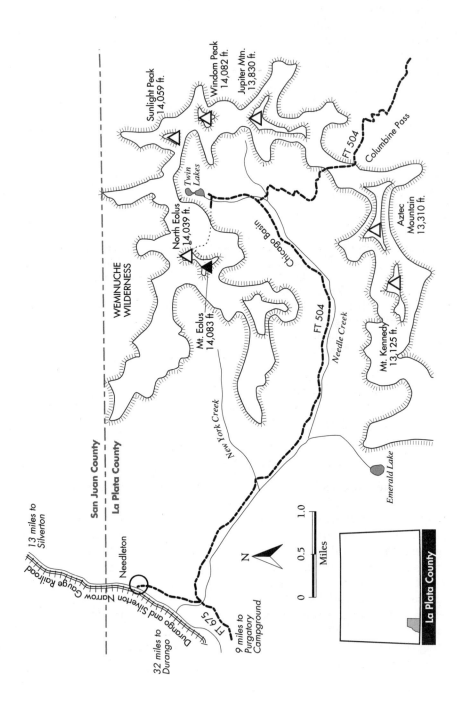

Key points:
- 0.8   Needle Creek
- 7.0   Junction of Forest Trail 504 and trail to Twin Lakes
- 7.7   South end of hanging valley
- 8.8   Mount Eolus and North Eolus ridge
- 8.9   Southwest end of "Sidewalk in the Sky"

The hike: Begin the hike by crossing the Animas River to the east over a fine wooden bridge, turn right (south), and walk parallel with the river for 0.8 mile to the trailhead on the north side of Needle Creek. Turn left (east) onto FT 504 and begin the long haul up Needle Creek into the Chicago Basin. The basin is home to three Fourteeners. Because of their presence, quite a few hikers are likely to be on the trail. At mile 7, leave FT 504 as it turns south to Columbine Pass and follow a distinct use trail north up the steep hillside to a hanging valley in which Twin Lakes are located. Many hikers camp in this eastern section of the lower valley; however, we recommend that you hump up the 1,300-foot wall ahead of you to the north via a steep but well-worn trail. This will place you in a hanging valley in the upper Chicago Basin.

After an overnight camp, rise early and watch for a herd of mountain goats. Leave camp, contour west on good trail, and enter a small basin with Mount Eolus forming its west ridge. Bear right (northwest) and climb toward the saddle between Mount Eolus and North Eolus at about mile 8. Once in the basin, stay to your left just enough to avoid slabs of rock, but eventually take a high, broad ledge to your right (northeast). Gain the saddle closer to North Eolus than Mount Eolus by scrambling west over looser rock. The next stretch of trail is legendary. The ridge connecting Mount Eolus and North Eolus is a rock ridge, at times no more than 3 feet wide, which climbers have dubbed "Sidewalk in the Sky." Do not be surprised if some hikers drop to all fours to cross this spine.

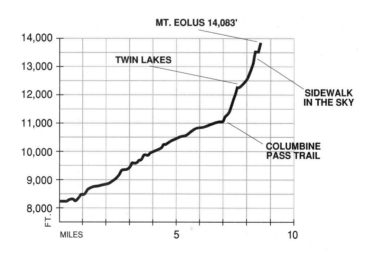

Reach the southwest end of the ridge at mile 8.1 and begin the final summit push by immediately climbing up ledges in front of you and to the left (southeast) side of Mount Eolus. Do not contour around to your left as you will cliff out. These ledges should be fun and no more than class 3 in difficulty. You will reach the summit ridge farther south and will have to come back north on the ridge to reach the highest point. This happens to be a collection of boulders that protrude high into the atmosphere. Sign the register and either return directly to camp or take a side trip by climbing north to capture North Eolus. Given the effort you've invested so far, you may wish to spend a few days climbing Sunlight Peak and Windom Peak. Officially, Windom Peak is only a foot or two lower than Mount Eolus and just misses being the highpoint of the county. Return back down Needle Creek to the train pickup at Needleton. Be sure to arrive well before the last scheduled train of the day passes by.

The best time to attempt to enter the Chicago Basin is July through September to avoid snow. Take advantage of the drier days of late August and September. By late September or early October, snow will turn this into a technical route. The ledges on Mount Eolus are no place to be during precipitation or lightning. Mount Eolus seems to be named "God of the Winds" for the storm clouds that congregate over the Needle Mountains. The original spelling may have been "Mount Aeolus."

County highlights: Durango is the county seat of La Plata County, which was established in 1874. The county name is Spanish for "silver" and is used in naming both a river and mountain range in the region. Various Spanish expeditions explored the San Juan Basin, and Coronado himself may have entered this region as early as 1540, although no archaeological evidence has been found to support this claim. Juan Maria de Rivera is known to have been in the region in 1765. With the discovery of silver in the San Juans, the entire region came to be known as "La Plata." In 1776, the Escalante Expedition traveled through the region, seeking an overland route from Mexico to the Spanish missions established in California. By the mid-1820s, a number of French and American trappers had established a thriving trade in the region. By 1861, miners began arriving from the mining camps of the Front Range in search of the purported mineral wealth in the San Juan area. The mining boom was short-lived, but a number of permanent settlements remained. Other industries such as agriculture, ranching, and timber figured prominently in the county's early years. The Denver & Rio Grande Railroad established a line in Durango in the early 1880s, and Durango has continued to serve as a marketing and distribution center for the county ever since. In more recent years, the focus of La Plata County's economy has shifted toward tourism, as thousands of visitors flock to the area to ride the narrow-gauge train, hike the mountains, tour the cliff dwellings of Mesa Verde National Park, and ski at Purgatory Resort. Durango hosts the Ironhorse Motorcycle Rally each Labor Day weekend. Be sure to visit the Steamworks Microbrewery 2 blocks north of the train depot for terrific burgers, quesadillas, and award-winning beer.

The narrow Sidewalk in the Sky leads to a series of cliffs and ledges below the summit of Mount Eolus.

Camping and services: Camping is permitted along the route to Mount Eolus, although Forest Service wilderness regulations apply. When camping in the huge Weminuche Wilderness, set tents at least 100 feet from trails and water sources.

The Forest Service maintains several campgrounds along U.S. Highway 550 between Durango and Silverton. You can hike south from Needleton along the Animas River to Cascade Creek and hike west up to US 550 and Purgatory Campgound.

Only snacks are available on the narrow-gauge train. Full services are provided in Durango and in Silverton,which cater to tourists and hikers; their many gift shops and unique restaurants make for a fun day or night.

For more information: Durango and Silverton Narrow Gauge Railroad, 479 Main Avenue, Durango, CO 81301, 970-247-2733.

36 Mineral County: Gwynedd Mountain

General description:	Rising above historic Creede, this Centennial Peak requires orienteering skills and a long hike and bushwack through grassy meadows and up tundra slopes.
Distance:	5.8 miles, one-way.
Difficulty:	Moderate.
Elevation gain:	4,175 feet.
Summit elevation:	13,895 feet.
Maps:	USGS Quads—Halfmoon Pass and San Luis Peak (required), DeLorme p. 78.
Access/permits:	La Garita Wilderness in Rio Grande National Forest.
Best months:	July–September.

Location: South-central Colorado in the La Garita Mountains, about 30 miles northwest of South Fork, and 12 miles northeast of Creede.

Finding the trailhead: From South Fork, west of Alamosa, go west on Colorado Highway 149 for about 22 miles to Creede, a small but thriving community. One of Colorado's most historic mining towns, Creede is accessed by CO 149, which enters the town, turns back sharply, and exits to the south. At the apex of this turn, where the road crosses Willow Creek, continue straight and pass through town. At the northern edge of town, notice the Creede Fire Department, which is housed in a tunnel in the side of the mountain. Continue north on Forest Road 503. This good gravel road passes through a narrow canyon at the edge of town and continues uphill to the north. Continue for 0.7 mile north from Creede to a fork in the road. Turn right on FR 502 and drive through the narrow canyon along East Willow

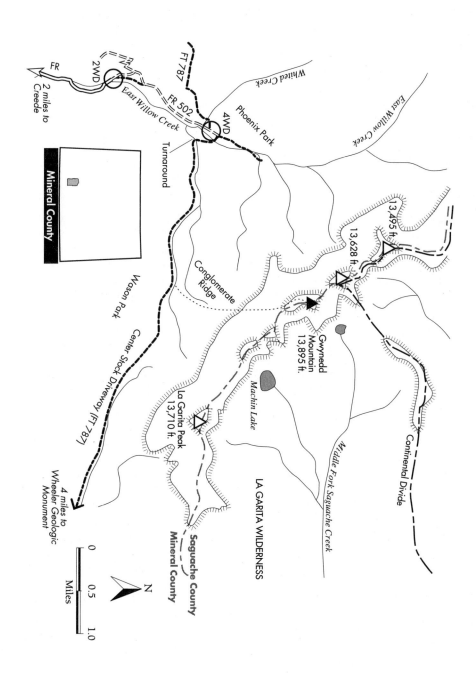

Creek and cross to the west side of the creek at mile 3 at two small tailing ponds. Park here. Be sure to get all the way off the road.

If you have four-wheel-drive, you can continue on FR 502 to mile 4.5, where Whited Creek enters the Willow Creek drainage from the west. This area is known as Phoenix Park, and the flat-bottomed valley, complete with beaver ponds, is a stark contrast to the narrow rock canyons below. Park here.

Key points:
- 0.2 Switchback on FR 502 uphill from trailhead
- 0.3 Intersection of FR 502 with cuttoff trail
- 1.2 Cross Whited Creek
- 1.8 Junction on Forest Trail 787
- 3.6 Depart FT 787 toward conglomerate ridge
- 3.9 Small, distinct conglomerate ridge with cliff face
- 5.2 Saddle

The hike: Starting from the two-wheel-drive parking area near the tailing ponds, walk uphill on gravel FR 502 for 0.2 mile to a prominent left switchback. At this turn, take a four-wheel-drive road to the right (north) and follow that road as it winds through trees and heads north up the valley created by East Willow Creek. You may notice a cutoff trail at mile 0.3 on the right (east) side of FR 502. This cutoff trail heads back through mine tailings, close to the creek, to the two-wheel-drive parking area. Continue on FR 502 along East Willow Creek and cross Whited Creek at mile 1.2. After crossing Whited Creek, continue on FR 502 for several hundred yards to mile 1.4 and park your four-wheel-drive vehicle. Leave the road by turning right (east) and walk along a worn route through the open grass of Phoenix Park down to East Willow Creek. This worn route, FT 787, is known as Center Stock Driveway and is used to drive livestock from higher grazing pastures.

Carefully cross East Willow Creek to the east side using the old beaver dams to stay high and dry. This route picks up on the creek's east bank as a four-wheel-drive route and heads east up the drainage of an unnamed creek

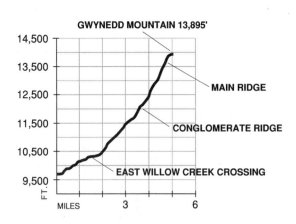

that flows down from Wason Park, a broad meadow at 11,600 feet. At mile 1.8, just up from East Willow Creek, the road ends at a spacious, flat turnaround with a prominent USDA Forest Service message board. Follow FT 787 out of the end of the turnaround and along the south side of the unnamed creek. This route is distinct but

The tuff deposit at Wheeler Geologic Monument near Gwynedd Peak are eroded into fantastic pillars and cliffs. PHOTO BY CHASE CURTIS

narrow and does not resemble a four-wheel-drive route. Continue to mile 3.6 and look for a rough cliff face on the north side of the creek. This cliffside heads away from the creek toward Gwynned Mountain. Cross the creek drainage here and bushwhack up grassy slopes and through dispersed clumps of pine. At mile 3.9, a use trail develops along the east edge of the well-defined but small conglomerate ridge. The rough cliff face on your left (west) consists of coarse, red conglomerate that has weathered into interesting hoodoos.

For an interesting alternate route, which is extremely scenic but more complex, go west from South Fork for about 13 miles in the narrow Rio Grande canyon, past Wagon Wheel Gap, to a broad open field. Go right (north) here on FR 600, a good gravel road known as Pool Table Road, and continue 9 miles to Hanson Mills, now in ruins. This serves as a trailhead for two-wheel-drive vehicles. If you have four-wheel-drive and don't mind a bumpy two-hour ride, continue for about 15 miles to Wheeler Geologic Monument, which has several good campsites. Follow a trail toward the monument for 0.3 mile and take a trail to the left (west) for a short distance before ascending volcanic outcrops. Travel west for about 4 miles on a faint path across the broad, flat, grassy meadow known as Wason Park to the base of La Garita Peak. (La Garita Peak is the prominent landmark in front of you since you left the trailhead.) This path disappears into small stands of trees several times, but eventually continues past wooden posts that mark Center Stock Driveway. When in doubt of the course, stay north near the base of the mountain ridge. Refer to your compass often. Continue about 2 miles past La Garita Peak to the conglomerate ridge at the base of Gwynedd

Peak and proceed as described above. This long trek, best done as a full-day hike from a camp at the monument, is not for inexperienced hikers.

The best time to visit is July through September to avoid snowpack. This peak is in remote country with few visitors, so plan your trip accordingly.

Gwynedd Peak misses the Continental Divide by a mere half mile. The odd name of this peak is referenced in Winners' book as "4,000 Meters." The name "Creede Crest" is also applied to this peak. We speculate that these names commemorate the mining history of the area, although the exact origins of both names remain uncertain. The Colorado Mountain Club simply refers to this peak as "Unnamed 13,895" in recognition of no official name on the USGS quad. This area is part of the enormous Creede Caldera, a volcanic remnant 20 miles across that is clearly visible from anywhere in the open valley floor by Creede itself.

Wheeler Geologic Monument was first made a national monument by President Theodore Roosevelt in the early 1900s, but the lack of visitors led to its demotion to "geologic area" status. Today, only serious four-wheel-drive buffs, hunters, and the odd peakbagger venture here. There are no rangers or facilities present.

Gwynedd Peak is a hiking goal in Colorado because of its status as a Centennial Peak, being in the highest 100 peaks in the state. In fact, it is the seventy-third highest peak in Colorado.

For extra credit, ascend La Garita Peak, located on the ridge to the south. For double extra credit, continue along the rim northwest for about 5 miles to San Luis Peak, the only Fourteener in the eastern San Juan Mountains. This may be accomplished best as a backpack in from the Cochetopa Creek access to the north. For still more extra credit, hike or drive a mile farther along Willow Creek to an old cabin, where the road dies. Continue a short distance to a drainage on the right (east) where a waterfall is visible about 250 feet above you.

County highlights: Creede is the county seat of Mineral County, which was established in 1893. The county name is a descriptive term recognizing the extreme mineralization that resulted from the volcanic activity that formed the Creede Caldera.

Nicolas Creede discovered the area's first silver lode in 1889. A late-comer to the silver bonanza, the new town of Creede was soon attracting 300 newcomers a day and nearing a population of 10,000. Boomtown status attracted a special breed of men and women whose names have survived the passage of time. Bat Masterson was the marshal of Creede for a short while. Bob Ford was another of Creede's first residents, famous only because he killed Jesse James with a shot to the back. He was in turn gunned down with a double-barreled shotgun. Champagne, wine, and song flowed freely at Ford's funeral. He will be forever remembered in a ballad as "the dirty little coward." Though Creede was once the leading producer of silver in the state, the repeal of the Silver Act in 1893 caused the area's economy to collapse. On top of that came many catastrophic fires and a number of flash floods. Boom had turned into bust in less than five years. Even with all this adversity, the town was able to rebuild and, over the years it has attracted an eclectic bunch of locals. Today the town is a relaxed haven for writers and artists as much as it is for retired folk and outdoorsmen.

The town of Creede is famous for its annual Fourth of July celebration. Reserve a room early at the Creede Hotel or one of several other small motels. Continue past Creede on CO 149 to Lake City over Slumgullion Pass, and observe the enormous movement of an earth slide on the west side of the pass.

Camping and services: National forest camping is available along CO 149 at Palisade Campground near Wagon Wheel Gap southeast of Creede and Marshall Park and Rio Grande campgrounds southwest of Creede. Creede offers full services.

37 Montezuma County: Hesperus Mountain

General Description:	This alpine peak—requiring a strenuous day hike, mostly off trail on talus and scree, with a final scramble on a ridge—requires orienteering skills.
Distance:	2.5 miles, one-way.
Difficulty:	Strenuous.
Elevation gain:	2,792 feet.
Summit elevation:	13,232 feet.
Maps:	USGS Quads—La Plata (required) and Rampart Hills (recommended), DeLorme p. 86.
Access/permits:	San Juan National Forest.
Best months:	July–September.

Location: Southwest Colorado in the La Plata Mountains, about 25 miles northwest of Durango, and 15 miles northeast of Mancos.

Finding the trailhead: From Mancos, leave U.S. Highway 160 and go north in the center of town on Colorado Highway 184 for 0.4 mile. Turn right (east) on County Road 42, and follow it northeast for 5.1 miles to the national forest boundary, where it becomes Forest Road 561. Continue northeast for an additional 5 miles to Transfer Campground, a major campground for the area; signs there will guide you to nearby Mancos Overlook. This point offers stunning views to the east of the La Plata Mountains.

Set your trip odometer and continue on FR 561 for 1.8 miles to FR 350, which veers to the right (east) just past the Aspen Guard Station and about a mile past the turnoff to FR 560. Turn right (east) here on FR 350 (Spruce Mill Road) and go to mile 5.6 on a fair dirt road to the junction with FR 351. Continue straight on FR 350 to mile 8.0 to the Y-intersection with FR 346.

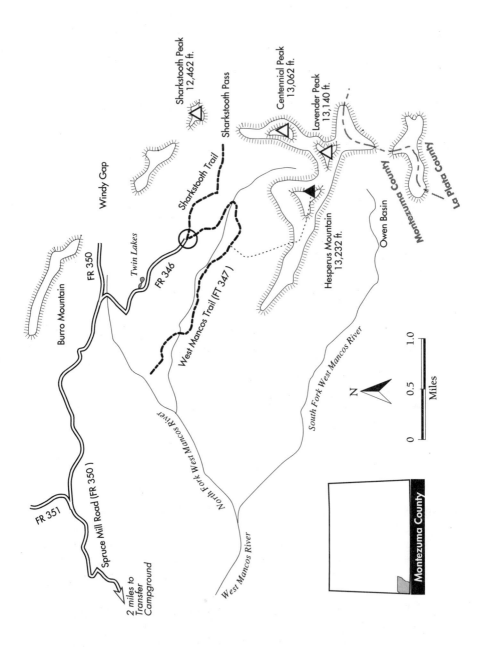

Sharkstooth Peak 12,462 ft.

Sharkstooth Pass

Centennial Peak 13,062 ft.

Lavender Peak 13,140 ft.

Windy Gap

Sharkstooth Trail

Hesperus Mountain 13,232 ft.

Owen Basin

Montezuma County

La Plata County

Burro Mountain

FR 350

Twin Lakes

FR 346

West Mancos Trail (FT 347)

North Fork West Mancos River

South Fork West Mancos River

West Mancos River

Spruce Mill Road (FR 350)

FR 351

2 miles to Transfer Campground

N

Miles

0   0.5   1.0

Montezuma County

Take the right-hand fork (FR 346), also known as the Aspen Loop Trail. Continue on FR 346 southeast to mile 8.7 at tiny Twin Lakes. The road ends at Sharkstooth Trailhead at mile 9.5.

The road quality deteriorates for about the last 2 miles to a point where a passenger car may have trouble if there has been any recent precipitation. Park at Sharkstooth Trailhead and look for the faint trail heading south. Do not follow the more established trail east toward Sharkstooth Pass, as this will lead you north and away from Hesperus Mountain.

Key points:
0.4 Cross North Fork West Mancos River
0.5 Leave West Mancos Trail, head south
1.3 Shallow saddle at 12,140 feet

The hike: Begin the route to Hesperus Mountain by following a faint road southeast and down toward the North Fork West Mancos River. This road ends, and a faint trail can be picked up that will wind down the remainder of the way to the river at mile 0.4. Cross the drainage and continue along the distinct trail as it follows the south bank in a westerly direction. Your goal is to gain the ridge to your left (south). There is no trail to the summit, so you will have to scramble 1,500 feet up one of the many gullies the ridge. The farther west you follow the trail, the easier the ascent to the ridge will be. The downside to this is that you will gain the ridge farther from the summit. If you choose to leave the trail sooner, farther east, and take the first gully that appears to reach the ridge, you will have a steeper climb to gain the ridge. Choose your poison: Either hike farther west to gain the ridge in an easier but longer fashion or charge up the ridge in a shorter but exhaustingly steeper manner.

We suggest a happy medium by following the stream for 1,000 feet before heading up a black shale gully that will gain the ridge at a shallow saddle, just right (west) of the final slopes to the summit. The entire route—peak and ridge—is visible from the trailhead, so take advantage of this and scout your route as you hike. There is no wrong way, just personal preference. Once on the ridge, follow it uphill to the east toward the summit. The trail alternates between loose talus and broken rock ledges that require some scrambling, although nothing too serious. Just when you think you've lost the trail, look up to the left and head up through ledges, regaining the trail.

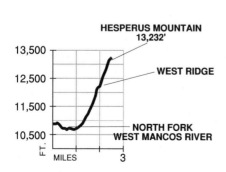

HESPERUS MOUNTAIN
13,232'

WEST RIDGE

NORTH FORK
WEST MANCOS RIVER

13,500
12,500
11,500
10,500
FT.
MILES   3

This will occur several times on the summit ridge. The trail bears to the right (south) of the summit and disappears as it approaches the rude pile of rocks that characterizes this peak. You are rewarded with a small summit area. There is no register. Return by the same route, enjoying the steep descent off the ridge. Seasoned hikers might wear gaiters for this portion of the hike.

Hesperus Mountain is clearly seen near Sharkstooth Trailhead.

The best time to visit is July through September. The dirt forest roads do not get plowed or cleared of debris until very late spring. Scrambling up the gullies to the ridge crest may be difficult or downright dangerous if there is too much snow and ice in them.

Hesperus Mountain is one of the four sacred mountains of the Navajo Nation and represents a northern corner. The other three mountains are Humphreys Peak near Flagstaff, Arizona, Mount Taylor near Grants, New Mexico, and Blanca Peak in Colorado. It is interesting to note that all are county highpoints. Hesperus is one of only a few county highpoints in Colorado that require a you to lose elevation prior to beginning the ascent. The trailhead, at 10,900 feet, is surprisingly close to timberline. The ruggedness of the other peaks in the area, most notably Lavender Peak to the east, reminds you of the fact that, while detached, the La Plata Mountains are definitely part of the rugged San Juans. Notice the interesting formation to the north known as Sharkstooth Peak as you make your way up the gullies and along the ridge. Hunting is possible in this area in the fall, so be cautious and wear orange. There is very little distance to go before you leave timberline behind, so this may make for a nice early fall hike.

County highlights: Cortez is the county seat of Montezuma County, which was established in 1889 and named for the Aztec chief Montezuma, who was conquered by Cortez and killed in 1520. Hesperus is Greek for "evening star," and the peak was named for the ship in Longfellow's "The Wreck of the Hesperus." The name Hesperus is also applied to the low-key ski area on US 160 near the town of Hesperus. The La Plata Mountains are named with the Spanish word for "silver." Montezuma County anchors the southwest

196

corner of Colorado and represents the state at famous Four Corners, where Arizona, Colorado, New Mexico, and Utah meet.

The county contains a variety of landscapes, including semiarid plains, mountains, agricultural valleys, and canyons. The county also boasts of Mesa Verde National Park and Hovenweep National Monument. The Ute Mountain and Southern Ute Indian reservations are home to Colorado's only Indian casinos, located in Towaoc and Ignacio. Not to be missed is the Ute Indians' dance performance held in Cortez City Park on weekday summer evenings at no charge.

Camping and services: Primitive camping is allowed throughout the national forest. The USDA Forest Service maintains Transfer Campground on the approach to Sharkstooth Trailhead. Campgrounds can be found at Mancos State Recreation Area just south of the national forest boundary on CR 42. The town of Mancos on US 160 offers the closest services to this peak. Full services are available along US 160 in Cortez, about 18 miles to the west, and Durango, about 28 miles to the east.

38 Montrose County: Castle Rock

General description:	A moderate day hike requires bushwhacking through evergreens to a flat, wooded ridge.
Distance:	2.6 miles, one-way.
Difficulty:	Moderate.
Elevation gain:	1,433 feet.
Summit elevation:	11,453 feet.
Maps:	USGS Quad—Buckhorn Lakes (required), DeLorme p. 67.
Access/permits:	Montrose County, City of Montrose, Bureau of Land Management.
Best months:	June–October.

Location: Southwest Colorado on the Cimarron Ridge, about 15 miles southeast of Montrose and 15 miles north of Ouray.

Finding the trailhead: Access to this highpoint is through Buckhorn Lakes Park. Reach this Montrose city park by going south from the junction of U.S. Highway 50 and US 550 in Montrose for about 13 miles to the Montrose-Ouray county line. Cross this line and turn left (east) onto Buckhorn Road at the north edge of the hamlet of Colona. If you are coming from the south, leave Ridgway at Colorado Highway 62 and go north on US 550 for 13.5 miles to Colona and turn right (east) onto Buckhorn Road. Proceed north and east on Buckhorn Road for 1.1 miles and turn right (east) at the junction with Uncompahgre Road. Continue east on Buckhorn Road as it rises through chaparral on the west slope of Cimarron Ridge. At 10.8 miles you reach the

Montrose County: Castle Rock

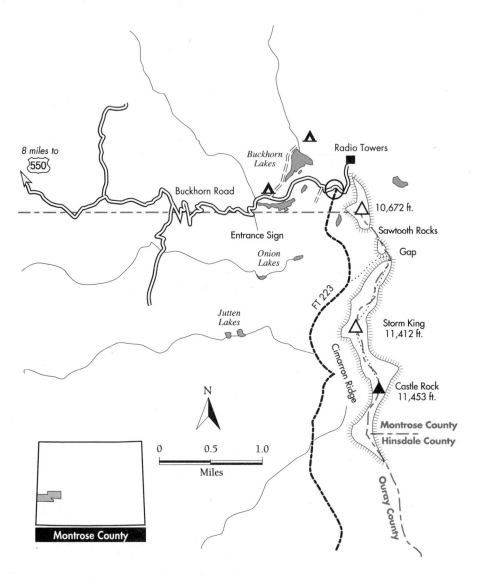

8 miles to
550

Buckhorn
Lakes

Radio Towers

Buckhorn Road

10,672 ft.

Entrance Sign

Sawtooth Rocks

Gap

Onion
Lakes

FT 223

Jutten
Lakes

Storm King
11,412 ft.

Cimarron Ridge

N

Castle Rock
11,453 ft.

Montrose County

Hinsdale County

0   0.5   1.0

Miles

Ouray County

Montrose County

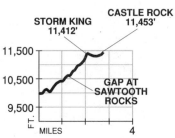

STORM KING
11,412'

CASTLE ROCK
11,453'

11,500

10,500

GAP AT
SAWTOOTH
ROCKS

9,500

FT.

MILES   4

entrance sign for Buckhorn Lakes Park on a prominent ridge. Consider leaving your vehicle here if the spring thaw has left the roads muddy, as your vehicle may not be able to regain the rise back up the ridge. If conditions are dry, descend to the left down the road and pass by several lakes owned by the city of Montrose. Proceed between the lakes, noting several poor dirt roads to the left. Reach mile 12, just after cresting a bench and passing a fair dirt lane, 1.3 miles from the Buckhorn Lakes entrance sign, at elevation 10,020 feet. Proceed an additional 1,000 feet and park where the road curves to the left (northeast). A second rough dirt road heads right (south) from the curve where you parked. This is the trailhead for most vehicles. If you continue on the road to the northeast you will dead-end in a half mile at a radio facility. Depending on conditions, the road to the south may be passable farther along the west face of the ridge.

Key points:
- 1.0   Leave Forest Trail 223 at elevation 10,400 feet
- 1.3   Gap between Sawtooth Rocks and Cimarron Ridge
- 2.0   Storm King
- 2.6   Castle Rock

The hike: From your parked vehicle, hike the road (FT 232) as it rises among the evergreens just west of the flat rock formations known as the Sawtooth Rocks. Walk 1 mile to an elevation of 10,400 feet, due west of the southern end of the Sawtooth Rocks, turn off FT 232, and bushwhack across very uneven terrain through the forest. Note any landmarks useful for route finding during your return. Take compass bearings—and time your travel between key points! At mile 1.3 you will breach the ridge between the Sawtooth Rocks to the north and Cimarron Ridge to the south. Pass completely through this gap and turn right (south) to the gentle eastern side of Cimarron Ridge. Begin your ascent of this ridge through a dense forest of large evergreens. Try to follow a faint trail close to the edge of the western cliff face of the ridge, but be careful of the dangerous drop-off. At mile 2 you will welcome the flat plateau of Storm King, knowing that you will have a relatively easy stroll from here. Bushwhack through the forest of this flat, wooded ridge that narrows considerably before spreading out into the summit rise at mile 2.6. This rise is named Castle Rock and contains television broadcast towers. If you continue south several hundred feet onto an exposed ridge, you will find the South Castle Peak benchmark anchored into the rock. This benchmark does not have an elevation and is dated 1958. Be cautious with the loose rock on these cliffs, and certainly avoid the temptation to chuck stones into the forest below as there may be people traveling there. Respect property rights and avoid electrical dangers by staying clear of the towers and their power source. Return by the same route, taking care to retrace your exact route after you leave the gap between Sawtooth Rocks and Cimarron Ridge.

The best time to visit is June through September. The gravel roads and bushwhack route will hold snow far longer than the hot adjacent valleys, as we found out one Memorial Day weekend!

From the summit, the broad valley of the Uncompahgre River presents itself to the west, and the sharper valley of the Cimarron River lies to the east. To the south, Cimarron Ridge develops into some of Colorado's classic rock-climbing peaks as it builds toward the high peaks in the Uncompahgre (formerly Big Blue) Wilderness. The ridge provides a scenic backdrop as you travel US 550 between Ouray and Montrose. This seldom-visited peak is fairly remote and lacks sufficient water sources. Take supplies and notify others of your hiking goal. The lands around the peak are privately owned, although your entire route is on land owned by the Bureau of Land Management. The actual summit is recorded as county property. We discovered that few people at Montrose City Hall or at the county courthouse realized that this unassuming peak is their home county's highpoint.

County highlights: Montrose is the county seat of Montrose County, which was established in 1883. The county was named after the novel *The Legend of Montrose*, penned by Sir Walter Scott, because the region bears a similarity to descriptions in the book. Montrose benefits as the busy crossroads of US 50 and US 550. The county's economic base is in agriculture. The town of Olathe hosts a sweet corn festival every August and provides over 80,000 ears of delicious corn to the lucky attendees. Visitors to the Black Canyon of Gunnison National Monument just east of Montrose can view Castle Rock from CO 347 as it rises to the high rim of this spectacular gorge.

The Whole Enchilada in Montrose serves great Mexican cuisine. Cap off a hike at the Red Barn on the east end of Montrose on US 50, with its signature dish, peanut butter ice cream pie.

Castle Rock dominates the prominent ridge along the highway from Montrose to Ouray.

Camping and services: The city of Montrose allows camping at Buckhorn Lakes Park. All amenities can be found in Montrose and Ridgway, and limited services can be found in Colona and along US 550.

39 Ouray County: Mount Sneffels

General description:	A day hike up a steep couloir requires rock scrambling near the top of an alpine peak.
Distance:	4 miles, one-way.
Difficulty:	Strenuous.
Elevation gain:	3,400 feet.
Summit elevation:	14,150 feet.
Maps:	USGS Quads—Mount Sneffels and Telluride (recommended), Ironton (optional), DeLorme p. 66, Trails Illustrated #141.
Access/permits:	Mount Sneffels Wilderness in Uncompahgre National Forest.
Best months:	July–September.

Location: Southwest Colorado in the San Juan Mountains, about 6 miles west of Ouray, and 4 miles north of Telluride.

Finding the trailhead: Head south on U.S. Highway 550 from Ouray for about 0.5 mile and turn right (south) onto County Road 361 at the outside of the first of two major hairpin curves that US 550 makes as it leaves Ouray. Drive 4.8 miles on CR 361 on good gravel road to a junction at Camp Bird, an abandoned mine site. CR 361 becomes Forest Road 853 as you pass into the national forest. Stay right (uphill) and pass by the base of an impressive cliff for about 0.5 mile to another abandoned mining site called Sneffels at mile 6.1. At mile 6.8 you reach a point that may be gated, depending on conditions. The road rapidly deteriorates beyond this point. Park between the ghost town of Sneffels and here, staying well off the road, as rangers may need to access the gate.

Key points:
2.2 Wright's Lake
2.7 Junction of Forest Trail 201 and trail to Mount Sneffels
3.4 Saddle between Kismet and Mount Sneffels at 13,500 feet
3.8 Top of summit couloir

The hike: The trail to Mount Sneffels is well used and easy to follow and is, in fact, a jeep road for about the first 2 miles. Off-road driving in Yankee Boy Basin forced the Forest Service to restrict access into this scenic basin. Hike or drive the road to the right along the north bank of Sneffels Creek. The left-hand fork by the gate leads to Governor Basin, a center of mining activity a century ago. Continue up to the right as the road degrades into a

Ouray County: Mount Sneffels

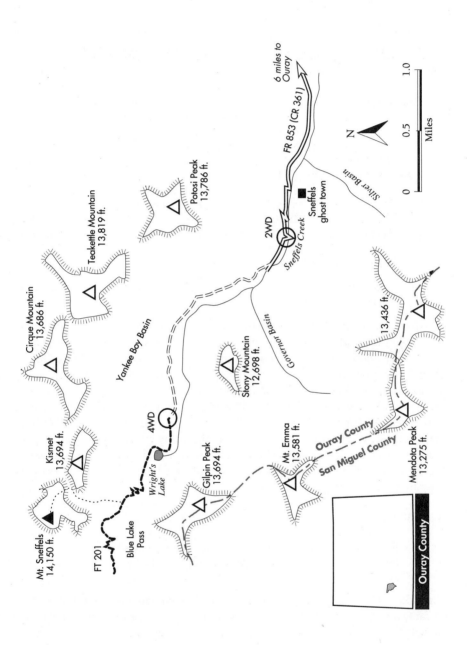

6 miles to Ouray

FR 853 (CR 361)

2WD

Sneffels Creek

Sneffels ghost town

Silver Basin

Potosi Peak
13,786 ft.

Teakettle Mountain
13,819 ft.

Cirque Mountain
13,686 ft.

Yankee Boy Basin

Stony Mountain
12,698 ft.

Governor Basin

13,436 ft.

Kismet
13,694 ft.

4WD

Wright's Lake

Gilpin Peak
13,694 ft.

Mt. Emma
13,581 ft.

Ouray County

San Miguel County

Mendota Peak
13,275 ft.

Mt. Sneffels
14,150 ft.

FT 201

Blue Lake Pass

N

0   0.5   1.0
Miles

Ouray County

two-track jeep trail to a small lake nestled in the upper reaches of Yankee Boy Basin at mile 2.2. Trek past this pond, known locally as Wright's Lake, and head northwest to Blue Lake Pass. At the base of the switchbacks up to the Pass, veer right at mile 2.7 and head north on a less worn but discernible trail that heads up the long, steep gully to a saddle between Mount Sneffels and her 13,694-foot eastern sister, Kismet Mountain. A good crowd is likely to be on this popular Fourteener on any summer weekend. Be careful if there are hikers above or below you in this gully, as the talus and scree are extremely loose and tumbling rocks are a constant hazard. Many hikers enjoy glissading down the steep scree slopes, oblivious to the presence of peakbaggers below. Heads up!

When you reach the saddle at mile 3.4, head to your left up the narrow and steep summit couloir, which ascends northwest to the summit plateau. This couloir is filled with very large boulders, which will slow you down as you make your way around them but provide a margin of safety by minimizing your exposure to the chute straight below. Exit the couloir a few yards from the top via a narrow weakness in the rock wall forming the left edge of the couloir. Scramble up and head across the interesting ledges to the flat summit area. The rocks are relatively solid in the couloir, especially after snowmelt in July. Expect to encounter snow and ice in June. It may be easier to scramble up the rocky ridge to the left side of the couloir if conditions within inhibit travel. Several prominent rock windscreens and a summit register are on top. Return via the same route.

The best time to visit is July through September. The gravel roads are plowed to Camp Bird, but it is a long hike in from there. June is beautiful in Yankee Boy Basin, with an abundance of snow still in evidence, but the ground can be soggy. This may be the definitive place to view wildflowers in the state of Colorado. Columbine, the state flower, appears to grow in thick, uninterrupted blankets across the basin, with a hue, intensity, and size unmatched elsewhere. The view from the summit is spectacular, with a few hundred jagged San Juan peaks visible. Numerous county highpoints can be identified, including Uncompahgre Peak, Vermilion Peak, Mount Wilson, Wilson Peak, and Castle Rock. Watch out for the omnipresent jeep tours on the roads in this area. Look east along the ridge past Kismet Mountain to Potosi Peak and Teakettle Mountain, which bears a strong resemblance to its namesake. Stay clear of tunnels, shafts, and abandoned structures, as they are unstable and a constant danger to the unwary hiker. It is illegal to drive your vehicle off road in Yankee Boy Basin. Use low gear while descending the steep but relatively smooth gravel road back into Ouray.

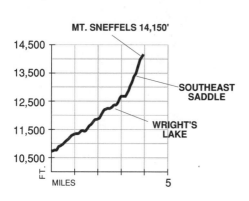

A hiker exits the summit couloir via a notch just below the top of the couloir.

County highlights: Ouray is the county seat of Ouray County, which was established in 1877. In February 1883, the area of present-day Ouray County seceded and called itself Uncompahgre County. In March 1883, the legislature broke the remainder of Ouray County into several other counties and changed the name of Uncompahgre County to Ouray County after Chief Ouray of the Arapaho tribe. A high Thirteener just south of US 50 near Monarch Pass also bears the name of this American Indian leader. The zenith of the county's mining occurred in 1883 when 400 mining claims were listed. Tourism has surpassed mining as the county's chief industry. Although small in size, Ouray offers many fine restaurants and galleries as well as a fine assortment of lodging.

Ouray County is home to many natural wonders, and its economic base reflects this. Tourism and mining are dominant industries in this small county of just over 2,000 residents. Be sure to visit Box Canyon Waterfall at the southwest edge of Ouray. The city of Ouray is known as the "Gem of the Rockies," and Mount Sneffels is frequently called the "Queen of the San Juans." Uncompahgre Peak is higher, but the abrupt rise of Sneffels from the surrounding Uncompahgre River valley and majestic grandeur have captured the hearts of visitors for over a century. An early visitor to the mountain named Mount Sneffels for the peak that explorers to the center of the earth had to pass by in Jules Verne's novel *Journey to the Center of the Earth*. If you don't mind spending a few dollars, try the Pinion in Ouray for great steaks and its famous escargot.

Camping and services: There is a fine campground in Ouray, just east of town against the tunnel-strewn cliff walls of Wild Horse Peak. The Amphitheatre Campground is large and provides a good view down into the town of Ouray. Ouray offers full services. The region is well-known for hot springs, and Orvis Hot Springs in Ridgway, about 8 miles north of Ouray, is open to the public. Primitive camping is available in Yankee Boy Basin, but you must be more than 0.25 mile from Sneffels Creek or the tributary flowing from Governor Basin. This doesn't leave much room on the sides of the valley, but it may be worth checking out.

40 Rio Grande County: Bennett Peak

General description:	Entirely above timberline, this half-day walk follows a dirt road to a gentle, grassy tundra summit with an unusually large rock cairn.
Distance:	2 miles, one-way.
Difficulty:	Easy.
Elevation gain:	1,573 feet.
Summit elevation:	13,203 feet.
Maps:	USGS Quad—Jasper (recommended), DeLorme p. 89.
Access/permits:	Rio Grande National Forest.
Best months:	June–October.

Location: South-central Colorado at the eastern edge of the San Juan Mountains, about 15 miles southwest of Monte Vista, and 10 miles northeast of Summitville.

Finding the trailhead: The mining and logging industries have left their legacy on the eastern San Juans, and access is its name: Bennett Peak can be approached from nearly every compass direction. Blowout Pass serves as the highest trailhead to the summit, and we have approached this pass from both the south and north sides. Although winding, we found the north approach, via Forest Road 14 and FR 329, to be a well-graded and well-maintained route. The approach from the south to the pass, via a road along Spring Creek off FR 250, requires four-wheel-drive in all but the best weather. From the south you will encounter a gate across the road that the Forest Service rangers ensure remains unlocked. Many hikers also take FR 265 east from the Forest Service's Comstock Campground, accessible from south of Monte Vista.

For the primary route to Blowout Pass, take County Road 14 south off of U.S. Highway 160 at the west edge of Del Norte, immediately west of the hill by the highway. At mile 11.1, the pavement ends and the road becomes FR 14, although some maps show it as FR 330. FR 14 is a good gravel road that enters the Rio Grande National Forest at mile 11.6. Observe Bennett Peak at mile 13.5. Continue south, climbing 2,600 feet to mile 17.6 at the junction of FR 14 (to the north), FR 329 (to the east), and FR 330 (to the south). Turn left (east) onto FR 329 and proceed east, noting Fuchs Reservoir at mile 20.1 and several unmarked roads to the left and to the right. At mile 28.3, FR 329.10 veers to the left and another road heads to the right with a sign indicating Blowout Pass. Stay right at this intersection.

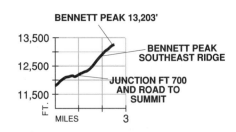

BENNETT PEAK 13,203'

BENNETT PEAK SOUTHEAST RIDGE

JUNCTION FT 700 AND ROAD TO SUMMIT

Rio Grande County: Bennett Peak

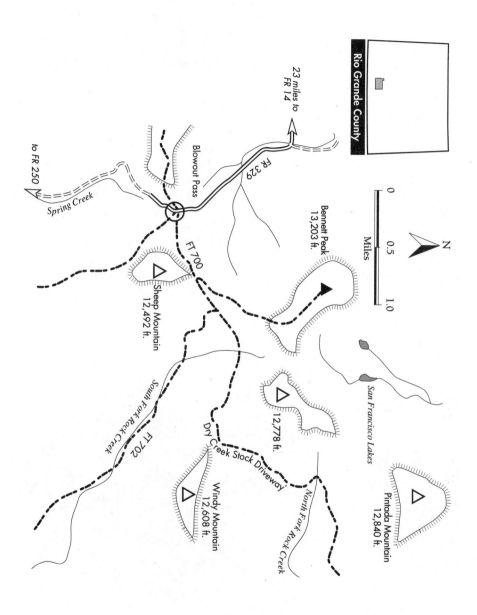

Rio Grande County

23 miles to
FR 14

FR 329

Blowout Pass

to FR 250

Spring Creek

N

0   0.5   1.0

Miles

FT 700

Bennett Peak
13,203 ft.

Sheep Mountain
12,492 ft.

San Francisco Lakes

South Fork Rock Creek

12,778 ft.

FT 702

Dry Creek Stock Driveway

Pintada Mountain
12,840 ft.

Windy Mountain
12,608 ft.

North Fork Rock Creek

At mile 29.1 a logging road goes uphill to the right. Do not go left since you would enter a logged area and cross over Bennett Creek and come to a four-wheel-drive road. Instead, turn right (south) on the logging road that serves as FR 329 and reach Blowout Pass at mile 30.6. This pass is a gentle saddle at timberline between Sheep Mountain to the east and Marble Mountain to the west. The last mile of your approach is a rough dirt road that may be unsuitable for passenger cars in wet weather. If you have a passenger car, park at mile 30 at a bend in the road and hike east toward Bennett Peak.

Key points:
    0.7   Junction of Forest Trail 700 and road to Bennett Peak
    0.9   Southeast ridge

The hike: The hiking route to Bennett Peak is on old roads, although nearer the summit the route deteriorates into a rutted jeep trail. Begin on the east side of Blowout Pass by following a worn road steeply uphill at first and then flat as it contours around the north slope of Sheep Mountain. This road is labeled FT 700 by the Forest Service and is known as Dry Creek Stock Driveway, used for driving cattle from the upper mountain pastures in the summer. After 0.7 mile, FT 700 reaches the saddle between Bennett Peak and Sheep Mountain. FT 702 goes right (east) to Comstock Campground and beyond, while the rocky road to Bennett Peak continues left (north) and gains altitude over three benches. At the ridge connecting Bennett Peak with well-defined Windy Mountain 1.5 miles due east, the road turns left (west) and follows the ridge uphill to the summit. The highest point on the broad, rounded summit of Bennett Peak might be difficult to determine

Gentle slopes make Bennett Peak a pleasure to hike.

were it not for a 4-foot cairn and a nearby register. This hike is one of the shortest hikes to a county highpoint that is over 10,000 feet in elevation.

From the summit, stroll over to the northeast cliffs for a spectacular view of the San Francisco Lakes, 1,000 feet below you. Substantial logging occurs in this area, and the view from the summit will confirm this. Indeed, as you approach the mountain from the north, you will witness the effects of the logging industry on the landscape. The hike is entirely above timberline and exposes you to the elements, including lightning strikes. No water is available en route. Be careful of the loose, rocky surface of the old roads, especially the steep sections.

The best time to visit this highpoint is from June to October. Once the snow melts in spring, it is an easy stroll to the summit, although several stretches are steep. About 8 miles to the southwest is the Summitville Mine, which was declared a Superfund site by the U.S. Environmental Protection Agency in 1992. To date, nearly $100 million has been spent in a major ongoing cleanup effort. Heavy metals flow out of the earth via this abandoned mine and are carried by the Alamosa River to the south into Terrace Reservoir where they precipitate, creating vivid hues of teal and orange.

County highlights: Del Norte is the county seat of Rio Grande County, which was established in 1874. The county name is Spanish for "large river," a term applied to the famous river that flows eastward out of the central San Juan Mountains. The Rio Grande flows around Bennett Peak to the north and east, turning south to flow through the San Luis Valley into New Mexico, eventually reaching the Gulf of Mexico in Texas. Although Del Norte is a small town, essential services are available. It serves the region's outdoor industries and offers arts and crafts gift shops to visitors.

Camping and services: Camping is allowed along FR 329 on the approach to Blowout Pass. More comfortable sites are available at the national forest campgrounds of Comstock, southeast of the peak, and at Stunner, about 10 miles to the southwest. The closest town with full services is Del Norte, about 30 miles to the north. Some facilities are available in scenic Platoro to the southeast.

41 San Juan County: Vermilion Peak

General description:	A strenuous, off-trail, day hike on class-3 rotten talus and scree to a high basin and alpine peak with a small, airy summit.
Distance:	5.3 miles, one-way.
Difficulty:	Strenuous.
Elevation gain:	4,034 feet.
Summit elevation:	13,894 feet.
Maps:	USGS Quad—Ophir (required), DeLorme p. 76, Trails Illustrated #141.
Access/permits:	San Juan National Forest.
Best months:	July–September.

Location: Southwest Colorado in the San Juan Mountains, about 50 miles north of Durango, and 7 miles west of Silverton.

Finding the trailhead: From the southern edge of Silverton, take U.S. Highway 550 north about 2 miles toward Ouray to Forest Road 585 (County Road 7). Turn left (west) and follow this good gravel road for 4.1 miles along South Fork Mineral Creek to South Mineral Campground. Park just west of the campground at the Ice Lakes Trailhead.

Key points:
- 2.2 Lower Ice Lake Basin
- 3.5 Ice Lake in Ice Lake Basin
- 5.0 Fuller-Vermilion saddle

The hike: The route to Vermilion Peak follows a good but steep trail from the trailhead to the high basin below the peaks. The trail gains 1,500 feet to Lower Ice Lake Basin and another 900 feet to reach Ice Lake Basin. After passing Ice Lake at elevation 12,257 feet, the trail turns southwest, staying to the left (east) of the drainage. Gain the small ridge northwest of Fuller Lake and head up toward Fuller Peak. Follow this trail up the north shoulder of Fuller Peak, elevation 13,761 feet. Fuller Peak is a rounded and gentle little brother to its more northerly neighbors. Descend 261 feet to the Fuller-Vermilion saddle on an easy scree slope. Cross the saddle and carefully follow the trail as it winds up the southeast shoulder of Vermilion Peak. The trail stays to the left (west) of the main

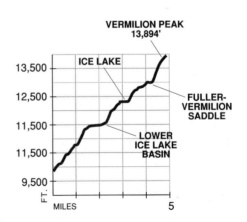

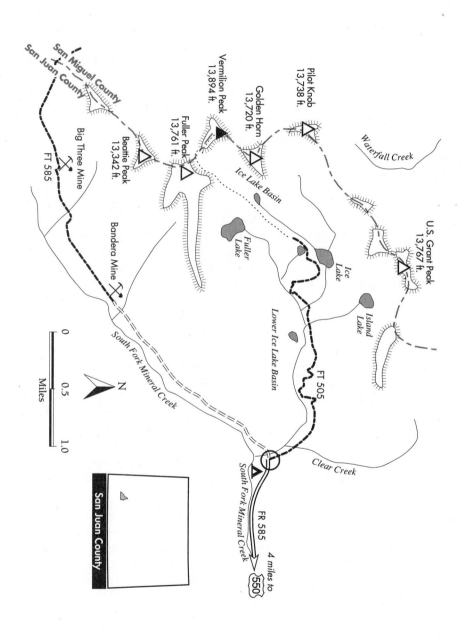

San Miguel County

San Juan County

Big Three Mine

FT 585

Beattie Peak
13,342 ft.

Fuller Peak
13,761 ft.

Vermilion Peak
13,894 ft.

Golden Horn
13,720 ft.

Pilot Knob
13,738 ft.

Waterfall Creek

Ice Lake Basin

U.S. Grant Peak
13,767 ft.

Fuller Lake

Ice Lake

Island Lake

Bandera Mine

Lower Ice Lake Basin

South Fork Mineral Creek

FT 505

0   0.5   1.0

Miles

N

Clear Creek

South Fork Mineral Creek

FR 585   4 miles to   550

San Juan County

ridgeline to avoid prominent turrets along the ridge. The trail becomes less distinct as it reaches the bottom of a prominent summit couloir. Carefully scramble up the couloir, watching for loose rocks. Once at the top of the couloir, turn right (southeast) and scramble a few yards up across small boulders to the final summit plateau, an area the size of your kitchen table. Pull up a seat and enjoy the spectacular surroundings as you make your well-earned lunch disappear.

We first ascended this peak by driving past South Mineral Campground and continuing southwest on FR 585 for another 2.2 miles to Bandera Mine, an abandoned site. The road is impassable farther by vehicle but provides easy access all the way to the 12,445-foot saddle southwest of Beattie Peak. From this point you can follow the narrow ridge crest 1.2 miles to Beattie Peak and another 0.5 mile to Fuller Peak. This route is a scramble on small boulders in places but is generally straightforward. Compared to South Mineral Campground, the starting elevation of this route is a thousand feet higher and about the same distance; however, an additional 600 feet of elevation gain is required on two subpeaks along the ridge. These peaks are seldom visited, and the summit registers date back over a decade.

The best time to visit is July through September. If there is any snow at all near the summit, the final approach to the couloir will be hazardous.

While on the summit, several peaks to the northeast capture your attention. Golden Horn, Pilot Knob, and U.S. Grant Peak, all bicentennial peaks— in the top 200 in elevation in Colorado—are very jagged and appear at first glance to be unclimbable. It is interesting to note that San Juan County, nestled in the heart of the great San Juan Mountains and accessible only via high mountain passes, contains no Fourteeners. Each of the counties that surround San Juan County is indeed summited by a Fourteener.

The rugged beauty of Ice Lake Basin was carved less than 20,000 years ago by the last glacial episode, leaving a hanging valley. The range consists of volcanic rock, and the loose talus is characterized by flat slabs, which are quick to slide out from underfoot if a climber is not wary. Vermilion Peak is on the southwest edge of one of the world's great mining districts, the Silverton Caldera. Silverton itself lies within a collapsed volcano, which was discovered to be rich in silver ore and other minerals before the turn of the century.

County highlights: Silverton is the county seat of San Juan County, which was established in 1876 and named for Saint John the Baptist of biblical fame. Although one of the smallest counties in the state, San Juan has the highest average elevation, with a low point of 8,600 feet. It is also the only county in the Centennial State that was established in 1876, making it the centennial county.

Once the exclusive domain of the Ute Indians, all of San Juan County was officially "granted" to them in an 1868 treaty. Gold fever set in a few years later, and a steady stream of miners poured into the area. A short, bitter struggle for the land ensued, and the Utes, under the direction of

The summit of Vermilion Peak is known for exposed ledges and loose rock.

Chief Ouray, surrendered 3 million acres of mineral-rich mountains to the U.S. government.

Silverton boomed until the demonetization of silver in 1893. Mining remains a bread-and-butter industry, and Silverton still sustains itself with income from the Sunnyside Mine, but tourism and occasional moviemaking have contributed. Residents of Silverton form a community of people who truly appreciate a simple and isolated lifestyle.

Camping and services: Lodging and RV camping are available in Silverton, and camping is permissible in South Mineral Campground. Primitive backcountry camping is allowed in Ice Lake Basin, and we recommend this not only to minimize distance traveled in one day but also to enjoy the unique splendor of this cluster of rugged peaks. Silverton is a resurgent mining and tourism locale and the northern terminus of the famous Durango and Silverton Narrow Gauge Railroad, which follows the Animas River south through some of the most rugged mountains in the state.

Northern Plains

This region is noted for its lack of topographic relief, always a concern to highpointers seeking a definitive summit to a county. Farming and ranching dominate the landscape, with bluffs and sand hills breaking up an otherwise flat landscape. These are among the easiest counties to summit, with reasonable dirt-road access and modest walks involved. These four counties can all be summited together in one long day by enthusiastic highpointers. We suggest you plan Phillips and Sedgwick counties together as a single outing. Permission in advance is required for all but Phillips. An added bonus is the close proximity to over a half dozen other county highpoints in Nebraska and Kansas, as well as the highest points of both those states. See Andy Martin's book *County High Points* (Old Adit Press) for information and research.

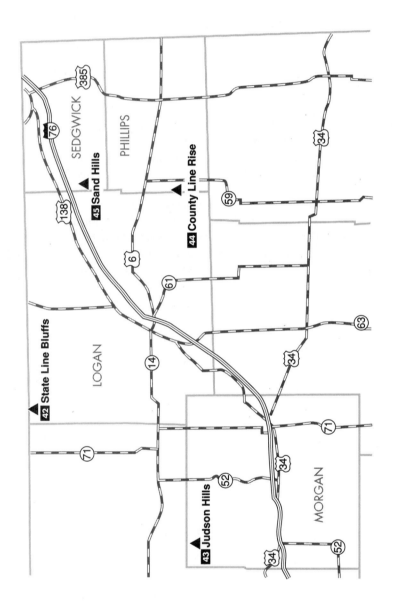

42 Logan County: State Line Bluffs

General description:	An easy 3-mile round-trip walk along a ranch road and over rangeland just south of the Nebraska state line.
Distance:	1.5 miles, one-way.
Difficulty:	Easy.
Elevation gain:	60 feet.
Summit elevation:	4,940 feet.
Maps:	USGS Quads—Dipper Spring (CO) and Kimball SE (NE) (required), DeLorme p. 94 (Colorado) and p. 56 (Nebraska).
Access/permits:	Private property.
Best months:	March–May and October–November.

Location: Northeast Colorado, about 25 miles northwest of Sterling, at the northwest corner of the county on the Colorado-Nebraska border.

Finding the trailhead: This highpoint is on ranchland owned by a private grazing association. Please contact the owner in advance and ask permission to visit the site. As with private property anywhere, please respect the land as it provides the rancher's livelihood.

From Interstate 76 in Fort Morgan take exit 80 onto Colorado Highway 52. Head north on CO 52 across the South Platte River and continue on CO 14 for about 23 miles to CO 14. Go right (east) and go 6.5 miles to CO 71. Turn left (north) and continue for about 26 miles to the Colorado-Nebraska state line. Drive 2.1 miles north into Nebraska and turn right (east) onto County Road 6 at the bend in what is now Nebraska Highway 71. Go east on CR 6 for 4.9 miles and turn right (south) on CR 49. An abandoned radio tower complex is just east of here. Go south 1.2 miles into Sidney Draw and pass through an oil and gas field. Be watchful for oil-field truck traffic. Continue south across the state line at the 2-mile mark. At 2.3 miles you come to a missile silo, and the gravel road deteriorates into a poor two-track lane. Park at the locked gate on the left (east) side of the road.

Key points:
0.5	Two-track lane bends around gullies
1.0	Fence line at corner of section
1.2	Low spot of gully
1.4	Ridge north of gully

The hike: A two-track lane leads east from this gate. Carefully cross through the gate or fence and walk about a mile to the east, following this lane. The lane bends slightly north at the 0.5-mile mark, around a small wash. At the far section line at mile 1 you encounter a north-south fence line. Pass to the east side of this fence, then follow it north for 0.5 mile. As you follow this fence line you walk down into a shallow gully, then up 50 feet to a small

Logan County: State Line Bluffs

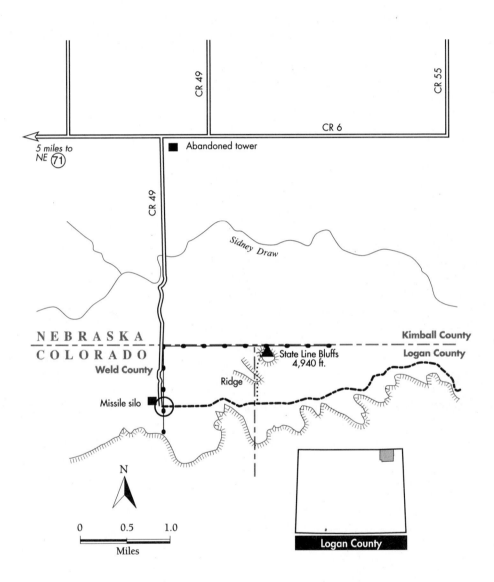

CR 49

CR 55

CR 6

5 miles to
NE 71

■ Abandoned tower

CR 49

Sidney Draw

NEBRASKA
- - - - - - - -
COLORADO
Weld County

Kimball County
Logan County

▲ State Line Bluffs
4,940 ft.

Ridge

■ Missile silo

N

0   0.5   1.0
Miles

Logan County

ridge. Stop and compare this elevation to that of the small barren mound 200 yards northeast. Walk to the mound and look back to the spot by the fence line you just left. We determined by handlevel that the mound is a few feet higher than the ridge by the fence. You will notice higher ground directly to the north, but the elevation is higher across the state line in Nebraska. Return to your vehicle by the same route.

The best time to visit is later in spring after the roads dry out but before the heat of summer sets in or later in the fall when cool temperatures return. There is private property along CR 49; please respect the rights of property owners by not attempting to access the highpoint across their land. Stay on established roads. Hunting is possible in this area in the fall, so be cautious and wear orange. Avoid livestock. Watch for cactus. Note the hard white caprock on the highpoint mound and other ridges. This material is caliche, a hard calcium residue that builds in the soil through evaporation. From the "summit" cairn made of caliche, you are afforded a modest view south into Colorado ranchland. The highpoint of this county lies about 0.5 mile north of a prominent bluff line that extends many miles along the Colorado-Nebraska border. The relief of the actual highpoint, however, is too minimal to have been named by early settlers. These bluffs are referred to locally as "the Breaks."

County highlights: Sterling is the county seat of Logan County, which was established in 1887 and named for John Alexander Logan (1826–1886), who rose from lieutenant in the Mexican War in 1847 to twice serving as U.S. senator from Illinois. Described as the "rainbelt of Colorado," Sterling is surrounded by irrigated farm country. It is known as a regional hub for many industries, such as agriculture (Great Western Sugar) and construction (Ready Mix Cement). While you drive through town be sure to notice the "living tree" sculptures.

Although not in Colorado, a must-visit goal for any peakbagger is the highest point in Nebraska, only 22 miles west of the Logan County highpoint. To go there, drive south 4 miles on CO 71 from the Colorado-Nebraska border, turn right (west) on CR 32 for 5 miles, turn right (north) on CR 135 for 1 mile, turn left on CR 134 for 12 miles, and turn right (north) on CR 111 for 3 miles to the state line. The turnoff lane to the Nebraska state highpoint is just north of the state line on your left (west).

Camping and services: The general area surrounding this highpoint is privately owned, and there are no campsites. The nearest full-service town is Kimball, Nebraska, located about 25 road miles north of the trailhead at the junction of I-80 and NE 71 (CO 71).

Owner contact: Chimney Canyon Grazing Association, c/o Dick Rogers, 970-522-3627.

43 Morgan County: Judson Hills

General description:	A short walk across gently rolling cropland leads to a small rise on a bluff edge.
Distance:	1.4 miles.
Elevation gain:	25 feet.
Summit elevation:	4,935 feet.
Difficulty:	Easy.
Maps:	USGS Quads—Sunken Lake and Keota SE (required), DeLorme p. 94.
Access/permits:	Private.
Best months:	March–May and October–November.

Location: Northeast Colorado, about 15 miles northwest of Fort Morgan, and 8 miles north of Jackson Lake State Recreation Area.

Finding the trailhead: The owner of the Morgan County highpoint accommodates those who wish to enjoy the unique physical terrain in this area. Please contact the owner in advance and ask permission to visit the site. As with private property anywhere, please respect land as it provides the rancher's livelihood.

From Interstate 76 in Wiggins take exit 66, onto Colorado Highway 39. Head north on CO 39 for 6.7 miles, cross the South Platte River, and continue for 1 mile to CO 144. Go right (east) 0.7 mile to County Road 5. Hang a left (north) for 3.7 miles, skirting the east edge of Jackson Reservoir. Arrive at CR CC, turn left (west), and continue 0.7 mile to CR 4. Turn right (north) and travel 6.5 miles to the top of the bluff. On the left (west) side of the road look for an abandoned farm site consisting of trees and a foundation. Park your vehicle completely off the county road on the western side. This trailhead is located 9.3 miles south of CO 14, on CR 4 (CR 105 in Logan County). You may wish to use a compass to help you determine your direction and a handlevel to ascertain the highest ground.

Key points:
0.2 East-west fence
0.6 Slight bend in fence with high ground immediately to the south
0.9 Very sharp bend in fence with depression to the east
1.1 Gully

The hike: From your vehicle, cross to the east side of gravel CR 4 at a double row of fence. Locate a gap in the fence, about 100 feet south of the farm site. Pass through this gap and immediately turn right (south) on a distinct dirt farm road. The dirt road to the windmill shown on the USGS quad does not exist, so be observant of the route described here. Begin your walk on the farm road by going 0.2 mile south from the gap, staying parallel to CR 4. Turn left (east) when you come to a wooden-post, three-strand barbwire fence. At this point you are at the top of a gentle bluff. Follow the

Morgan County: Judson Hills

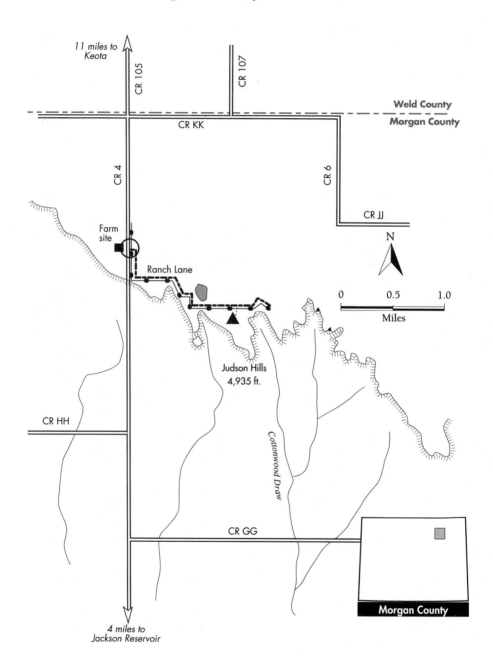

11 miles to
Keota

CR 105

CR 107

Weld County
Morgan County

CR KK

CR 4

CR 6

CR JJ

N

Farm
site

Ranch Lane

0   0.5   1.0
Miles

Judson Hills
4,935 ft.

CR HH

Cottonwood Draw

CR GG

Morgan County

4 miles to
Jackson Reservoir

221

road along the north side of the fence as it winds east, away from CR 4, to the highpoint. At mile 0.6, the fence (and road) bends slightly right. High ground rises to the right (south) on the other side of the fence. At mile 0.8, the fence bends sharply left. The fence bends very sharply to the right at mile 0.9 where a large depression to the left (east) may be filled with water. Continue along the fence to mile 1 where the route bends sharply to the left and continues east. At mile 1.1 the fence and road pass down into the head of a gully that drains to the right (south). To the southwest, you may observe part of the bluff jutting out to the south, ending in a small but distinct hillock. Continue east along the fence as it rises up a broad gentle hill and begins a descent at mile 1.4.

Carefully pass under the fence to the right (south). Do not stress or damage the fence wires in any way. On the north side of the fence is cropland and on the south side is rangeland. Walk south on this rangeland for 40 feet to an almost imperceptible rise. Look for the benchmark marked "VABM Shannon Elevation 4,935" on a cement block that protrudes almost a foot out of the ground. Do not confuse this benchmark with a similar-sized horizontal control marker, 20 feet west of the benchmark, on a cement block that has been broken off at ground level. The actual highest ground appears to be 30 yards to the northwest of the benchmark. South of the highpoint, the land drops off dramatically southward into the Cottonwood Draw drainage. To the west, the bluff has gentle, rounded slopes and to the east the bluff is steep and consists of broken rock. Return to your vehicle by the same route.

For extra credit, visit the slight rise near the bluff, at mile 0.6 along the fence. You passed just to the north of this rise as you walked along the fence on your way to the highpoint. On the USGS quad this slight rise is the same elevation as the elevation on the Shannon VABM, but we determined by handlevel that this rise is actually a few feet lower.

The best time to visit is in the spring and fall to avoid the snows and storms of winter and the relentless heat of summer; however, antelope and deer hunting may make this locale dangerous in the fall. This highpoint is a bit off the beaten path, so have a vehicle in good operating condition. Be on the lookout for rattlesnakes and watch for cactus, especially as you roll under the fences. Even though this hike is not demanding, sturdy hiking boots are recommended as they privide better protection from thorns than casual shoes. Stay clear of any livestock in the area.

County highlights: Fort Morgan is the county seat of Morgan County, which was established in 1889 and named for Colonel Christopher A. Morgan. A fort was built near the county seat as a refuge from Native Americans. Called "Junction" at first, Fort Morgan was renamed in 1866 to honor Colonel Morgan, who died that year.

Northeastern Colorado was first occupied by Plains Indians as a hunting ground. Fossil remains and other artifacts indicate that these early people hunted the vast bison herds living in this region.

Locating a benchmark may be important when determining the location of a county highpoint.

Fort Morgan, the agricultural and ranching center of the county, is widely recognized for its production of seed used throughout Colorado. The town of Brush is famous for its Fourth of July rodeo, billed as the largest amateur rodeo in the state.

Camping and services: There are no campsites in the general area of this hike. Camping is permitted at Jackson Reservoir, about 7 miles south of the highpoint. Full services are available in Fort Morgan to the south, and limited services are available along CO 14 to the north.

Owner contact: Don Wickstrom, 970-656-3676.

44 Phillips County: County Line Rise

General description:	A small rolling hill along the county-line road marks this highpoint.
Distance:	Drive-up.
Difficulty:	Drive-up.
Elevation gain:	None.
Summit elevation:	4,120 feet.
Maps:	USGS Quad—Rockland (required), DeLorme p. 95.
Access/permits:	Logan-Phillips county-road right-of-way.
Best months:	April–May and October–November.

Location: Northeast Colorado, about 30 miles east of Sterling, and 18 miles west of Holyoke, on the Logan-Phillips county line.

Finding the trailhead: From Sterling on Interstate 76 take exit 125 to U.S. Highway 6 and go east on US 6 about 18 miles to Fleming. Continue on US 6 for 6.4 miles to Dailey. Stay on US 6 for another 2.9 miles (27.3 miles from I-76). Turn right (south) on County Road 1 (CR 97 in Logan County) and go south for 6.7 miles. CR 1 follows the trace of the county line. Note that the county road numbering system is a bit unique in Phillips County, as each road is numbered two higher than the road to the south. The highpoint appears to be at mile 6.7 as the gentle ridge crosses into Phillips County from the west. This is the only place where the 4,120-foot contour actually reaches the Phillips County line. Park your vehicle well off the road and be watchful of speeding rural traffic when handleveling.

The hike: This highpoint is a drive-up on the county-line road with no hiking required. However, careful monitoring of your odometer is essential to locate this county highpoint. This highpoint is accessible year-round, unless there has been substantial recent snowfall. Park your vehicle and stand on the east edge of the county road to claim the highest point in Phillips County.

There are ten separate areas where the 4,110-foot contour exists in Phillips County. All are along CR 1, and within about 4 miles north and south of the

Phillips County: County Line Rise

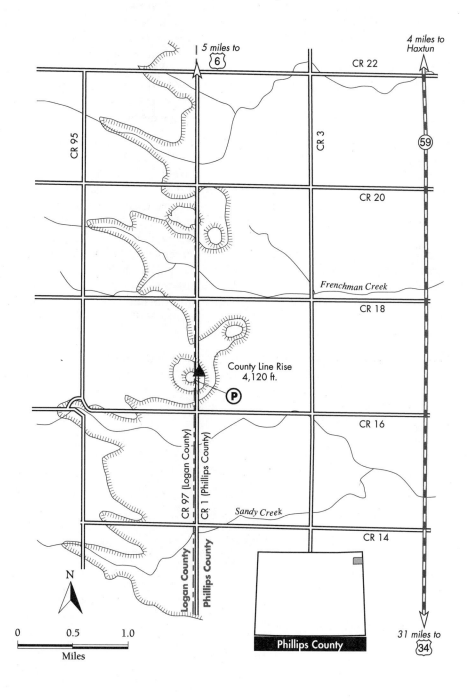

actual highpoint located at mile 6.7. We have determined by careful field observations that this rise at mile 6.7 is indeed higher than the other nine contours. The USGS quad's topographic contours would suggest this. Some county highpoint purists would be sure to visit all ten possible areas. The fact that the 4,120-foot contour actually touches the county line at this location (although it doesn't enter Phillips County from the higher land to the west in Logan county), indicates that while another area may possibly be equally high, certainly none is higher. Visitors to this highpoint can compare the elevation at mile 6.7 with the rise in the land located a quarter mile to the northeast and practice determining relative elevations.

County highlights: Holyoke is the county seat of Phillips County, which was established in 1889 from a strip cut from the southern part of Logan County that was, in turn, formerly a part of Weld County. The county was named for Mr. R. O. Phillips, secretary of the Lincoln, Nebraska, Land Company that established a number of towns in eastern Colorado along the surveyed Burlington and Missouri Railroad route. Sheep became a big industry along the railroad, and the Standard Sheep Company north of Holyoke was formed. Beatrice (Foods) built cream stations at Holyoke and Haxtun. A glance at any road map will reveal a square grid pattern to Phillips County's road system, suggesting that the county remains an agricultural area. Irrigation, which did not come into wide practice until the late 1960s, has doubled gross farm income in the 1980s in Phillips County. Phillips County also has a small amount of natural gas production.

Camping and services: There are no campsites in this farming region. The nearest services are available in Haxtun, about 8 road miles to the north.

45 Sedgwick County: Sand Hills

General description:	A short walk leads to a grassy sand dune amid a series of sand hills.
Distance:	0.8 mile, one-way.
Difficulty:	Easy.
Elevation gain:	40 feet.
Summit elevation:	4,120 feet.
Maps:	USGS Quad—Tamarack Ranch (recommended), DeLorme p. 95.
Access/permits:	State of Colorado private lease.
Best months:	April–May and October–November.

Location: Northeast Colorado in the Sand Hills, about 25 miles southwest of Julesberg, and 9 miles north of Haxtun, on the Logan-Sedgwick county line.

Finding the trailhead: The highpoint of Sedgwick County is located on state of Colorado land that is leased to local ranching interests. To reach the highpoint you walk along the edge of a private ranch. Please contact the ranch owners in advance by mail to let them know of your desire to visit this site and to gain their permission.

From Interstate 76 west of Julesberg take exit 165 south on Colorado Highway 59. Go south 8 miles on CO 59 to County Road 10. Turn right (west) on CR 10 and proceed 3 miles to CR 5. Turn left (south) on CR 5 and go 1 mile. Turn right (west) on CR 8 and go 1 mile to the intersection of CR 8 and CR 3. Turn left (south) and proceed 0.5 mile to a sand lane that extends right (west) to a farm site. Trees line the right (north) side of this lane. Drive a quarter mile down the lane. The lane will curve to the right (north) and continue for only 200 feet at a clearing on the east side of a barn. Park here.

To reach this trailhead from the south from Phillips County, leave Haxtun at the intersection of U.S. Highway 6 and CO 59 and proceed north on CO 59. Go 4 miles north on CO 59 to a sweeping curve to the east. At the curve turn left (west) onto CR 38 and go 0.3 mile. Turn right (north) onto CR 3 and go 5.5 miles to the sand lane described above. You will pass the Sedgwick County line at mile 3. Drive west on the lane and park at the barn.

Key points:
0.0   Barn
0.8   Fence on county line

The hike: From the tree-surrounded clearing on the east side of the barn, walk back south for 200 feet to the east-west fence line. Follow this fence line west, in the same direction that the sand lane led you away from it to the farm site. Hike 0.75 mile to a prominent north-south fence line that

Sedgwick County: Sand Hills

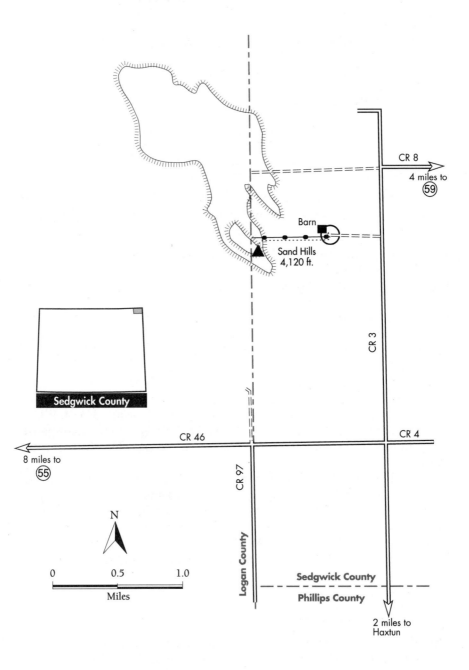

marks the Logan-Sedgwick county line. The highpoint is along this county-line fence, several yards to the left (south) at a rise in the land. Observe the relative relationship of fence posts to determine the highest point. You should be able to spot the highest fence posts from the barnyard. Return by the same route, being careful to avoid any cattle in the field. Watch for cactus.

The best time to visit is in the spring and fall to avoid the snows and storms of winter and the relentless heat of summer. The county roads may be passable earlier, but the drive on the sand lane and the hike along the fence may be messy with any snow present. Take plenty of water. The sand dunes of western Sedgwick County were created by ice-age (Pleistocene) sand from the Front Range mountains. This sand was carried by streams and wind to their present position along the South Platte River valley. Be sure to empty your shoes when you get back to your car.

County highlights: Julesburg is the county seat of Sedgwick County. The county was established in 1889 and named for Fort Sedgwick, which was located across the river from present-day Ovid. The fort was named in honor of Major General John Sedgwick, who was killed in the battle of Spottsylvania in 1864 after having led Indian campaigns into the Colorado region in 1857 and 1860. Sedgwick is the sixth smallest county in Colorado but commands the northeast corner position in the state. Agriculture dominates the economy. The county receives economic and recreational benefits from the South Platte River and I-76 as they pass from west to east through the county. Oil and gas exploration began in 1949, and in 1952 the *Grit-Advocate* newspaper headlined, "Big Gas Well Struck Here!" Gas and oil continue to add to the county's economy, but agriculture remains the basic industry.

Camping and services: There is little in the way of camping in the area. The nearest services are available in Haxtun, about 9 miles to the south. Full services can be found about 20 miles to the north along US 138 on the north side of the South Platte River and in Julesburg.

Owner contact: S&D Starkebaum, County Road 26, Haxtun, CO 80731, 970-774-6436.

Central Plains

This region is wide-open rangeland, and the county summits are on privately owned land where a county road is not involved. This land is sparsely populated, with fewer people in all of these counties than in a midsized city elsewhere in the state. The hikes are easy, with minimal gain and distance required. Watch for cattle and antelope when navigating the confusing roads, and be aware that roads on a published map may no longer exist. Permission is required on several summits. We suggest combining Lincoln and Crowley counties. Washington and Yuma counties are less than an hour drive apart. The walk to the summits of Cheyenne and Kit Carson counties should be done together, to minimize disruption to ranchers.

Central Plains

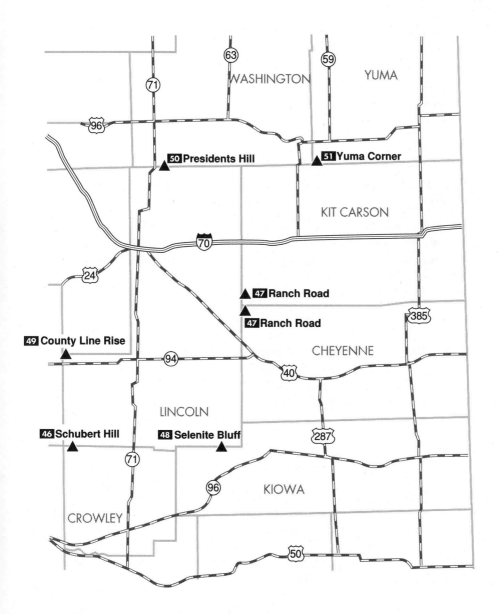

46 Crowley County: Schubert Hill

General description:	Walk to a remote but gentle plains hill on Colorado ranchland.
Distance:	2.5 miles, one-way.
Difficulty:	Easy.
Elevation gain:	10 feet.
Summit elevation:	5,220 feet.
Maps:	USGS Quads—Truckton SE and Grandview School (optional), DeLorme p. 98.
Access/permits:	Private property.
Best months:	October–November.

Location: Southeast Colorado, about 45 miles northeast of Pueblo, and 25 miles northwest of Ordway.

Finding the trailhead: The highpoint of Crowley County is located on a private ranch; however, advance permission is not required to visit this site. Please stop at the ranch house and introduce yourself before proceeding through the gate on the left (west) side of the ranch complex.

Access to the Crowley County highpoint is reached through the Schubert Ranch, about 2 miles south of the actual highpoint. To reach the ranch from the south, leave U.S. Highway 50 at Main Street in Fowler and go north on Colorado Highway 167 for about 2 miles until it ends at CO 96. The road that continues north of CO 96 is County Road 3. Head north on CR 3 up the prominent bluffs of the Arkansas River valley for 3 miles to CR F. Turn left (west) and proceed 2 miles to CR 1 on the Crowley-Pueblo county line. Turn right (north) and continue 18 miles to the end of CR 1. A slight jog in the road appears at the 4-mile mark. Go right (east) on CR AA (Highland Road) for 1 mile and turn left (north) on CR 2, which reaches the ranch house in 2 miles. Soft, sandy shoulders on the county roads can cause your vehicle to overturn, so please drive slowly.

To reach the ranch from the north, turn off CO 94 south onto CR 2 about 1 mile east of the El Paso-Lincoln county line. Continue south and enjoy the wonderful views of Pikes Peak and Greenhorn Mountain at about the 9 mile mark. After 10 miles, watch for a sharp jog in the road. At 11 miles turn left (east) onto CR M and at 12 miles turn right (south) onto CR 3. Continue south past Kendrick Church at CR K, near mile 14. Between 18 and 19 miles, follow CR 3 as it jogs east on CR E, becoming CR 4 as it resumes south. At about 23 miles, notice the fence line marking the Crowley-Lincoln county line. At about 25 miles, CR CC is a lane heading west to the Schubert Ranch. At about 27 miles, turn right (west) on CR AA and proceed 2 miles to CR 2. Turn right (north) on CR 2 and proceed 2 miles to the ranch.

Crowley County: Schubert Hill

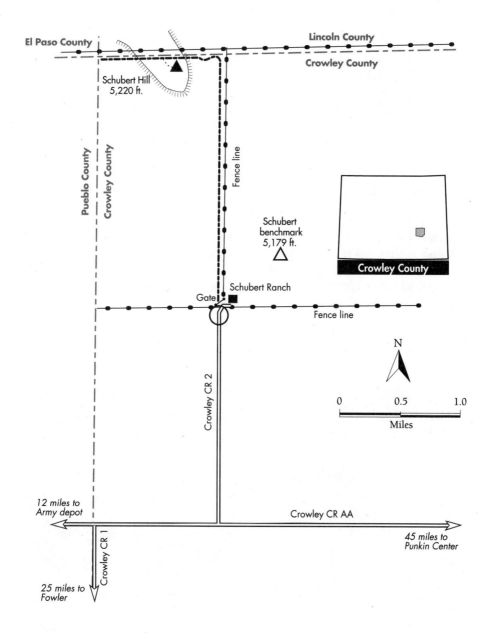

El Paso County

Lincoln County

Crowley County

Schubert Hill
5,220 ft.

Pueblo County

Crowley County

Fence line

Schubert
benchmark
5,179 ft.

Crowley County

Schubert Ranch

Gate

Fence line

N

Crowley CR 2

0   0.5   1.0

Miles

12 miles to
Army depot

Crowley CR AA

45 miles to
Punkin Center

Crowley CR 1

25 miles to
Fowler

Key points:
- 0.4   Ridge to the east, Schubert Hill benchmark
- 0.9   Dug-out pond to the west
- 1.0   Fence line to the east
- 2.0   CR 2 ends at county-line fence
- 2.4   Rise along county-line fence

The hike: Contact the owner in the ranch house to the right (east) side of the ranch complex. Drive to the left (west) side of the ranch complex and park your vehicle in the spacious dirt parking area. Pass through a gate and proceed north along the west side of a fence on CR 2 for about 2 miles to the Crowley-Lincoln county line, marked by a fence. CR 2 is an ungraded ranch road north of the ranch. At mile 0.4 look right (east) to see the ridge on which the "Schubert Hill VABM 5,179'" benchmark is located. At 0.9 mile watch for a dug-out pond on your left and shortly thereafter the fence line to your right that marks the section line about 1 mile north of the ranch. Upon reaching the county-line fence, turn left (west) on CR A, an obvious two-track lane through grassland, and proceed 0.4 mile along a fence line to a gentle rise. The highpoint lies 100 yards south. We have determined by handlevel that this is the highest of the three closed contours at 5,220 feet. The open rangeland has cactus and cattle. Watch for both. Please be considerate of all cattle operations, especially in spring during the calving season. Do not drive on rangeland and leave all gates as you find them, whether open or closed.

The highpoint can be visited year-round, but to avoid the snowdrifts and summer heat we recommend the moderation of spring or fall. The fall months

John visits the Schubert benchmark with the owner, Walter Schubert.

will avoid calving season. Before visiting Crowley County, make sure your vehicle has plenty of fuel and carry drinking water as you would on a mountain hike. Antelope hunting is possible in this area in the fall, so wear orange. The owner, Mr. Walter Schubert, escorted us to the Schubert benchmark on the distinct rise to the northeast of his ranch house. He was quite certain this was the highest point of land around and related a story of the military surveying the Pueblo Chemical Depot, about 12 miles to the west, from his property. As you travel along CR 2 north of the ranch, imagine it as it once was; a busy rural mail route for local residents. There is a nice view from Schubert Hill, and three county highpoints are clearly visible: Pikes Peak to the northwest, Greenhorn Mountain to the west, and West Spanish Peak to the southwest.

County highlights: Ordway is the county seat of Crowley County, which was established in 1911 and named for John H. Crowley, a Colorado senator at the time when this area was part of Otero County. Crowley County's highest point of land existed unnamed and largely unrecognized until 1995 when we began referring to the highpoint with the name inscribed on the nearby benchmark, "Schubert Hill," in honor of the family that works this ranch. Crowley County is one of the least populous counties in Colorado and had fewer than 3,000 residents at the last census. There once were many more residents in rural Crowley County, but like most plains counties the population has dwindled. Ordway hosts the Crowley County Fair the last weekend in July each year. The lakes along the Arkansas River attract numerous waterfowl, including sandhill cranes, Canada geese, bald eagles, and American white pelicans.

Camping and services: There are no campgrounds in the general area. Services can be found in Fowler and other towns along US 50 south of the highpoint.

Owner contact (not required): Schubert Ranch, 719-263-5486.

47 Cheyenne and Kit Carson Counties: Ranch Roads

Cheyenne County

General description: A half-day hike across open rangeland reaches a gentle rise at the northwestern corner of the county.
Distance: 1.3 miles, one-way.
Difficulty: Easy.
Elevation gain: 195 feet.
Summit elevation: 5,255 feet.

Kit Carson County

General description: A half-day hike across open rangeland reaches a gentle rise at the southwestern corner of the county.
Distance: 2.6 miles, one-way.
Difficulty: Easy.
Elevation gain: 240 feet.
Summit elevation: 5,290 feet.
Maps: USGS Quads—Bledsoe Ranch (required) and Bellyache Creek (formerly Hugo 4 SE) and Sanders Ranch (recommended), DeLorme p. 97.
Access/permits: Private property.
Best months: October–November.

Location: East-central Colorado, about 40 miles southeast of Limon, and 15 miles south of Flagler.

Finding the trailhead: These highpoints are on private ranchland and require advance permission from the owners to gain access. As with private property anywhere, please respect the landowners' rights; you may not hunt, harvest, collect, or trespass on posted property. This land provides their livelihood and you must treat it with respect.

Reach this ranch from the south by locating the intersection of County Road 2 and U.S. Highway 40-287, 7.2 miles northwest of Wild Horse and 0.2 mile northwest of the junction of Colorado Highway 94 and US 40-287. Proceed north on CR 2 for 2 miles, turn right (east) on CR X for 1 mile, and turn left (north) on CR 3. After driving about 9 miles, stay left at the intersection of CR DD. At mile 9.5, observe the Smoky Hill monument commemorating the old Montana-to-Texas cattle drives. Take the left fork at mile 10.6, and at mile 11.7 stop at the ranch. The highpoints are 1.3 and 2.6 additional miles north across ranchland.

Cheyenne and Kit Carson Counties: Ranch Roads

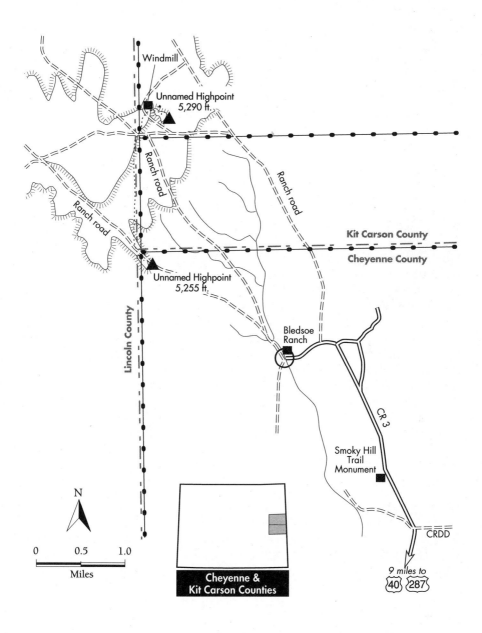

Windmill

Unnamed Highpoint
5,290 ft.

Ranch road

Ranch road

Ranch road

Kit Carson County

Cheyenne County

Unnamed Highpoint
5,255 ft.

Lincoln County

Bledsoe
Ranch

CR 3

Smoky Hill
Trail
Monument

CRDD

9 miles to
40 287

N

0   0.5   1.0
Miles

Cheyenne &
Kit Carson Counties

Key points:
 0.3   Road ascends ridge
 1.3   Cattle-guard fence crossing
 2.6   Cattle-guard fence crossing

The hike: If you have secured permission in advance from the owners, hike the dirt road through the ranch complex along Wild Horse Creek. Stay left at a faint fork in the ranch road. After 0.3 mile the road begins an ascent to the high land about 2 miles northwest of the ranch. As you gain elevation, this ridge becomes very remote and devoid of trees. At mile 1.3 the road comes to a cattle guard where it intersects the fence line marking the Cheyenne-Lincoln county line. The land 100 yards southeast of this cattle guard is the highest in Cheyenne County. You remembered your handlevel and compass, didn't you?

You can reach the highpoint of Kit Carson County by following the west side of the fence line on foot due north for 1.25 miles to another road crossing through the fence. The highpoint of Kit Carson County as determined by handlevel observations and backsighting appears to be 0.3 mile northeast of the fence crossing on a gentle rise. High ground also lies 200 yards north of the crossing, between the windmill and fence crossing. Return to the ranch and thank the owners for your visit.

The fence crossing at Kit Carson's highpoint can also be reached by walking ranch roads as follows. Cross the cattle guard at the highpoint of Cheyenne County and hike northwest along the southwest-facing bluff edge to mile 2.5. Watch carefully for a faint range road and take that right (northeast) to the cattle guard and fence crossing at the Kit Carson County highpoint at mile 2.7. Please avoid traversing the range needlessly and instead stay on the ranch roads or walk close to the fence line. Do not involve yourself with the livestock, and minimize the stress on them from your presence.

The best time to visit is spring or fall to avoid the snowstorms of winter and the burning summer sun. There is no water or shade on this hike. If you desire to add this county highpoint to your list of life achievements, we suggest you avoid calving season in the spring and plan a trip in the more hospitable weather of fall.

County highlights: Cheyenne Wells is the county seat of Cheyenne County, which was established in 1889 and named for the Cheyenne Indian tribe. Prospectors heading for the gold fields of California and Colorado traveled through the region, and the inception of the Kansas Pacific Railroad began to attract farmers. The discovery of oil near the town of Kit Carson in the 1930s guaranteed that all of the components of the county's present-day economy were in place. Note that the town of Kit Carson is not in Kit Carson County!

Burlington is the county seat of Kit Carson County, which was also established in 1889. The county was named for Christopher Carson (1809–1868), who gained knowledge of the area as a guide on Fremont's exploratory expeditions in the mid-1840s. Carson served as an Indian agent and later fought the Indians during the Civil War era. The county's association with the famous scout stems from a rock formation found in the northern part of the county that bears his signature and the date of 1847, making it one of the earliest indications of the presence of trappers and traders in the region.

Camping and services: Camping is not permitted near the trailhead. This is very remote plains country, and you are advised to have a vehicle in top working condition with a full fuel tank and plenty of drinking water. The nearest services are in the town of Kit Carson, about 20 miles to the southeast on US 287, and in Limon, about 40 miles to the northwest at the junction of US 287 and Interstate 70.

Owner contact: Beldsoe Ranch, 719-962-3598.

48 Kiowa County: Selenite Bluff

General description:	A short, easy hike leads to a plains bluff on remote grazing land.
Distance:	1.3 miles, one-way.
Difficulty:	Easy.
Elevation gain:	15 feet.
Summit elevation:	4,690 feet.
Maps:	USGS Quads—Bluff Spring (required) and Haswell and Galatea SW (recommended), DeLorme p. 99.
Access/permits:	Private.
Best months:	April–May and October–November.

Location: East-central Colorado, about 30 miles north of La Junta, and 7 miles northwest of Haswell.

Finding the trailhead: The highpoint of Kiowa County is on the eastern edge of the expansive Davis Ranch and, as with most western ranching operations, it is advisable to let the owners know of your intentions to travel the ranch. Contact a ranch foreman (see "Owner contact" below), identify your intentions, and request permission to visit the site on a specific day. Please honor your welcome by respecting the rules governing the ranchland, which provides the ranchers' livelihood. Avoid driving on range vegetation, travel only on ranch roads, do not climb on fences, and leave all gates in the position you found them, whether open or closed. Under no circumstances should you bother the livestock.

Although you can approach this high bluff from the east, west, or north, we recommend the simpler eastern approach. To approach from the east, drive to the hamlet of Haswell on Colorado Highway 96 between Eads and Ordway. From Haswell, leave CO 96 and go due west on County Road P, also known as Fourth Street, north of the railroad tracks. After 0.3 mile, turn right (north) on CR 19 and continue for 5 miles. Turn left (west) on CR V, which is unmarked to the west and follows the Kiowa-Lincoln county

Kiowa County: Selenite Bluff

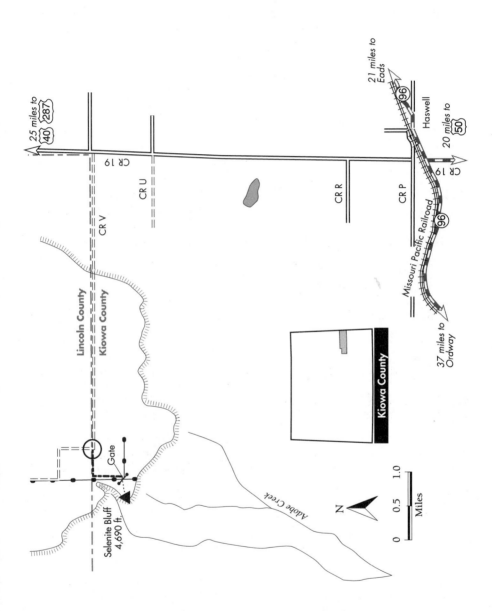

line. The road's counterpart to the east, offset by a hundred feet to the north, is well-signed as CR V. Go 4.5 miles west on CR V, which is a bladed dirt road, manageable by most vehicles in good weather. At mile 4.5 CR V turns right (north) and goes into Lincoln County. Park at this corner, being careful to stay off the road and away from traffic. There are plowed fields along CR 19, and north and south of CR V for about the first 3 miles to the west, beyond which you pass through open rangeland.

Key points:
    0.5   North-south fence line
    1.0   Manmade mound near gate

The hike: Leave your vehicle and hike 0.5 mile due west from the corner on CR V, proceeding straight to a fence. The trail is a very faint two-track, which crosses through tall scrub grass and range vegetation. Turn left (south) at the fence line, and continue along the east side of the fence, generally on another faint two-track, to mile 1. Please do not take a shortcut, as the rangeland is fragile and you will be trespassing if you do not stay close to the county-line right-of-way. You are approaching the southern edge of the bluff, and you will encounter a manmade mound trending east-west, about 5 feet high and a hundred feet long. This mound is the result of human activity and cannot be considered a candidate for the highest ground. A wire gate is at this mound. Pass through carefully, and proceed straight west to the southwest edge of the bluff to mile 1.3. The land on the west side of the fence is quite flat and is home to an extensive prairie-dog colony. Continue through the prairie-dog mounds to the west, where the edge of the bluff is slightly higher than the surrounding land. The rise at bluff's edge is 200 yards west of the dirt ridge. We have determined by handlevel that the rise due west of the dirt ridge is higher than the rise you may notice 300 yards to the north. When hiking to this bluff, be aware of your compass direction. Although the bluff edge is prominent and the dirt ridge near the fence line is fairly obvious, it would serve you well to bring a compass, topo map, and handlevel to assist you in pinpointing the highpoint.

The highpoint can be visited year-round, but to avoid the snowdrifts and summer heat we recommend the moderation of spring or fall. Antelope season begins around the first weekend in October, and you don't want to be anywhere near here during the hunt. This region of Colorado contains some of the most remote land in the state with a population density of one person per square mile. It is critical that you come here with a well-maintained vehicle fully fueled and that you have essential emergency gear. Take heed of the day's weather forecast. This is no place to be caught in a blizzard, lightning storm, or cloudburst, which can turn the dirt roads into slippery mud trails. The view from the bluff edge is expansive, and you should easily spot Pikes Peak and the Spanish Peaks on the western horizon. We have given the name "Selenite Bluff" to this highpoint in recognition of the mineral found in the gullies along the bluff.

County highlights: Eads is the county seat of Kiowa County, which was established in 1889 and named for the Kiowa Indian tribe. The name "Kiowa" is a corruption of the Indian "ka-i-gwu," meaning "principal people." Nearly treeless, Kiowa County can boast of several large warm-water lakes that lure boating and fishing recreationists, the nearest being Adobe Creek Reservoir (Blue Lake) about 11 miles south of Haswell. Oil and gas production assumed an important role in the county's economy in the 1970s. Today, wheat, corn, hay, sorghum, and dry beans are the major crops produced in the county. History buffs should stop in Haswell for the Kiowa County Museum and "the nation's smallest jail," which was built in 1921 with the dimensions of 10 feet by 12 feet. In the town of Sheridan Lake you may visit a 1929 schoolhouse that features a three-lane bowling alley on its second floor.

Eastern Kiowa County holds two historic sites. The Sand Creek Massacre site northeast of Chivington remains in a natural state as it did in 1864 when this controversial event took place. The Towner Bus Tragedy of 1931 is marked by a large stone monument 15 miles south of Towner on CO 89. Six people lost their lives in a school bus when it became stranded during a vicious blizzard. On a more positive note, this county enjoys Colorado's lowest crime rate, lowest divorce rate, and lowest unemployment rate, and it is fourth in per capita spending for education.

Camping and services: There are no campgrounds in the immediate area, although camping is permitted at the recreational lakes about 15 miles to the south, along the southern edge of the county. Limited services are available in Haswell, Eads, and Ordway along CO 96. Come well stocked for this highpoint!

The wide-open rangeland of Kiowa County is perfect habitat for pronghorn antelope.

242

Owner contact: D4 Ranch, Denny Wall, 719-446-5381, or Larry Leonard, 719-446-5204.

49 Lincoln County: County Line Rise

General description:	A series of rises follows a county road among gently rolling plains in a rural neighborhood.
Distance:	None.
Difficulty:	Drive-up.
Elevation gain:	None.
Summit elevation:	5,960 feet.
Maps:	USGS Quad—Rush (optional), DeLorme p. 98.
Access/permits:	County-road right-of-way.
Best months:	Year-round.

Location: East-central Colorado, about 30 miles east of Colorado Springs in the northwest corner of the county.

Finding the trailhead: From the west, take exit 139 at the intersection of Interstate 25 and U.S. Highway 24 in central Colorado Springs and go east on US 24 for 8.5 miles to the junction of US 24 and Colorado Highway 94. Be aware that US 24 jogs to the north around the Colorado Springs Municipal Airport. Follow the signs for US 24, and turn left (north) on Powers Road and right (east) on Platte Avenue to reach the junction of US 24 and CO 94. Turn right (east) on CO 94 and go about 32 miles to the small community of Rush. Continue east through Rush on CO 94 for 2 miles to the El Paso-Lincoln county line. Turn left (north) on unpaved County Road 1 (Holtwood Road) and go 2 miles to CR 2B, which extends east. Turn right (east) and proceed slowly for 0.4 mile to a slight rise. Lincoln County is on your right (south). This is the highest point in Lincoln County. Be sure to park off the road on the shoulder. There is a good spot for parking a few yards east of the actual highpoint.

The hike: This highpoint is a drive-up on the county-line road with no hiking required. Four areas in Lincoln County have an elevation of 5,960 feet. We have determined by extensive handlevel work that the rise along CR 2B, 0.4 mile east of CR 1, is the highest spot in the county. The highest point appears to be on the south side of the road along a fence. This situation is an excellent example of a highpoint being located on higher ground that enters a county from another county without forming a peak within the highpoint county. In such cases, the highest spot is usually found along the county line, the road in this instance. The highpoint is on the county right-of-way, so avoid private property by not crossing any of the fences along the road.

Lincoln County: County Line Rise

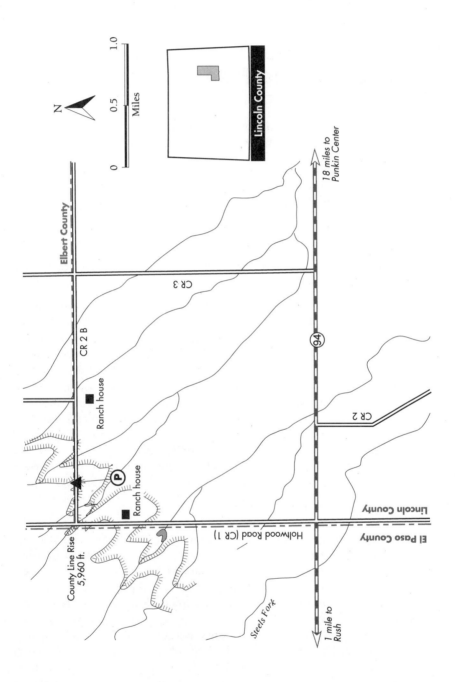

This highpoint can be visited year-round. The roads may be passable in winter, but scrambling along the edge of the road in deep snowdrifts may be hazardous, especially if there is oncoming traffic. The surrounding area is grazing land. The view would be considered minimal from this highpoint were it not for a nice vista due west of Pikes Peak. The area to the east along CO 94 through Punkin Center and on to Aroya is one of the least-traveled roads in Colorado. Be sure to have plenty of fuel and confidence in your vehicle if you plan to traverse Lincoln County to the east. The highpoint lies along the southern edge of the Palmer Divide as it extends 70 miles eastward from Colorado Springs toward Limon.

County highlights: Hugo is the county seat of Lincoln County, which was established in 1889 and named for Abraham Lincoln, the sixteenth president of the United States, and known as the "Great Emancipator." Lincoln was assassinated in 1865 as the Civil War drew to a close, and today there are 18 states with a Lincoln County named in tribute to this great leader. Only Jackson, Jefferson, Madison, and Washington are more represented in the United States by county names.

Limon is a well-known truck-stop town along I-70. It is not uncommon to see hundreds of travelers and truckers stranded there during the area's famous winter and spring blizzards. The townspeople always extend a helping hand and even open their own homes to families in need during these times. Limon endured one of the most devastating tornadoes in the history of the state in 1988, as a twister tore through town and leveled many buildings. Hugo has a medical facility that treats those who live in the area. The drive from Limon to Kit Carson on US 287 along Big Sandy Creek is rather

View of Pikes Peak due from the Lincoln County highpoint.

scenic. Lucky birders may catch a glimpse of bald eagles as they nest along the creek in large cottonwood trees.

Camping and services: It is not permissible to camp at highway rest stops in the county, and there are no recognized campgrounds near the highpoint. The nearest services are in Rush, about 4 miles south and west of the highpoint. Full services can be found in Limon and Hugo to the northeast, along US 24 to the north, and in Colorado Springs to the west. The "coldest beer in Colorado" is available at Ellicot's drive-through liquor store, about 20 miles west on CO 94. There is no development to speak of in Punkin Center to the east.

---

50 Washington County: Presidents Hill

General description:	An imperceptible rise sits on a county-line road.
Distance:	None.
Difficulty:	Drive-up.
Elevation gain:	None.
Summit elevation:	5,420 feet.
Maps:	USGS Quad—Lusto Springs (optional), DeLorme p. 96.
Access/permits:	Lincoln-Washington county-road right-of-way.
Best months:	April–May, and October–November.

Location: Northeast Colorado, about 17 miles northeast of Limon, and 12 miles southeast of Last Chance on the Lincoln-Washington county line.

Finding the trailhead: From the junction of U.S. Highway 36 and Colorado Highway 71 in the town of Last Chance, go south on CO 71 for 11.8 miles. Watch for the landmark hill called Flat Top just to the west of the highway as you approach the Lincoln-Washington county line. As the highway jogs slightly to the west, look for the county-line sign. Turn sharply left (east) and proceed on County Road 0 for 2.2 miles. The road dips slightly before heading up and out of a draw at about the 1-mile mark. The road crests at mile 2.2, and this spot is the highpoint. If you travel 0.5 mile farther east, you reach CR 28, which turns south. Use your judgment, and your handlevel if you have one, to determine the exact highest point, as the rise is rather gradual.

From exit 361 from Interstate 70 in Limon, go north on CO 71 for about 10 miles. The highway jogs 3 miles east and then continues about 11 miles north to the Lincoln-Washington county line. Turn right (east) at the county line and continue as described above.

Washington County: Presidents Hill

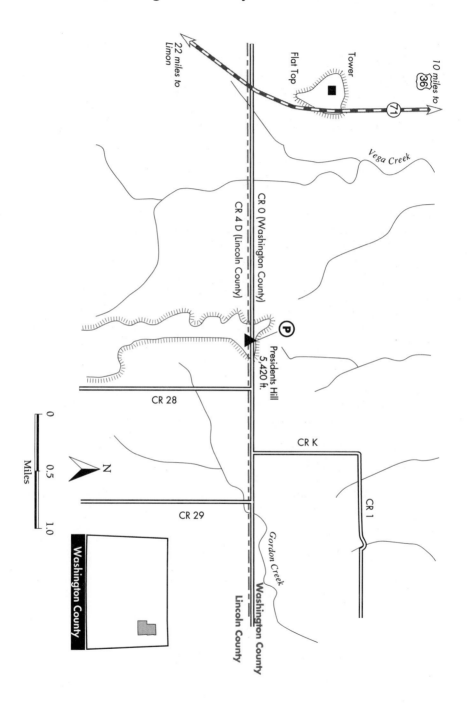

22 miles to Limon

Flat Top

Tower

10 miles to (36)

71

Vega Creek

CR 0 (Washington County)

CR 4 D (Lincoln County)

P

Presidents Hill 5,420 ft.

CR 28

CR K

CR 29

CR 1

Gordon Creek

Washington County

Lincoln County

0   0.5   1.0
Miles

N

Washington County

The hike: This highpoint is a drive-up on the county-line road with no hiking required. Carefully park your vehicle at the side of the county road and watch for rural traffic as you walk to the fence line on the north side of the road.

The best time to visit is spring and fall. Snowstorms in the winter can make these roads impassable within minutes. Be sure to have enough fuel and drinking water when exploring this area in the summer as distances are long between towns. We named this highpoint in recognition of the two adjacent counties named for the first and sixteenth presidents of our country. This highpoint lies on the crest of a broad, gentle rise that extends in a northeast-southwest trend and forms the divide between the South Platte River to the north and the Arikaree River to the east.

County highlights: Akron is the county seat of Washington County, which was established in 1887 and named for George Washington, the first president of the United States from 1789 to 1797. George was a rather popular fellow, as seen by the fact that 31 U.S. counties have been named for him, more than any other county namesake.

Akron was laid out in 1882 by the Lincoln Land Company, as were many of the towns of eastern Colorado. Until 1886 it was scarcely more than a vacant town site. Situated on the Burlington and Missouri Railroad, it gained population rapidly as waves of immigrants from Kansas and Nebraska settled the region beginning in the late 1880s. The railroad payroll served as a stable economic base for Akron as the region was beset with droughts and other unfavorable weather conditions that affected its agricultural base. Agriculture continues to be the economic base of Washington County, and it has led the state in wheat production virtually every year since records have been kept. Oil and natural gas production have of late also become important aspects of the county's economy.

Camping and services: There are no campgrounds in the general area. Limited daytime services are available in Last Chance, about 14 miles to the north at the junction of US 36 and CO 71. Full services are available in Limon, about 22 road miles to the south.

51 Yuma County: Yuma Corner

General description: An imperceptible rise at the southwestern corner of the county sits along a county-line road.
Distance: None.
Difficulty: Drive-up.
Elevation gain: None.
Summit elevation: 4,440 feet.
Maps: USGS Quad—Cope SE (optional), DeLorme p. 97.
Access/permits: Kit Carson–Yuma county-road right-of-way.
Best months: April–May and October–November.

Location: Northeast Colorado, about 37 miles northwest of Burlington, and 24 miles northeast of Flagler, at the common corner of Washington and Yuma counties along the Kit Carson county line.

Finding the trailhead: From the south, take Interstate 70 exit 405 in Seibert and go north on Colorado Highway 59 for about 19 miles to the Kit Carson-Washington county line. Turn right and go east on County Road 0 for 3.2 miles. You encounter a slight jog in the road to the left at the 1.7-mile mark. At mile 3.2, a fence runs north from CR 0 at the Yuma-Washington county line. This fence marks the far southwestern corner of Yuma County. The intersection of the fence with the road is the highest point in Yuma County.

From the north, at the intersection of CO 59 and U.S. Highway 36 in Cope, proceed south for about 6 miles on CO 59. This highway curves to the right as it approaches the county line. Before reaching the county line, you will see a gravel road to the left that actually continues straight south to the county line. Take this gravel road to the left and drive straight for 0.2 mile to the county line. Turn left and go east on CR 0 as above. The highest spot appears to be 10 to 15 feet north of the gravel county road at the fence corner.

The hike: This highpoint is a drive-up on the county-line road with no hiking required. If you desire a photo recording your presence at this dubious highpoint, be sure to park to the side of the road and watch for rural traffic.

The highpoint can be visited year-round, but to avoid the snowdrifts and summer heat we recommend the moderation of spring or fall. The highest ground in Yuma County lies on a broad, gentle ridge trending north-south, but because this feature has no known name, we refer to this highpoint simply as "Yuma Corner" in honor of its unique location. This is one of only three county highpoints—along with Blanca Peak and James Peak—that are at a tri-county junction. Several others are very close but not quite on a junction. The Arikaree River and North Fork Republican River drain the county to the east. North of Wray, sand hills dominate the county landscape. This area is ranching and farming country. Hunting is possible in this area in the fall, so be cautious and wear orange if you get out of your car.

County highlights: Wray is the county seat of Yuma County, which was established in 1889 and named for the Yuma Indian tribe. The region served as the hunting grounds for many of the Plains Indian tribes of the region, notably the Cheyenne, Arapaho, Sioux, Pawnee, and Arikara. Fur trappers and traders were in the area by the 1780s, although permanent settlement did not begin until 1859. In 1882 the Burlington and Missouri Railroad was completed and other towns were then established along the route. By 1890 a number of towns were flourishing. Cattle raising was the principal industry of Yuma County preceding World War I. By the 1920s, ranching had given way to agriculture. During the 1930s oil exploration began, and oil production and refining became an important aspect of the county's economy until the 1960s. Today, Wray is a marketing and distribution center for the farming and livestock industries. Wheat, corn, sugar beets, and grain sorghum are the principal crops, along with cattle raising and feedlot operations.

Be sure to visit the Beecher Island battle site about 15 miles south of Wray. This nine-day engagement in 1868 was one of the last major encounters between the U.S. Cavalry and American Indians. Of special note to peakbaggers is the tri-state point of Colorado, Kansas, and Nebraska only about 5 miles south of US 34 east of Wray. There are 62 such junctures throughout our country, and a growing number of geography buffs are determined to visit each site.

Camping and services: There are no campgrounds in the immediate area of this highpoint, although camping is permitted at Bonny Reservoir, about 30 miles to the east. To the south, varying services can be found along I-70 in the towns of Flagler, Seibert, Stratton, and Bethune. Full services are offered in Burlington. To the north, limited services are found along US 36 in this region. This is remote agricultural country. Venture out only with a well-maintained vehicle and a full tank of gas.

The highest land in Yuma County is in the exact corner of the county along the county road.

Yuma County: Yuma Corner

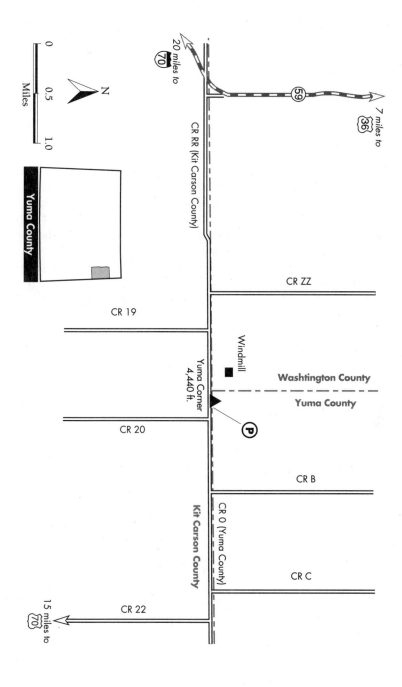

0 0.5 1.0

Miles

N

20 miles to 70

CR RR (Kit Carson County)

59

7 miles to 36

Yuma County

CR ZZ

CR 19

Windmill

Yuma Corner 4,440 ft.

Washington County

Yuma County

P

CR 20

CR B

Kit Carson County

CR O (Yuma County)

CR C

15 miles to 70

CR 22

Southern Plains

The Southern Plains are characterized by a great deal more relief than can be found in the Central and Northern Plains. The hikes here are short but interesting and include mesas, buttes, and bluffs. These summits are farther apart than one would think when first looking at a map, and you should be satisfied with visiting two in a single day. This region is hot and dry, and you should take along water on all hikes, no matter how short the distance. The Bent County highpoint, San Jose Ranch Mesa, is ideally situated between the other three in a triangle, and can be combined with any of them easily in a day. However, advance permission is required before visiting the ranch. Consider making a weekend of it and staying in Lamar, La Junta, or Springfield. The Oklahoma state highpoint is just south of Carrizo Mountain in Baca County, and the volcanoes of eastern New Mexico are just to the southwest.

Southern Plains

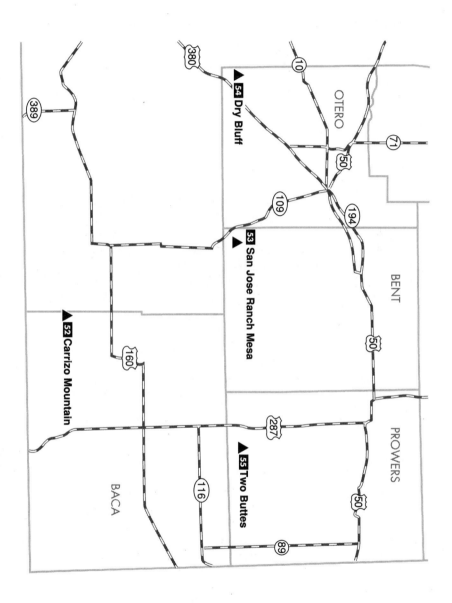

52 Baca County: Carrizo Mountain

General description:	A broad rise marks an otherwise classic flat mesa top.
Distance:	None.
Difficulty:	Drive-up.
Elevation gain:	None.
Summit elevation:	5,280 feet.
Maps:	USGS Quad—Carrizo Mountain (recommended), DeLorme p. 101.
Access/permits:	Private property.
Best months:	April–May and October–November.

Location: Southeast Colorado, about 45 miles southwest of Springfield, and 10 miles north of the Colorado-Oklahoma state line.

Finding the trailhead: The owners of the ranch on which the highpoint is located assured us that no permission is required to visit the mesa top. Please honor this generous allowance by respecting their property. Avoid driving on range vegetation, only travel on ranch roads, do not climb on fences, and leave all gates as you found them, whether open or closed. Under no circumstance should you bother the livestock.

Located on remote ranchland in southeastern Colorado, the highpoint of Baca County (pronounced Back-ah by locals) is typically approached from the north by U.S. Highway 160. Although the USGS quad indicates several possible routes to the mesa top, field research indicates only two are feasible.

From the city of Springfield at the junction of US 287 and US 160, drive west on US 160 for about 29 miles to County Road 3, passing through the town of Prichett along the way. About 6 miles west of Prichett, scan the southern horizon for the round form of Potato Butte, which crowns Carrizo Mountain near the highpoint. At the junction of CR 3 and US 160, turn left (south) and proceed 6.5 miles on CR 3. Turn right (west) on CR P and drive 2.3 miles. CR P becomes CR Q as the dirt road crosses East Carrizo Creek along the way. Turn off CR Q to the left (south) and drive on a ranch road as it negotiates the cliff of the mesa. After 0.8 mile of ranch road that is rough in places, you end your climb and reach the mesa top. You may consider parking your low-clearance vehicle before reaching this rough stretch. Follow this faint road for 0.2 mile south until it turns right (west) and follows a fence line 0.4 mile west to the county line. Turn left (south) and follow the fence line of the section on open rangeland for 0.1 mile to Carrizo Mountain.

To approach the mesa top from the south, you must have a four-wheel-drive vehicle. From Springfield, drive south on US 287 for about 17 miles and turn right (west) on CR M. Continue west for 26.5 miles. As you travel CR M, watch for CR 539 at mile 22, which leads to the Carrizo Picnic Area. At mile 23.3, CR M crosses East Carrizo Creek and soon passes the junction with CR 3.1, which leads north to the Everett Ranch. At mile 26.5, leave CR M to the right (north) on a ranch road that angles to the northwest toward

Baca County: Carrizo Mountain

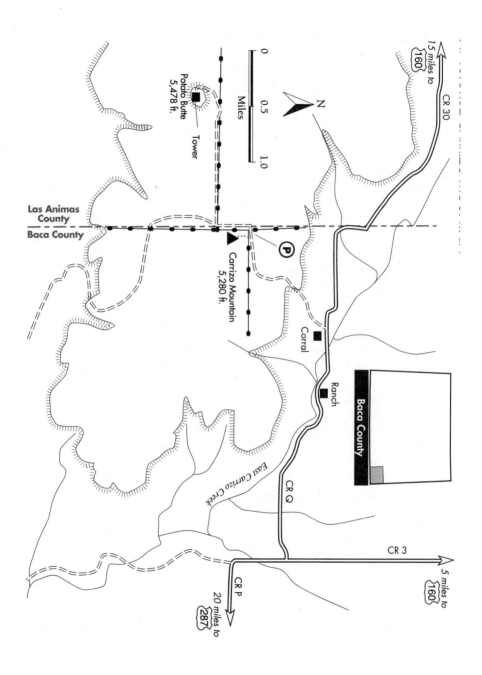

stock tanks, 0.6 mile from CR M. Continue north and east for 0.5 mile as the road passes through rocky basalt cliffs to reach the flat mesa top. Follow the faint road for 1.1 miles as it curves to the left (west) to the fence line marking the Baca–Las Animas county boundary. Carefully pass through the fence gate and follow the road right (north) for 0.4 mile to a Y-intersection at stock tanks. Angle to the right (northeast) for 0.2 mile to the fence line that forms the southeast corner of section 12. The highpoint lies 0.2 mile north along this fence line on the right (east) side of the fence.

If approaching this area from the west, simply locate the junction of CR 3 and US 160, about 18 miles east of the junction of US 160 and Colorado Highway 109 near the town of Kim. Follow directions as explained above.

The hike: This highpoint is a drive-up on the county-line road with no hiking required. The highpoint is along the fence line that traces the Baca–Las Animas county boundary, but because the mesa top is so flat the actual highest ground may not be obvious. We advise you to park your vehicle and walk the fence line, noting the relative heights of the fence posts as they indicate the curvature of the land. You may have to walk north and south along the fence to determine the true highest ground. The ground continues to rise on the other side of the fence, which is actually Las Animas County.

Potato Butte rises prominently to the west of the highpoint. To visit this anomaly, drive south from the highpoint along the fence for 0.2 mile, turn right (west), and follow the fence for 1.2 miles. At this point the ranch road peels left away from the fence line. Continue for 0.2 mile and stay left on a dirt road that provides access to Potato Butte. Although the road to the summit is narrow and steep, there is plenty of room on top for you to turn around; just be very careful of the steep drop-off along the roadside. From the top of Potato Butte, it is difficult to discern the edge of the mesa as it blends in with the distant countryside. During fair-weather days, look to the horizon to the southwest to see the small rounded form of Capulin Volcano, a national monument, just right of the larger and wider Sierra Grande, a county highpoint in New Mexico. The Raton volcanics are visible to the south and southwest. The grain towers in Prichett are on the northeastern horizon.

The highpoint of Baca can be visited year-round, but to avoid winter snowstorms and summer heat we recommend the moderation of spring or fall. The gravel roads may be passable earlier. Hunting is possible in this area in the fall, so be cautious and wear orange.

County highlights: Springfield is the county seat of Baca County, which was established in 1889 and named for Don Felipe Baca, a respected and prosperous businessman in Trinidad. The agricultural and livestock industries have been mainstays of the county's economy since its inception. Baca County was once the "broomcorn capital of the world." Over the past decade Baca County has seen the rise of the American Agricultural Movement, an organization originally meant to draw attention to the plight of America's farmers. Although at first nonviolent, the organization has become militant in recent years, due in no small part to the continuing slump of the agricultural industry.

The Forest Service maintains 203,393 acres in the county as Comanche National Grassland. The grassland preserves dinosaur tracks, petroglyphs, scenic canyons, and historic pioneer sites. For detailed information about these, visit the office on US 287 at the south edge of Springfield. The Works Project Administration (WPA) authorized construction of unique stone buildings throughout the area. Built in the mid 1930s, good examples of these can be found about 3 miles south of US 160 at CR 3 and CR 24 and about 5.5 miles south of US 160 on CR 219.1 just south of CR 30. While in the area, be sure to visit the highest point in the state of Oklahoma, only about 20 miles south of Carrizo Mountain. From CR M at Carrizo Canyon Picnic Area, take CR M east about 5 miles to CR 8, which takes you south to The Nature Conservancy's road to the Oklahoma highpoint located on top of Black Mesa, one of the largest mesas in the world. On the way you may wish to visit the tri-state point of Colorado, New Mexico, and Oklahoma.

Camping and services: Comanche National Grassland maintains primitive campsites at Carrizo Canyon Picnic Area about 2 miles southeast of the Carrizo Mountain mesa off CR M about 2 miles west of CR 6. Camping is not permitted on the mesa. Full services are available in Springfield, about 40 miles to the northeast. We recommend the restaurant the Hill at the intersection of US 160 and US 287. The town of Prichett on US 160 has no services. The town of Kim, about 18 miles to the west, has limited services.

Owner contact (not required): Carrizo Ranch Company, c/o Miles Mizer, 719-643-5473.

Stone structures near the Baca County highpoint were constructed in 1938 by WPA workers.

53 Bent County: San Jose Ranch Mesa

General description:	Beautiful plains buttes offer a half-day hike in juniper forest to sandstone mesa caps.
Distance:	0.8 mile, one-way.
Difficulty:	Easy.
Elevation gain:	335 feet.
Summit elevation:	4,855 feet.
Maps:	USGS Quads—Corbin Canyon (recommended) and Rock Canyon (optional), DeLorme p. 101.
Access/permits:	Private property.
Best months:	April–May and October–November.

Location: Southeast Colorado, about 25 miles southeast of La Junta, and 2 miles from the southwest corner of county.

Finding the trailhead: This highpoint is on private ranchland and access requires advance permission from the owners. As with private property anywhere, please respect the landowners' rights; you may not hunt, harvest, collect, or trespass on posted property. This land provides their livelihood and you must treat it with respect.

From La Junta, head south on Colorado 109 at the south edge of town. After about 12 miles, begin the drop into the Purgatoire River valley. At mile 13.5 take note of County Road 802 on your right, which provides access to Vogel and Picket Wire canyons in the Comanche National Grassland. At mile 15 descend into the McMahon Arroyo. Cross the Purgatoire River at mile 18.6 and continue south to the Bent-Otero county line at mile 24.5. Continue an additional 1.5 miles and find a spot to pull off the highway.

Seven separate buttes in Bent County have elevations that exceed 4,840 feet. From your turnout, six are northeast of Colorado Highway 109 and one is due south. Field inspection indicates the northernmost, and largest, area is likely to contain the highpoint. The relative relief of this area is greater than any of the other six areas, and a handlevel sighting does not refute this observation.

Key points:
- 0.2   Base of mesa slope
- 0.6   Narrow neck between two mesas

The hike: From the highway hike about 0.25 mile northeast across flat ranchland to the base of the closest mesa. Hike 200 feet up a grassy slope to the top of this mesa. Scramble through the sandstone caprock and reach the relatively flat, tree-covered surface of the mesa. Follow the mesa northeast. At mile 0.6, a narrow neck between this mesa and the larger one to the northeast requires some boulder hopping. Take care in this remote country. Permission is granted only to visit the highpoint and not to rock climb. From

Bent County: San Jose Ranch Mesa

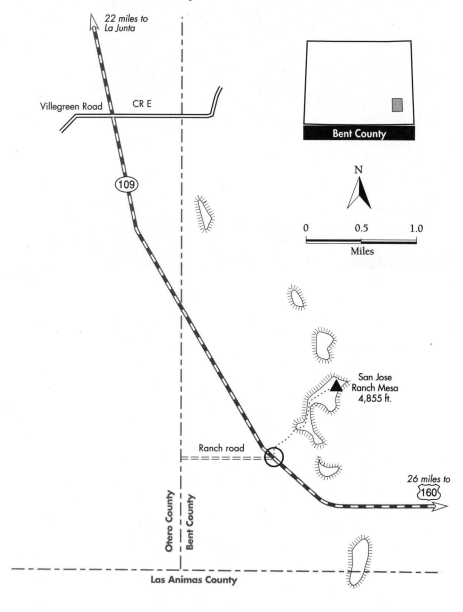

22 miles to
La Junta

Villegreen Road   CR E

109

N

0   0.5   1.0
Miles

Bent County

San Jose
Ranch Mesa
4,855 ft.

Ranch road

26 miles to
160

Otero County

Bent County

Las Animas County

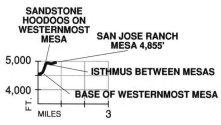

SANDSTONE
HOODOOS ON
WESTERNMOST
MESA

SAN JOSE RANCH
MESA 4,855'

5,000

ISTHMUS BETWEEN MESAS

4,000

BASE OF WESTERNMOST MESA

FT.

MILES   3

A hiker ascends the short but steep side of San Jose Ranch Mesa.

the neck continue to mile 0.8 to the center of the mesa and the probable highest point. We determined that the 4,855-foot spot elevation on the USGS quad is probably on a small bare rock that protrudes 1 or 2 feet from the ground.

The best time to visit is in the spring and fall to avoid the snows and storms of winter and the relentless heat of summer. No water is available on this hike, so take plenty. Watch for snakes and use caution when negotiating steep slopes and bare rock. Time and weather have eroded the exposed sandstone into tall and fascinating hoodoo structures. Stand at the edge for wonderful views of the desolate mesa country of southeastern Colorado and you'll know why this makes our favorite highpoints list.

County highlights: Las Animas is the county seat of Bent County, which was established in 1870 and named for William Bent, the settler and fur trader who, in 1859, became the government agent for the Arapaho, Cheyenne, Comanche, and Kiowa tribes. The trading stockade he built in 1828 along the Arkansas River just east of La Junta is now Bent's Old Fort National Historical Monument. A visit to this site provides an understanding of the European settlement in this region and the famous Santa Fe Trail, which brought immigrants west to the continent's frontier.

Bluffs, canyons, and mesas mark the southern portion of the county. A number of railroad lines were established in the county, making Las Animas a principal shipping point for livestock from southern Colorado and northern New Mexico. The Arkansas River valley developed into a productive agricultural region. Many prominent cattle trails passed through the county, and a number of large cattle ranches were established. The agriculture and

260

livestock industries have continued to play dominant roles in Bent County's economy; however, drought and other forms of extreme weather have not been without influence. During the dust bowl of the late 1920s, and again during the mid-1980s, episodes of drought have been followed by economic hardship. Farm foreclosures were many during both periods. In September 1986, Bent County, along with the counties of Baca, Prowers, Kiowa, Otero, and Crowley, was designated part of Colorado's first enterprise zone. While the economic hardships have eased somewhat over the past few years, continuing hard times for farmers and the need to attract industry remain primary concerns.

Camping and services: Camping is not permitted in this area. Vogel Canyon in the Comanche National Grassland has a limited number of primitive campsites. La Junta, about 28 miles to the north, is a full-service town. Limited services are available in the town of Kim, about 30 miles to the south, but there are no services in Ninaview, about 7 miles east along the Bent–Las Animas county line.

Owner contact: San Jose Ranch, c/o the Ericksons, 719-384-9706.

54 Otero County: Dry Bluff

General description: An easy hike on gentle slopes to the top of a remote bluff, part of a national grassland, rewards with mountain views to the west.

Distance: 1.2 miles, one-way.

Difficulty: Easy.

Elevation gain: 135 feet.

Summit elevation: 5,260 feet.

Maps: USGS quads—Delhi and Bloom (required), DeLorme p. 100.

Access/permits: Comanche National Grassland.

Best months: April–May and October–November.

Location: Southeast Colorado, about 30 miles southwest of La Junta, and 5 miles north of the southwest corner of the county.

Finding the trailhead: The trailhead can be reached from three directions. From U.S. Highway 50 in La Junta, look for Barnes Avenue and follow it south out of town; it becomes US 350 at the edge of town. Follow this highway southwest for about 30 miles to Bloom. The only feature that marks the presence of Bloom is the stone foundations on the south side of the highway, across from a gravel county road that leads north across railroad tracks. Turn right (north) onto this road, County Road 801, zero out your trip odometer, and proceed across the tracks and through grazing land for 0.7 mile. The road goes down into a drainage and fords Timpas Creek. The

Otero County: Dry Bluff

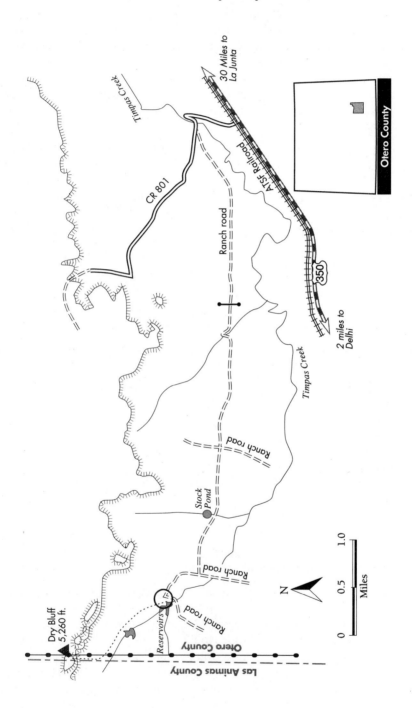

Otero County

30 Miles to La Junta

Timpas Creek

CR 801

ATSF Railroad

Ranch road

350

2 miles to Delhi

Timpas Creek

Ranch road

Stock Pond

Ranch road

N

0   0.5   1.0
Miles

Ranch road

Reservoirs

Dry Bluff
5,260 ft.

Otero County

Las Animas County

road climbs back out of the drainage. Immediately take the left, less-used dirt road. At this point you will be driving mostly through Comanche National Grassland. Rangers request you to leave gates as you find them, whether open or closed, and do not approach or bother livestock. Drive only on the roads. Proceed west on this dirt road for 2.1 miles to a gate at mile 2.9.

Continue west 0.2 mile to a hairpin jog to the right, around a gully. Travel 1.4 miles farther to a junction with an unmarked ranch road at mile 4.5. Pass straight through this intersection and continue to mile 5 and a small stock pond on the right (north). At mile 5.7, an unmarked ranch road branches to the left and crosses a drainage; stay on a westerly heading. At mile 6.2 park at the first of two small reservoirs. It is possible to continue past this lower reservoir, but national grassland rangers prefer that you spare the vegetation by not driving across it.

From Trinidad take US 350 northeast about 38 miles to Delhi, continue another 4.8 miles to Bloom, and follow the directions from La Junta above.

From Rocky Ford on US 50, take Twelfth Street south to the edge of town where it becomes Colorado Highway 71. Continue south about 14 miles to US 350. Watch for the half-mile jog to the west at the intersection of CO 10 about 5 miles south of Rocky Ford. Drive about 17 miles southwest to Bloom. Follow the directions from La Junta above.

Key points:
0.4   Gate at upper reservoir
0.9   Barbwire fence line along county line

The hike: Five areas in Otero County have elevations that exceed 5,260 feet. All are along the south edge of Dry Bluff. From the lower reservoir walk northwest on the faint road for 0.4 mile to the gate by the upper reservoir. Pass through the gate and head northwest along the base of the bluffs for a half mile to the county line, marked by a good barbwire fence. You will have left the faint road behind near the upper reservoir, as it turns right and heads northeast onto the bluffs. Follow the fence line north 0.3 mile up the slope of the bluffs to the top. The highest point of this bluff is to the west in Las Animas County, across the fence. Field observation and handleveling indicate that the highest point in Otero County appears to be here, at the east side of the fence line, at the crest of the bluff. A very small rock cairn is here. Return by the same route, or earn extra credit by continuing east along the bluff for 1.2 miles, passing over several barely perceptible rises that also exceed 5,260 feet. You encounter the faint road again between the fourth and fifth rises, and you can descend via this road to the upper reservoir. We strongly recommend that you obtain the topo map for this hike.

The best time to visit is from April through May and from October through November. Otherwise, summer heat and winter snows make this remote hike unpleasant and possibly dangerous. Do not be fooled: This is isolated ranch country, and you should be well prepared before venturing into these wilds.

Otero County's highpoint is a rise along a fence on the top of a bluff. PHOTO BY DAWN HOWARD

The highpoint and nearly all of the approach road are within the boundaries of the Comanche National Grassland, one of only two federally designated grasslands in Colorado. The Bankhead-Jones Farm Tenant Act of 1937 gave the U.S. Department of Agriculture the authority to manage the land for restoration and protection. In 1960 Congress designated these lands as the Comanche National Grassland, named for the Indian tribe that once called this land home.

The Santa Fe Trail roughly parallels US 350 in Otero County. This wagon trail carried many pioneers west to New Mexico and beyond from 1821 to 1880. Iron Springs Historic Area, about 2 miles northeast of Bloom on US 350, offers access to the trail and is a recommended side trip. Another good stopping point is Sierra Vista Overlook, just north of US 350 on the west side of CO 71. This bluff afforded early pioneers their first good view of the Rocky Mountains, about 50 miles to the west.

County highlights: La Junta is the county seat of Otero County, which was established in 1889 and named for Miguel Otero, one of the founders of La Junta. He was appointed the territorial governor of New Mexico in 1897. Rocky Ford and La Junta are well-known for the melons grown in the Arkansas River valley. Numerous roadside stands populate US 50 between Manzanola and Swink. If you come from the west and are heading south from Rocky Ford, watch for the Suto family stands at the intersection of CO 71 and CO 10. Reward your highpointing efforts with a melon, pride of Otero County. Bent's Old Fort National Historical Monument, established in 1833, provides an interesting look back into the early history of the southeastern Colorado plains.

Camping and services: Primitive camping is allowed on Comanche National Grassland. No facilities are available between La Junta and Trinidad on US 350. We recommend stopping at the tiny store known as One Stop, 0.1 mile south of the Las Animas county line on US 350 near Delhi, offering vending-machine goodies around the clock in the middle of nowhere. No commercial camping facilities are available in the vicinity of Dry Bluff.

55 Prowers County: Two Buttes

General description: An unusual isolated hill, visible from miles around, offers an easy hike across rangeland and a short, steep pitch to a rock summit.

Distance: 0.4 mile, one-way.

Difficulty: Easy.

Elevation gain: 306 feet.

Summit elevation: 4,711 feet.

Maps: USGS Quad—Two Buttes Reservoir (optional), DeLorme p. 101.

Access/permits: Private property.

Best months: April–May and October–November.

Location: Southeast Colorado, about 30 miles south of Lamar, and 12 miles northwest of the town of Two Buttes.

Finding the trailhead: This highpoint is privately owned as a "wildlife refuge," and the owner allows those who wish to hike and view nature to visit this unique hillock. Please respond to this generous allowance by respecting the property. Use only the wood fence for accessing the land and do not disturb the vegetation and rock formations. Hunting is not permitted.

From Lamar, go south on U.S. Highway 287-385 for about 26 miles to County Road C and turn left (east). From Springfield, go north on US 287-385 for about 17 miles to CR C and turn right (east). Note that the actual town of Two Buttes is located about 10 miles southeast of the highpoint, in Baca County. Proceed east on CR C for about 4 miles, passing a cemetery at mile 3.5. Turn right (south) and follow this gravel road south 0.5 mile and locate a wooden section of the fence surrounding Two Buttes. Park well off the road.

Key points:

0.2 Base of slope
0.3 Saddle between two buttes

The hike: Carefully cross over the wooden section of fence, being careful not to bend or injure the tension of the wire. Hike 0.2 mile across rangeland to the base of the steep hillside. Follow a faint trail up the southwest slope of

Prowers County: Two Buttes

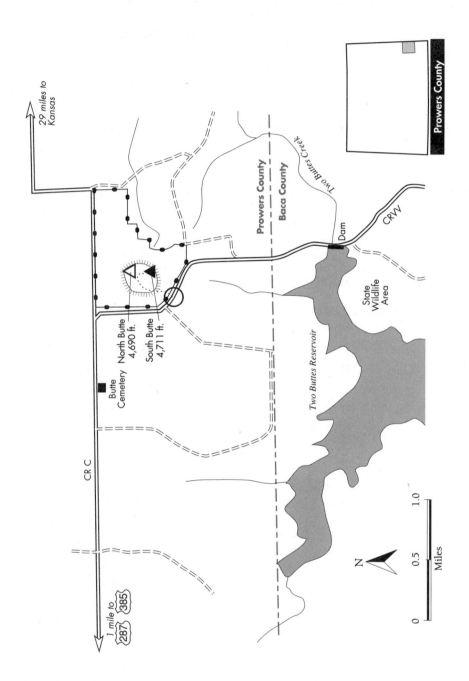

Prowers County

29 miles to Kansas

Two Buttes Creek

Prowers County

Baca County

Dam

CRVV

State Wildlife Area

Two Buttes Reservoir

North Butte 4,690 ft.

South Butte 4,711 ft.

Butte Cemetery

CR C

1 mile to 287 385

N

0   0.5   1.0

Miles

The twin peaks of Two Buttes rise sharply from the flat plains and offer a rare climb in southeastern Colorado.

the hill and at 0.3 mile gain the saddle between the north butte and the south butte. Watch for cactus and loose footing on the steep, stony slope. The southern butte is more than 20 feet higher than the northern butte, so stay right and scramble over rocks to the blocky summit. Notice the evidence of picnics and late-night parties. (Please collect and remove trash if you can.) Consider it extra credit to visit the northern butte before descending the route you used to ascend. Few plains counties in Colorado require this much elevation gain to reach the summit and offer such an expansive view of the surrounding countryside. Take care that vertigo does not overcome you on such lofty heights!

This highpoint can be visited year-round, although the best time to visit is in the more moderate weather of spring and fall. Sudden winter snows and blistering summer heat on the plains can turn a simple outing into a treacherous situation. Although fairly close to US 287, all visitors should make sure their vehicles are in proper working condition and carry full fuel in this remote country. Take water and sunshade on this hike.

Two Buttes was undoubtedly a navigation aid and landmark to early pioneers and travelers in the region. Early maps referred to this prairie mountain as Twin Buttes. This unusual feature is considered a lacolith, an igneous intrusion that did not break the earth's surface. After centuries passed, the surrounding countryside was eroded away, leaving this plug exposed. The resistant

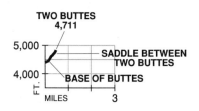

sandstone layer that the intrusion did not penetrate is still present on the Two Buttes summit. It is blocky on the southern butte and smooth on the northern butte. In 1914, gold and silver were discovered in the igneous rock, and three tunnels were dug to recover a nominal amount of precious metals before the venture failed.

Two Buttes is visited frequently by area residents and has served as a gathering place for Easter sunrise services, according to townsfolk in Springfield. A petrified forest is about 3 miles northwest of Two Buttes near the head of North Butte Creek. Fossil oyster shells can be found about 5 miles east and 8 miles northeast of Two Buttes in creek drainages. Be sure to drive about a mile farther southeast to Two Buttes Reservoir. Numerous vultures reside in the canyon just below the dam, and they are seldom observed as closely as here.

County highlights: Lamar is the county seat of Prowers County, which was established in 1889 and named for pioneer John W. Prowers. Prowers County is known as the "goose hunting capital of the nation" as it serves as a wintering ground for Canada and snow geese. Hunting is allowed in the reservoir area, so be cautious and wear orange during the fall hunting season.

Lamar is on the Santa Fe Trail and is the location of Big Timbers, a name that refers to a 25-mile stretch of huge cottonwood trees that once grew along the Arkansas River. Wilde was once a small town about 1 mile north and 1 mile west of Two Buttes, and Wilde's Butte Cemetery can still be seen on 3 acres immediately west of the highpoint.

Camping and services: There are no services at Two Buttes Reservoir, and camping is not allowed in the immediate area. Full services are available in Springfield to the south and Lamar to the north.

Owner contact (not required): Robert G. Barnhardt Jr., 316-826-3837.

Appendix A: For More Information

In 1987, Jack Longacre formed the Highpointers Club so hikers who desired to visit the highest point in each of the 50 states could exchange ideas and information and stories. Since then the club has grown to over 1,700 members. The club produces an excellent quarterly magazine, *Apex to Zenith*, and hosts an annual convention near a state highpoint. In addition, the club issues awards for progress toward the goal and a handsome plaque for completing the 50 state summits. Members frequently exchange ideas regarding county highpointing, tri-state points, state low points, and highpoints of the world's nations, to name a few. Send annual dues of $10 per household to P.O. Box 6364, Sevierville, TN 37864, 423-428-7512, highpointers@hotmail.com. All other correspondence is accepted at P.O. Box 1496, Golden, CO 80402, 303-278-1915, HPerNews@diac.com. Visit their website at: www.highpointers.com.

Several other organizations provide information regarding Colorado's trails, mountains, and parks. Many are choosing to locate in the American Mountaineering Center, a beautifully renovated building on Tenth Street in Golden, about 17 miles west of Denver at the base of the foothills of the Rocky Mountains. Most notable of these organizations is the Colorado Mountain Club.

The Access Fund (Technical Climbing Preservation)
P.O. Box 17010
Boulder, CO 80308-9804
303-545-6772
www.accessfund.org
www.outdoorlink.com/accessfund

The American Alpine Club
710 Tenth Street
Golden, CO 80401-1022
303-384-0110
www.americanalpineclub.org

The Colorado Fourteeners Initiative
710 Tenth Street, Suite 220
Golden, CO 80401-1022
303-278-7525

The Colorado Mountain Club (CMC)
710 Tenth Street, Suite 200
Golden, CO 80401-1022
303-279-3080
800-633-4417
www.cmc.org/cmc/

The Colorado Trail Foundation
710 Tenth Street, Suite 210
Golden, CO 80401-1022
303-384-3729, ext. 113 (business)
303-526-0809 (information)
www.coloradotrail.org

A number of commercial firms serve as outlets for their own custom maps. Maps Unlimited also offers an outstanding inventory of maps, atlases, books, and guides. Outdoor gear and books can be obtained from a variety of wonderful stores in the Denver metropolitan area, including Bent Gate, EMS, Gart Brothers, Grand West Outfitters, Mountain Miser, Neptune Mountaineering (Boulder), and REI. Denver has a wide variety of bookstores that all carry a good selection of hiking and climbing references.

Maps Unlimited
800 Lincoln Street
Denver, CO 80203
303-623-4299
Full inventory of maps and books.
www.coloradomaps.com

Trails Illustrated (trail maps)
1-800-962-1643
www.trailsillustrated.com

Local and state government entities provide information and regulations on a variety of subjects. Most state offices are located immediately south of the capitol in Denver. The Denver Public Library Main Branch at Thirteenth Avenue and Broadway maintains a complete collection of all USGS quads for perusal.

Colorado Department of Natural Resources (parks, wildlife, geology)
6060 Broadway
Denver, CO 80216
303-297-1192
www.dnr.state.co.us

Colorado Division of Parks and Outdoor Recreation (state parks)
1313 Sherman Street, Room 618
Denver, CO 80203
303-866-3437
www.parks.state.co.us

Colorado Geological Survey
1313 Sherman Street, Room 715
Denver, CO 80203
303-866-3437
www.dnr.state.co.us/geosurvey

Colorado State Forest State Park
(Clark Peak in Jackson County)
2746 Jackson CR 41
Walden, CO 80480
970-723-8366
www.parks.state.co.us

Denver Public Library
Main Branch
10 W. 14th Avenue
Denver, CO 80203
303-640-6200
www.denver.lib.co.us

The U.S. Department of Agriculture's Forest Service maintains its Rocky Mountain Region offices about 10 miles west of Denver. Exit Sixth Avenue north on Simms Street to the large office buildings, where there is a map sales counter. Ranger districts (RD) can be critical sources of information concerning trail conditions, snow level, and current weather, so phone before you begin a trip. Information is vital when entering the backcountry. Arm yourself!

Park-Net, Inc.
877-444-6777
New campground reservation service as of October 1998.
www.reserveusa.com

USDA Forest Service
Rocky Mountain Region
11177 West Eighth Avenue
P.O. Box 25127
Lakewood, CO 80225
303-236-9431
303-275-5367 (recorded information)
303-275-5350 (map sales)
www.fs.fed.us

USDA Forest Service
Campground Reservations
800-280-2267

Arapaho and Roosevelt National Forests

Clear Creek RD
(James Peak in Gilpin County and Pettingell Peak in Grand County)
Idaho Springs, CO
303-567-2901

Estes/Poudre RD
(Clark Peak in Jackson County)
Fort Collins, CO
970-498-2770

Pawnee National Grassland
(conditions in northern plains counties)
Greeley, CO
970-353-5004

Grand Mesa, Gunnison, Uncompahgre National Forests

Collbran RD
(Leon Peak in Mesa County)
Collbran, CO
970-487-3534

Grand Junction RD
(Leon Peak in Mesa County)
Grand Junction, CO
970-242-8211

Norwood RD
(Wilson Peak in Dolores County)
Norwood, CO
970-327-4261

Ouray RD
(Uncompahgre Peak in Hinsdale County and Mount Sneffels in Ouray County
and conditions on Castle Rock on Cimarron Ridge in Montrose County)
Montrose, CO
970-240-5300

Paonia RD
(Mount Lamborn in Delta County)
Paonia, CO
970-527-4131

Medicine Bow and Routt National Forests

Hahns Peak/Bears Ear RD
(Mount Zirkel in Routt County—West)
Steamboat Springs, CO
970-879-1870

Parks RD—Kremmling
(Black Mountain in Moffat County)
Kremmling, CO
970-724-9004

Parks RD—Walden
(Mount Zirkel in Routt County—East)
Walden, CO
970-723-8204

Yampa RD
(Flat Top Mountain in Garfield County and northwest ridge of Orno Peak in
Rio Blanco County)
Yampa, CO
970-638-4516

Pike and San Isabel National Forests

Comanche National Grassland—Carrizo Unit
(conditions at Carrizo Mountain in Baca County)
Springfield, CO
719-523-6591

Comanche National Grassland—Timpas Unit
(Dry Bluff in Otero County)
La Junta, CO
719-384-2181

Leadville RD
(Mount Elbert in Lake County and Mount Harvard in Chaffee County)
Leadville, CO
719-486-0749

Pikes Peak RD
(Pikes Peak in El Paso County and Teller County)
Colorado Springs, CO
719-636-1602

San Carlos RD
(Greenhorn Mountain in Pueblo County and Crestone Peak in Custer County)
Canon City, CO
719-269-8500

South Park RD
(Mount Lincoln in Park County)
Fairplay, CO
719-836-2031

South Platte RD
(Buffalo Peak in Jefferson County)
Morrison, CO
303-275-5610

San Juan and Rio Grande National Forests

Columbine RD West
(Vermilion Peak in San Juan County and Mount Eolus in La Plata County
and Mount Wilson in San Miguel County)
Durango, CO
970-385-1283

Conejos Peak RD
(Conejos Peak in Conejos County and Summit Peak in Archuleta County)
La Jara, CO
719-274-8971

Del Norte RD
(Bennett Peak in Rio Grande County)
Del Norte, CO
719-657-3321

Divide RD
(Gwynedd Mountain in Mineral County)
Creede, CO
719-658-2556

Mancos/Dolores RD (Hesperus Mountain in Montezuma County)
Dolores, CO
970-882-7296

Saguache RD (Bushnell Peak in Fremont County and Crestone Peak in
Saguache County and Blanca Peak in Alamosa/Costilla/Huerfano Counties)
Saguache, CO
719-655-2547

White River National Forest

Aspen RD
(Castle Peak in Gunnison/Pitkin Counties)
Aspen, CO
970-925-3445

Holy Cross RD (Mount of the Holy Cross in Eagle County)
Minturn, CO
970-827-5715

Other federal government entities manage the land and provide regulations and information about the peaks.

Bureau of Land Management
Colorado State Office
2850 Youngfield Street
Lakewood, CO 80215
303-236-2100
www.blm.gov

National Park Service
Rocky Mountain Region
12795 West Alameda Avenue
P.O. Box 25287, DFC
Denver, CO 80225
303-969-2000
www.nps.gov

Rocky Mountain National Park
(Longs Peak in Boulder County and Hagues Peak in Larimer County)
Estes Park, CO 80517
970-586-1206 (general information)
970-586-1242 (backcountry office)
www.nps.gov/romo

U.S. Fish and Wildlife Service
P.O. Box 25486, DFC
Denver, CO 80225
303-236-7904
www.fws.gov

U.S. Geological Survey
Western Branch
USGS Information Service
Box 25286, DFC
Denver, CO 80225
303-202-4700
800-872-6277
800-435-7627
www.usgs.gov
Order USGS quads.

Weather

The Weather Channel:
www.weather.com

National Weather Service
www.wrh.noaa.gov/wrhq/nwspage.html

Appendix B: Further Reading

Boddie, Caryn, and Peter Boddie. *Hiking Colorado*. Helena: Falcon, 1991.

Borneman, Walter. *Colorado's Other Mountains: A Climbing Guide to Selected Peaks Under 14,000 Feet*. Evergreen: Cordillera Press, 1984.

Borneman, Walter, and Lyndon Lamper. *A Climbing Guide to Colorado's Fourteeners*. Boulder: Pruett, 1998.

Casewit, Curtis. *Colorado Off the Beaten Path*. Chester CT: The Globe Pequot Press, 1991.

Chronic, Halka. *Roadside Geology of Colorado*. Missoula: Mountain Press, 1988.

Colorado Historical Society. *Colorado County Histories Notebook*. Colorado Historical Society, 1997.

Dawson, J. Frank. *Place Names in Colorado*. Lakewood: Dawson Publishing Co., 1954.

Dawson, Louis. *Dawson's Guide to Colorado's Fourteeners* (2 volumes). Colorado Springs: Blue Clover Press, 1996.

Colorado Atlas and Gazetteer. Freehold: DeLorme Mapping, 1991.

Eichler, George. *Colorado Place Names*. Boulder: Johnson, 1977.

Fielder, John, and Randy Jacobs. *The Colorado Trail: The Official Guide*. Englewood: Westcliffe, 1994.

Fielder, John, and Tom Jones. *Colorado's Continental Divide Trail; The Official Guide*. Englewood: Westcliffe, 1997.

Garratt, Mike, and Bob Martin. *Colorado's High Thirteeners*. Evergreen: Cordillera, 1992.

Hart, John. *Fourteen Thousand Feet*. Golden: The Colorado Mountain Club, 1977.

Holmes, Don. *Highpoints of the United States*. Castle Rock: Holmes, 1998.

Huff, Paula, and Tom Wharton. *Hiking Utah's Summits*. Helena: Falcon, 1997.

Kane, Joseph. *The American Counties*. Metuchen, NJ: Scarecrow Press,1983.

Martin, Andy. *County High Points*. Tucson: Old Adit Press, 1999.

McTighe, James. *Roadside History of Colorado*. Boulder: Johnson Books, 1989.

Michael, Robert. *Colorado County Summits, Trail & Timberline,* Golden: The Colorado Mountain Club, 1976.

Noel, Thomas, Paul Mahoney, and Richard Stevens. *Historical Atlas of Colorado*. Norman: University of Oklahoma Press, 1993.

Ormes, Robert. *Guide to the Colorado Mountains*. Golden: The Colorado Mountain Club, 1992.

Roach, Gerry. *Colorado's Fourteeners: From Hikes to Climbs*. Golden: Fulcrum, 1996.

Rosebrough, Robert. *Climbing Colorado's San Juan Mountains*. Helena: Falcon, 1999.

State Historical Society of Colorado. *Point of Interest*. Denver: State Historical Society of Colorado, 1972.

Suttle, Gary. *California County Summits*. Berkeley: Wilderness, 1994.

Thompson, Jay and Therese Thompson. *Hiker's Guide to the Mount Zirkel Wilderness*. Boulder: Pruett Publishing Co., 1992.

Van Zandt, Franklin. *Boundaries of the United States and the Several States*. Reston: USGS Professional Paper No. 909, 1976.

Winner, Evans, and Ellen Winner. *Four Thousand Meters*. Denver: Eastwood 1977.

Zumwalt, Paul. *Fifty State Summits*. Vancouver: Jack Grauer, 1998.

Appendix C: A Hiker's Checklist

The "Ten Essentials" for every outing include the following:
- ☐ Bivouac gear: space blanket, twine, and duct tape
- ☐ Extra clothing: warm garments, rain gear, gloves, hat, neck gaiter
- ☐ Extra food
- ☐ Extra water
- ☐ First-aid kit
- ☐ Two sources of light: headlamp, flashlight
- ☐ Map and compass and guidebook directions
- ☐ Matches and fire starter
- ☐ Pocketknife
- ☐ Sunglasses, sunscreen, lip balm

We usually carry these additional items and consider them essential:
- ☐ Handlevel
- ☐ Note pad and pencil
- ☐ Personal identification
- ☐ Some money, including coins for phone calls

For day hikes, we recommend you carry or wear the following:
- ☐ Balaclava or neck gaiter
- ☐ Bandana
- ☐ Belt
- ☐ Boots, appropriate for a day hike, a backpack, or mountaineering
- ☐ Camera and film
- ☐ Cap with visor or wool hat
- ☐ Day pack
- ☐ Gaiters for snow, water, loose rock and dirt
- ☐ Insect repellent
- ☐ Outer wind shell
- ☐ Pants, long or short
- ☐ Parka or down vest
- ☐ Rain pants
- ☐ Shirts, long or short sleeve, cotton or wool
- ☐ Socks, wool and liner

- ☐ Timepiece
- ☐ Toilet paper
- ☐ Underwear, long or short, thermal
- ☐ Water containers
- ☐ Whistle

For overnight hikes, we recommend these items, too:
- ☐ Backpack
- ☐ Binoculars
- ☐ Camp shoes
- ☐ Cooking gear: pots, cups, plates, utensils, cleaning items
- ☐ Food for meals, snacks, drinks
- ☐ Groundcloth
- ☐ Light source for camp and tent
- ☐ Rope for campsite use
- ☐ Sleeping bag
- ☐ Stove
- ☐ Tent
- ☐ Toiletries
- ☐ Towel
- ☐ Trowel
- ☐ Water containers
- ☐ Water purifier

For mountaineering, you'll need these, too:
- ☐ Crampons
- ☐ Gloves
- ☐ Hardware: carabiners, slings, belay device
- ☐ Harness
- ☐ Helmet
- ☐ Ice axe
- ☐ Mittens, with overgloves
- ☐ Plastic boots
- ☐ Rope, climbing and prusik
- ☐ Shovel and avalanche hardware such as probes and beacons

Appendix D: In Case of Emergency

In case of any emergency, phone **911.**

Colorado County Sheriff Phone Numbers

Adams
Brighton 303-659-6400

Alamosa
Alamosa 719-589-6608

Arapahoe
Littleton 303-734-5101

Archuleta
Pagosa Springs 970-264-2131

Baca
Springfield 719-523-4511

Bent
Las Animas 719-456-1363

Boulder
Boulder 303-441-3600

Chaffee
Salida 719-539-2814

Cheyenne
Cheyenne Wells 719-767-5633

Clear Creek
Georgetown 303-534-5777

Conejos
Conejos 719-376-5921

Costilla
San Luis 719-672-3302

Crowley
Ordway 719-267-5555

Custer
Westcliffe 719-783-2270

Delta
Delta 970-874-2000

Denver
Denver 303-375-5629

Dolores
Dove Creek 970-677-2257

Douglas
Castle Rock 303-660-7505

Eagle
Eagle 970-328-8500

El Paso
Colorado Springs 719-520-7100

Elbert
Kiowa 303-621-2027

Fremont
Canon City 719-275-2000

Garfield
Glenwood Springs 970-945-0453

Gilpin
Golden 303-582-1060

Grand
Hot Sulphur Springs 970-725-3343

Gunnison
Gunnison 970-641-1113

Hinsdale
Lake City 970-944-2291

Huerfano
Walsenburg 719-738-1600

Jackson
Walden 970-723-4242

Jefferson
Golden 303-271-5444

Kiowa
Eads 719-438-5411

Kit Carson
Burlington 719-346-8934

La Plata
Durango 970-247-1157

Lake
Leadville 970-486-1249

Larimer
Fort Collins 970-498-5100

Las Animas
Trinidad 719-846-2211

Lincoln
Hugo 719-743-2426

Logan
Sterling 970-522-1373

Mesa
Grand Junction 970-244-3500

Mineral
Creede 719-658-2600

Moffat
Craig 970-824-4495

Montezuma
Cortez 970-565-8441

Montrose
Montrose 970-249-6606

Morgan
Fort Morgan 970-867-2461

Otero
La Junta 719-384-5941

Ouray
Ouray 970-325-7272

Park
Fairplay 719-836-2494

Phillips
Holyoke 970-854-3144

Pitkin
Aspen 970-920-5300

Prowers
Lamar 719-336-5234

Pueblo
Pueblo 719-583-6125

Rio Blanco
Meeker 970-878-5023

Rio Grande
Del Norte 719-657-4000

Rocky Mountain National Park
Estes Park 970-586-1206

Routt
Steamboat Springs 970-879-1090

Saguache
Saguache 719-655-2544

San Juan
Silverton 970-387-5531

San Miguel
Telluride 970-728-3081

Sedgwick
Julesburg 970-474-3355

Summit
Breckenridge 303-453-2232

Teller
Divide 719-687-9652

Washington
Akron 970-345-2244

Weld
Greeley 970-356-4015

Yuma
Wray 970-332-4805

Appendix E:
List of Summits by Elevation

	County	Highpoint	Elevation
18	Lake	Mount Elbert	14,433
15	Chaffee	Mount Harvard	14,420
20	Alamosa & Costilla	Blanca Peak	14,345
20	Huerfano	Blanca Peak NE Ridge	14,320
34	Hinsdale	Uncompahgre Peak	14,309
21	Saguache	Crestone Peak	14,294
19	Park	Mount Lincoln	14,286
10	Clear Creek & Summit	Grays Peak	14,270
17	Gunnison & Pitkin	Castle Peak	14,265
21	Custer	East Crestone Peak	14,260
9	Boulder	Longs Peak	14,255
33	Dolores	Mount Wilson	14,246
39	Ouray	Mount Sneffels	14,150
6	El Paso	Pikes Peak	14,110
35	La Plata	Mount Eolus	14,083
33	San Miguel	Wilson Peak	14,017
16	Eagle	Mount of the Holy Cross	14,005
36	Mineral	Gwynedd Mountain	13,895
41	San Juan	Vermilion Peak	13,894
23	Las Animas	West Spanish Peak	13,626
14	Larimer	Hagues Peak	13,560
12	Grand	Pettingell Peak	13,553
31	Archuleta	Summit Peak	13,300
11	Gilpin	James Peak	13,294
37	Montezuma	Hesperus Mountain	13,232
40	Rio Grande	Bennett Peak	13,203
32	Conejos	Conejos Peak	13,172
22	Fremont	Bushnell Peak	13,105
6	Teller	Devils Playground	13,060
13	Jackson	Clark Peak	12,951
26	Garfield	Flat Top Mountain	12,354
24	Pueblo	Greenhorn Mountain	12,347
30	Routt	Mount Zirkel	12,180
29	Rio Blanco	NW Ridge of Orno Peak	12,027
7	Jefferson	Buffalo Peak	11,589
38	Montrose	Castle Rock	11,453
25	Delta	Mount Lamborn	11,396
27	Mesa	Leon Peak	11,236
28	Moffat	Black Mountain	10,840
4	Douglas	Thunder Butte	9,836
5	Elbert	Elbert Rock	7,360
8	Weld	Bison Butte	6,380

2	Arapahoe	Smoky Hill Ridge	6,210
49	Lincoln	County Line Rise	5,960
3	Denver	Kipling near Belleview	5,680
1	Adams	DIA Ridge	5,665
50	Washington	Presidents Hill	5,420
47	Kit Carson	Ranch Road	5,290
52	Baca	Carrizo Mountain	5,280
54	Otero	Dry Bluff	5,260
47	Cheyenne	Ranch Road	5,255
46	Crowley	Schubert Hill	5,220
42	Logan	State Line Bluffs	4,940
43	Morgan	Judson Hills	4,935
53	Bent	San Jose Ranch Mesa	4,855
55	Prowers	Two Buttes	4,711
48	Kiowa	Selenite Bluff	4,690
51	Yuma	Yuma Corner	4,440
45	Sedgwick	Sand Hill	4,120
44	Phillips	County Line Rise	4,120

Appendix F: Hike Highlights

	COUNTY	SUMMIT	REMARKS
Nature—lakes	14 Larimer	Hagues Peak	Lawn Lake
	20 Alamosa/Costilla/ Huerfano	Blanca Peak	Lake Como
	21 Custer/Saguache	Crestone Peak	South Colony Lakes
	24 Pueblo	Greenhorn Mountain	Blue Lakes
	27 Mesa	Leon Peak	Many Grand Mesa ponds
	29 Rio Blanco	Northwest Ridge of Orno Peak	Mandall Lakes
Nature— Waterfalls	21 Custer/Saguache trail	Crestone Peak	30 feet, on Cottonwood
	30 Routt	Mount Zirkel	5 feet, along trail
	31 Archuleta	Summit Peak	30 feet, along trail
	34 Hinsdale	Uncompahgre Peak	10 feet, Upper Nellie Creek
	35 La Plata	Mount Eolus	10 feet, along trail
	55 Prowers	Two Buttes	30 feet, over Two Buttes Dam
Nature— geology	21 Custer/Saguache	Crestone Peak	Conglomerates
	23 Las Animas	West Spanish Peak	Radial dikes
	26 Garfield	Flat Top Mountain	Volcanic flows
	36 Mineral	Gwynedd Mountain	Volcanic tuff
	53 Bent	San Jose Ranch Mesa	Sandstone mesas
	55 Prowers	Two Buttes	Volcanic Stock
Nature—hot springs	10 Clear Creek/ Summit	Grays Peak	Idaho Springs
	15 Chaffee	Mount Harvard	Cottonwood Hot Springs
	17 Gunnison/Pitkin	Castle Peak	Conundrum Hot Springs
	30 Routt	Mount Zirkel	Strawberry Hot Springs
	38 Montrose	Castle Rock	Orvis Hot Springs
	39 Ouray	Mount Sneffels	Orvis Hot Springs
Nature—true wilderness	13 Jackson	Clark Peak	Colorado State Forest
	14 Larimer	Hagues Peak	Rocky Mountain National Park
	16 Eagle	Mount of the Holy Cross	Holy Cross Wilderness
	26 Garfield	Flat Top Mountain	Flat Tops Wilderness

	COUNTY	SUMMIT	REMARKS
	30 Routt	Mount Zirkel	Mount Zirkel Wilderness
	35 La Plata	Mt. Eolus	Weminuche Wilderness
Nature—wildlife	8 Weld	Bison Butte	Bison, Antelope
	10 Clear Creek/Summit	Grays Peak	Bighorn Sheep, Goats
	25 Delta	Mount Lamborn	Beaver
	35 La Plata	Mount Eolus	Mountain goats
	36 Mineral	Gwynedd Mountain	Elk, deer
	52 Baca	Carrizo Mountain	Antelope
Nature—wildflowers	17 Gunnison/Pitkin	Castle Peak	Entire Aspen area
	29 Rio Blanco	Northwest Ridge Orno Peak	Flat Tops
	32 Conejos	Conejos Peak	Saddle Creek
	34 Hinsdale	Uncompahgre Peak	Upper Nellie Creek Basin
	37 Montezuma	Hesperus Mountain	West Mancos Creek Basin
	39 Ouray	Mount Sneffels	Yankee Boy Basin
Exertion—four-wheel-drive recommended	17 Gunnison/Pitkin	Castle Peak	Four-wheel-drive—moderate
	20 Alamosa/Costilla/Huerfano	Blanca Peak	VDL (vehicle damage likely)
	22 Fremont	Bushnell Peak	Four-wheel-drive—easy
	34 Hinsdale	Uncompahgre Peak	Four-wheel-drive—easy
	36 Mineral	Gwynedd Mountain	Four-wheel-drive—easy
	52 Baca	Carrizo Mountain	Four-wheel-drive—moderate
Exertion—driveup	1 Adams	DIA Ridge	Gravel Road
	3 Denver	Kipling & Belleview	Paved 3-lane highway
	6 El Paso	Pikes Peak	Gravel road, cog railway
	44 Phillips	County Line Rise	Gravel road
	50 Washington	Presidents Hill	Gravel road
	51 Yuma	Yuma Corner	Gravel road
Exertion—gentle trail	6 Teller	Devils Playground	200 feet in 1 mile
	8 Weld	Buffalo Butte	100 feet in 1 mile
	28 Moffat	Black Mountain	Easy 1,000 feet in 3 miles
	43 Morgan	Judson Hills	100 feet in 1 mile
	45 Sedgwick	Sand Hills	50 feet in 1 mile
	54 Otero	Dry Bluff	300 feet in 1 mile

286

	COUNTY	SUMMIT	REMARKS
Exertion— **well-defined** **route**	9 Boulder	Longs Peak	Paint on rocks
	10 Clear Creek /Summit	Grays Peak	Trail to summit
	15 Chaffee	Mount Harvard	Trail to summit
	18 Lake	Mount Elbert	Trail to summit
	34 Hinsdale	Uncompahgre Peak	Trail to summit
	40 Rio Grande	Bennett Peak	Faint road to summit
Exertion— **bushwhack**	4 Douglas	Thunder Butte	2 miles of bushwhack
	7 Jefferson	Buffalo Peak	4 miles of bushwhack
	22 Fremont	Bushnell Peak	3 miles of bushwhack
	36 Mineral	Gwynedd Mountain	3 miles of bushwhack
	38 Montrose	Castle Rock	4 miles of bushwhack
	55 Prowers	Two Buttes	1 mile of bushwhack
Exertion— **half day**	4 Douglas	Thunder Butte	4 hours
	24 Pueblo	Greenhorn Mountain	4 hours
	28 Moffat	Black Mountain	4 hours
	38 Montrose	Castle Rock	5 hours
	40 Rio Grande	Bennett Peak	3 hours
	53 Bent	San Jose Ranch Mesa	2 hours
Exertion— **long day**	7 Jefferson	Buffalo Peak	Long Bushwhack
	15 Chaffee	Mount Harvard	12 miles, 4,000 feet
	17 Gunnison/Pitkin	Castle Peak	10 miles, 3,000 feet
	21 Custer/Saguache	Crestone Peak	Rock Scrambling
	30 Routt	Mount Zirkel	14 miles, 3,000 feet
	36 Mineral	Gwynedd Mountain	12 miles, off trail
Exertion— **overnight**	9 Boulder	Longs Peak	Over 8 hours, 5,000 feet
	14 Larimer	Hagues Peak	18 mile round trip
	16 Eagle	Mount of the Holy Cross	900 feet drop to river
	20 Alamosa/Costilla/ Huerfano	Blanca Peak	Over 12 hours
	33 Dolores/ San Miguel	Wilson Peak/ Mount Wilson	Pack in, get three Fourteeners
	35 La Plata	Mount Eolus	7 miles to Chicago Basin
Exertion— **mobility** **challenged**	1 Adams	DIA Ridge	Asphalt road
	3 Denver	Kipling near Belleview	Neighborhood sidewalk
	6 El Paso	Pikes Peak	Gravel road, cog railway
	44 Phillips	County Line Rise	Gravel Road

	COUNTY	SUMMIT	REMARKS
	50 Washington	Presidents Hill	Gravel road
	51 Yuma	Yuma Corner	Gravel road
Experience— exposure to heights	9 Boulder	Longs Peak	Narrow ledge, steep slabs
	21 Custer/Saguache	Crestone Peak	Steep couloirs near summit
	33 Dolores	Wilson Peak	Steep climbing at summit
	33 San Miguel	Mount Wilson	Very steep chute to summit
	35 La Plata	Mount Eolus	Narrow sidewalk in the sky
	41 San Juan	Vermilion Peak	Steep, loose summit couloir
Experience— alpine environment	9 Boulder	Longs Peak	Glaciation evident
	19 Park	Mount Lincoln	Trailhead above timberline
	21 Custer/Saguache	Crestone Peak	All rock, no tundra
	33 San Miguel	Mount Wilson	Far from timberline
	39 Ouray	Mount Sneffels	Climb a couloir 1,000 feet
	41 San Juan	Vermilion Peak	Volcanic talus for miles
Experience— ridge walks	12 Grand	Pettingell Peak	On extensive ridge system
	20 Alamosa/Costilla/ Huerfano	Blanca Peak	Sharp ridge from cirque
	22 Fremont	Bushnell Peak	On extensive ridge system
	32 Conejos	Conejos Peak	Long gentle ridge to summit
	36 Mineral	Gwynedd Mountain	Rounded but long caldera rim
	37 Montezuma	Hesperus Mountain	Long ridge to summit
Experience— few people	7 Jefferson	Buffalo Peak	Very remote bushwhack
	22 Fremont	Bushnell Peak	Obscure, low Thirteener
	27 Mesa	Leon Park	Seldom visited
	37 Montezuma	Hesperus Mountain	Obscure, low Thirteener
	38 Montrose	Castle Rock	Obscure, no trail
	40 Rio Grande	Bennett Peak	5 Visitors in last 10 years
Experience— lots of people	6. El Paso/Teller	Pikes Pk/Devils Playground	Hundreds by car, railway, foot

COUNTY	SUMMIT	REMARKS
9 Boulder	Longs Peak	Most summer weekends see 200
10 Clear Creek/ Summit	Grays Peak	Closest Fourteener hike to Denver
11 Gilpin	James Peak	Dozens on St. Marys Glacier
18 Lake	Mount Elbert	Highpoint of state
39 Ouray	Mount Sneffels	Most popular San Juan peak

Experience good for kids

COUNTY	SUMMIT	REMARKS
6 El Paso/Teller	Pikes Pk/Devils Playground	Stores, easy hills
24 Pueblo	Greenhorn Mountain	High alpine meadows
28 Moffat	Black Mountain	Easy wooded hike
29 Rio Blanco	Northwest Ridge of Orno Peak	Flat Top's mesa
40 Rio Grande	Bennett Peak	Easy hike
54 Otero	Dry Bluff	Open, rolling rangeland

Experience— photography

COUNTY	SUMMIT	REMARKS
9 Boulder	Longs Peak	Rocky Mountain National Park, Diamond Face
21 Custer/Saguache	Crestone Peak	Very rugged
34 Hinsdale	Uncompahgre Peak	Vertical north face
36 Mineral	Gwynedd Mountain	Wheeler Geologic Monument
39 Ouray	Mount Sneffels	Queen of the San Juans
53 Bent	San Jose Ranch Mesa	Plains buttes

Experience— locating actual highpoint

COUNTY	SUMMIT	REMARKS
28 Moffat	Black Mountain	1 large wooded area
44 Phillips	County Line Rise	10 spots over 4 miles
47 Cheyenne/ Kit Carson	Ranch Roads	3 spots on rangeland
48 Kiowa	Selenite Bluff	2 spots on bluff
53 Bent	San Jose Ranch Mesa	7 spots on 7 mesas
86 Weld	Buffalo Butte	2 spots on butte

Experience— good trailhead campgrounds

COUNTY	SUMMIT	REMARKS
9 Boulder	Longs Peak	Rocky Mountain National Park Campground
23 Las Animas	West Spanish Peak	Cordova Pass Campground
24 Pueblo	Greenhorn Mountain	Blue Lakes Campground
27 Mesa	Leon Peak	Weir & Johnson Campgrounds

	COUNTY	SUMMIT	REMARKS
	34 Hinsdale	Uncompahgre Peak	National forest campground
	52 Baca	Carrizo Mountain	Carrizo Picnic Area
Experience— scenic and quaint towns near base	9 Boulder	Longs Peak	Estes Park
	21 Custer/Saguache	Crestone Peak	Crestone
	23 Las Animas	West Spanish Peak	Cuchara
	36 Mineral	Gwynedd Mountain	Creede
	39 Ouray	Mount Sneffels	Ouray
	41 San Juan	Vermilion Peak	Silverton
Experience— best side trips along trail	19 Park	Mount Lincoln	Other Fourteeners
	20 Alamosa/Costilla/ Huerfano	Blanca Peak	Other Fourteeners, sand dunes
	35 La Plata	Mount Eolus	Other Fourteeners
	36 Mineral	Gwynedd Mountain	Wheeler Geologic Monument
	39 Ouray	Mount Sneffels	Yankee Boy Basin
	52 Baca	Carrizo Mountain	Canyons, Potato Butte
Experience— best summit views	9 Boulder	Longs Peak	Rocky Mountain National Park
	15 Chaffee	Mount Harvard	High peaks, Arkansas Valley
	21 Custer/Saguache	Crestone Peak	Nearby Fourteeners, South Colony Lakes
	23 Las Animas	West Spanish Peak	Radial dikes
	35 La Plata	Mount Eolus	Needle Mountains
	41 San Juan	Vermilion	Rugged ridgeline to the north
Authors' ten favorites	9 Boulder	Longs Peak	
	18 Lake	Mount Elbert	
	21 Custer/Saguache	Crestone Peak	
	24 Pueblo	Greenhorn Mountain	
	29 Rio Blanco	Northwest Ridge of Orno Peak	
	34 Hinsdale	Uncompahgre Peak	
	35 La Plata	Mount Eolus	
	41 San Juan	Vermilion Peak	
	53 Bent	San Jose Ranch Mesa	
	55 Prowers	Two Buttes	

Appendix G: Glossary

Alpine—a fragile ecological zone characterized by cold, treeless terrain typically covered with grasses and lichens.

Apex—the highest point.

Benchmark—an elevation survey marker installed by the government; useful for locating oneself.

BLM—U.S. Bureau of Land Management.

Blocky—rock outcrop with steep sides and flatter top.

Bluff—a bold headland overlooking flat countryside.

BM—benchmark.

Bushwhack—to travel across country without the use of a trail or road, typically over wilderness terrain.

Butte—an isolated, flat-topped landform bounded by steep slopes; smaller than a mesa.

C-470—Colorado highway around the south and west of Denver (links with E-470).

Cairn—manmade mound of rocks used as a guidepost in navigation.

Caliche—hard calcium residue that builds in the soil through evaporation.

CDT (Continental Divide Trail)—north-south trail along the Contintental Divide from Canada to Mexico.

Centennial Peak—one of the 100 highest peaks in Colorado; a popular climbing goal with Colorado climbers.

Cirque—steep-walled, crescent-shaped bowl at the head of an alpine valley, produced by glacial erosion.

Class—a rating that classifies the difficulty of a climb on a scale of 1 to 5; class 1 is simple walking, and class 5 is technical climbing.

Cliff out—to unexpectedly arrive at a precipice with no means of safe descent.

Cog railway—a series of teeth laid in a trackbed that a wheel travels over to impart motion to a railcar.

Colorado Trail—east-west trail across Colorado from Denver to Durango.

Conglomerate—sedimentary rock composed of coarse, cemented pieces of pre-existing rock.

Continental Divide—drainage divide between the Atlantic and Pacific watersheds.

Contouring—traveling on uneven terrain by remaining at a constant elevation without losing or gaining altitude.

Cornice—overhanging mass of snow at the top edge of a steep slope.

Couloir—steep, narrow gully.

County—administrative division of a state.

County seat—administrative capital of a county.

DeLorme—atlas of landscape showing manmade features and general topography; useful for trailhead approaches.

DIA—Denver International Airport.

Dike— tabular igneous intrusion that cuts across the bedding of the country rock.

Drainage—physical features in the landscape that discharge water from that area.

Exposure—a drop of sufficient height to cause injury; unprotected position relative to inclement weather.

Forest Service—USDA Forest Service.

Fourteener—a mountain with a peak elevation over 14,000 feet.

FR—United States Forest Service road.

FT—United States Forest Service trail.

Gap—a sharp opening on a ridgeline.

Grade—the inclination of the land surface.

Grazing association—a cooperative of independent livestock owners.

Gulch—narrow, deep ravine, with steep sides larger than a gully.

Handlevel—handheld device used to determine land elevations equal in altitude to your eye level.

Hanging valley—a remnant glacial valley that is cut off by a lower, larger valley so that it appears to be a high, isolated valley.

Highpoint—highest ground of a defined area, listed with other similar areas.

Highpointer—person interested in reaching the summit of various geographic points that are defined and listed.

Livestock—domestic animals, usually free roaming, that are raised for sale.

Mesa—an isolated flat-topped landform bounded by steep slopes.

Milepost—formal mileage marker on interstates and routes.

Narrow-gauge railroad—railroad with a track width less than 56 inches.

Notch—a deep, narrow pass.

Pass—saddle over which a path can lead from one drainage to another.

Peak—summit or highest point of a mountain.

Peakbagging—hobby of visiting different summits on a defined list.

Plains—relatively flat, grassy region; the plains in eastern half of Colorado.

Quad—an abbreviation of "quadrangle," the standard topographic map produced by the United States Geological Survey (USGS).

Range—named series of mountains in a generally linear trend.

Relief—vertical distance from summit to the surrounding lower area.

Roadless area—government-recognized land parcel with no roads.

Rope-up—act of securing a climbing party using rope and harness; done on terrain with vertical exposure.

Saddle—low point on ridgeline between peaks or between higher and lower ground.

Scrambling—climbing over rough terrain, generally without exposure.

Scree—small, unconsolidated rock collected at the base of, or on, a cliff or slope.

Shoulder—rounded lateral spur on a mountain.

Summit—highest point of a geographic feature; also a verb to reach the highest point.

Summit register—paper in waterproof container for hikers to sign in recognition of their visits.

Switchback—a zigzag bend in a trail up a steep slope, constructed so that hikers gain elevation at a more gentle grade.

Tailing ponds—settling impoundments for mining activity.

Talus—larger unconsolidated rock debris collected at the base of steep terrain.

Technical climbing—complex climbing using specialized maneuvers; requires protection against vertical exposure.

Thirteener—a mountain with a peak elevation over 13,000 feet.

Trailhead—established place to leave a vehicle and begin a hike.

Use trail—an informal trail that is obvious and established through the common use of many hikers.

Wilderness—an established area set aside by the government to be preserved in a natural state for scientific and recreational pursuits.

Index

Page numbers in italic type refer to maps.
*Page numbers in **bold** type refer to photos.*

About the Authors

The authors have been hiking in Colorado for the past two decades. They ran into each other at a party for the Highpointers Club and soon discovered that the counties of Colorado held a new challenge for them. County highpointing, or peakbagging taken to a new extreme, soon occupied their summer vacations, fall weekends, and spring and winter spare time. Once a list was discovered and verified, John and Dave were off and running, and the result, four years later, is this guidebook.

Dave Covill was born in Massachusetts and first discovered Colorado on a geology field trip in college. He soon moved to Colorado for good and works for an oil and gas company in Denver. He lives in Evergreen with his wife, Beckie, and teenage son, Chris, and has absolutely no spare time. Dave has summited most of the state highpoints and Colorado's Fourteeners and always has an eye out for a new list.

John Drew Mitchler was raised in rural Illinois where he gained an appreciation of nature on his parents' farm along the Fox River. After working as a geologist in the coalfields of Illinois, he came to Colorado as an employee of an environmental engineering firm. A fascination with maps and a love of traveling have taken him to the highpoints of 45 states—to date— and helped him become the first person to reach the highest peak of every Colorado county. John lives in Golden and has never met a highpoint he didn't like.

Dave perches on the airy summit of Vermilion Peak in San Juan County.

John reaches his final Colorado county summit, Longs Peak in Boulder County.

American Hiking Society

American Hiking Society is the only national nonprofit organization dedicated to establishing, protecting and maintaining foot trails in America.

Establishing...

American Hiking Society establishes hiking trails with the AHS National Trails Endowment, providing grants for grassroots organizations to purchase trail lands, construct and maintain trails, and preserve hiking trails' scenic values. The AHS affiliate club program, called the Congress of Hiking Organizations, brings trail clubs together to share information, collaborate on public policy, and advocate legislation and policies that protect hiking trails.

Protecting...

American Hiking Society protects hiking trails through highly focused public policy efforts in the nation's capital. AHS affects federal legislation, shapes public lands policy, collaborates with grassroots trail organizations, and partners with federal land managers to protect the hiking experience. Members become active with letter-writing campaigns and by attending the annual AHS Trails Lobby Week.

Maintaining...

American Hiking Society maintains hiking trails by sending volunteers to national parks, forests and recreation lands; organizing volunteer teams to help our affiliated hiking clubs; and publishing national volunteer directories. AHS members get involved, get dirty and get inspired by participating in AHS programs like National Trails Day, America's largest celebration of the outdoors; and Volunteer Vacations, our week-long work trips to beautiful, wild places.

American Hiking Society
1422 Fenwick Lane
Silver Spring, MD 20910
OR CALL: (888) 766 - HIKEx115
OR VISIT: www.ahs.simplenet.com

FALCONGUIDES ® Leading the Way™

FALCONGUIDES ® are available for where-to-go hiking, mountain biking, rock climbing, walking, scenic driving, fishing, rockhounding, paddling, birding, wildlife viewing, and camping. We also have FalconGuides on essential outdoor skills and subjects and field identification. The following titles are currently available, but this list grows every year. For a free catalog with a complete list of titles, call FALCON toll-free at 1-800-582-2665.

HIKING GUIDES

Hiking Alaska
Hiking Arizona
Hiking Arizona's Cactus Country
Hiking the Beartooths
Hiking Big Bend National Park
Hiking the Bob Marshall Country
Hiking California
Hiking California's Desert Parks
Hiking Carlsbad Caverns
    and Guadalupe Mtns. National Parks
Hiking Colorado
Hiking Colorado, Vol.II
Hiking Colorado's Summits
Hiking Colorado's Weminuche Wilderness
Hiking the Columbia River Gorge
Hiking Florida
Hiking Georgia
Hiking Glacier & Waterton Lakes National Parks
Hiking Grand Canyon National Park
Hiking Grand Staircase-Escalante/Glen Canyon
Hiking Grand Teton National Park
Hiking Great Basin National Park
Hiking Hot Springs in the Pacific Northwest
Hiking Idaho
Hiking Maine
Hiking Michigan
Hiking Minnesota
Hiking Montana
Hiking Mount Rainier National Park
Hiking Mount St. Helens
Hiking Nevada
Hiking New Hampshire

Hiking New Mexico
Hiking New York
Hiking North Carolina
Hiking the North Cascades
Hiking Northern Arizona
Hiking Olympic National Park
Hiking Oregon
Hiking Oregon's Eagle Cap Wilderness
Hiking Oregon's Mount Hood/Badger Creek
Hiking Oregon's Three Sisters Country
Hiking Pennsylvania
Hiking Shenandoah National Park
Hiking the Sierra Nevada
Hiking South Carolina
Hiking South Dakota's Black Hills Country
Hiking Southern New England
Hiking Tennessee
Hiking Texas
Hiking Utah
Hiking Utah's Summits
Hiking Vermont
Hiking Virginia
Hiking Washington
Hiking Wyoming
Hiking Wyoming's Cloud Peak Wilderness
Hiking Wyoming's Wind River Range
Hiking Yellowstone National Park
Hiking Zion & Bryce Canyon National Parks
The Trail Guide to Bob Marshall Country
Wild Country Companion
Wild Montana
Wild Utah

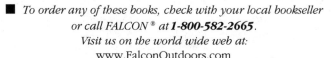

■ *To order any of these books, check with your local bookseller or call FALCON ® at **1-800-582-2665**. Visit us on the world wide web at:* www.FalconOutdoors.com

FALCON®

FALCONGUIDES® Leading the Way™

MOUNTAIN BIKING GUIDES
Mountain Biking Arizona
Mountain Biking Colorado
Mountain Biking Georgia
Mountain Biking New Mexico
Mountain Biking New York
Mountain Biking Northern New England
Mountain Biking Oregon
Mountain Biking South Carolina
Mountain Biking Southern California
Mountain Biking Southern New England
Mountain Biking Utah
Mountain Biking Wisconsin
Mountain Biking Wyoming

LOCAL CYCLING SERIES
Fat Trax Bozeman
Mountain Biking Bend
Mountain Biking Boise
Mountain Biking Chequamegon
Mountain Biking Chico
Mountain Biking Colorado Springs
Mountain Biking Denver/Boulder
Mountain Biking Durango
Mountain Biking Flagstaff and Sedona
Mountain Biking Helena
Mountain Biking Moab
Mountain Biking Utah's
   St. George/Cedar City Area
Mountain Biking the White
   Mountains (West)

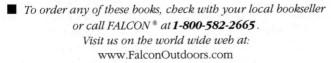

■ *To order any of these books, check with your local bookseller*
*or call FALCON ® at **1-800-582-2665**.*
Visit us on the world wide web at:
www.FalconOutdoors.com

FALCON®

WILDERNESS FIRST AID

By Dr. Gilbert Preston M.D.

Enjoy the outdoors and face the inherent risks with confidence. By reading this easy-to-follow first-aid text, all outdoor enthusiasts can pack a little extra peace of mind on their next adventure. *Wilderness First Aid* offers expert medical advice for dealing with outdoor emergencies beyond the reach of 911. It easily fits in most backcountry first-aid kits.

LEAVE NO TRACE

By Will Harmon

The concept of "leave no trace" seems simple, but it actually gets fairly complicated. This handy quick-reference guidebook includes all the newest information on this growing and all-important subject. This book is written to help the outdoor enthusiast make the hundreds of decisions necessary to protect the natural landscape and still have an enjoyable wilderness experience. Part of the proceeds from the sale of this book go to continue leave-no-trace education efforts. The Official Manual of American Hiking Society.

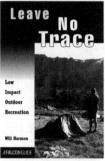

BEAR AWARE

By Bill Schneider

Hiking in bear country can be very safe if hikers follow the guidelines summarized in this small, "packable" book. Extensively reviewed by bear experts, the book contains the latest information on the intriguing science of bear-human interactions. *Bear Aware* can not only make your hike safer, but it can help you avoid the fear of bears that can take the edge off your trip.

MOUNTAIN LION ALERT

By Steve Torres

Recent mountain lion attacks have received national attention. Although infrequent, lion attacks raise concern for public safety. *Mountain Lion Alert* contains helpful advice for mountain bikers, trail runners, horse riders, pet owners, and suburban landowners on how to reduce the chances of mountain lion-human conflicts.

Also Available

*Wilderness Survival • Reading Weather • Backpacking Tips • Climbing Safely •
Avalanche Aware • Desert Hiking Tips • Hiking with Dogs • Using GPS •
Route Finding • Wild Country Companion*

To order check with your local bookseller or
call FALCON® at **1-800-582-2665.**
www.FalconOutdoors.com